What Teens Need to
SUCCEED

What Teens Need to SUCCEED

Proven, Practical Ways to Shape Your Own Future

Peter L. Benson, Ph.D., Judy Galbraith, M.A., and Pamela Espeland

free spirit
PUBLISHING®

Library of Congress Cataloging-in-Publication Data

Benson, Peter L.

    What teens need to succeed : proven, practical ways to shape your own future / Peter L. Benson, Judy Galbraith, and Pamela Espeland.

        p. cm.

    Includes bibliographical references and index.

    Summary: Describes forty "Developmental Assets" that teenagers need to succeed in life, such as family support, positive peer influences, and religious community, and suggests ways to acquire these assets.

    ISBN 1-57542-027-9

    1. Teenagers—United States—Life skills guides—Juvenile literature.   2. Teenagers—United States—Conduct of life—Juvenile literature.   [1. Life skills.   2. Conduct of life.]

    I. Galbraith, Judy. II. Espeland, Pamela. III. Title.

HQ799.U65B46   1998

646.7'00835—dc21

                       98-6036

                         CIP

                          AC

What Teens Need to Succeed is based on *The Troubled Journey: A Portrait of 6th–12th Grade Youth* by Peter L. Benson, Ph.D., published in 1993 by Search Institute and sponsored by RespecTeen, a national program of Lutheran Brotherhood; on "The Asset Approach: Giving Kids What They Need to Succeed," copyright © 1997 by Search Institute; and on other publications and continuing research by Search Institute.

Reading Level Grades 7 & up; Interest Level Ages 11 & up;
Fountas & Pinnell Guided Reading Level Z

20 19 18 17 16 15 14
Printed in the United States of America
S18860311

Free Spirit Publishing Inc.
217 Fifth Avenue North, Suite 200
Minneapolis, MN 55401-1299
(612) 338-2068
help4kids@freespirit.com
www.freespirit.com

CONTENTS

Building Internal Assets   167

Tools and Resources   333

INTRODUCTION

You've got the power

You might think you have little or no control over your life. Parents, teachers, and other adults seem to have all the power—at home, at school, in the community, in the world. Some adults might treat you with suspicion and look down on you just because you're a teenager. Factor in Circumstances Beyond Your Control—violence, prejudice, poverty, crime, injustice, ignorance—and you may feel as if there's nothing you can do about anything.

Not true. You've got the power—to take a look at your life, celebrate the good parts, identify the problem areas, plan your future, decide your direction, and shape your own success. Plus you've got the power to make a real difference in the lives of people around you. Ideally, you'll have help from caring adults who want the best for you. But even if you don't, there's a lot you can do yourself. This book tells you how.

What this book is about

What Teens Need to Succeed is about building assets. Not financial assets (though you can build those, too), but Developmental Assets—good things you need in your life and in yourself. Developmental Assets can give you the support, skills, and resources that will get you where you want to go.

What are Developmental Assets? They're not complicated or hard to understand. They're 40 basic, commonsense things like family support, a caring neighborhood, honesty, self-esteem, and resistance skills—the ability to stand up against negative pressure and avoid dangerous situations. If you read through the Contents, you'll be able to tell what most of them mean.

What's the connection between assets and power? That takes a bit of explaining.

The assets story

Starting in 1989, Search Institute—an organization that specializes in research on children and teenagers—surveyed more than 250,000 students in grades 6–12 in communities across the United States. Starting in 1996, another 100,000 students took a new survey. As we studied the survey results, we asked ourselves: Why do some kids have a fairly easy time growing up, while others struggle? Why do some get involved in dangerous activities, while others lead productive lives? Why do some beat the odds, while others get trapped?

The usual answers to questions like these focus on *problems.* Kids struggle, make poor choices, and lose their way because they're poor, or their families are messed up, or they're surrounded by bad influences, or the culture is too violent, or they've suffered traumatic events in their lives, or some other reason that's difficult to change.

We decided to look for other answers—answers that would tell us why some kids *prevail,* not fail. And we found that assets make the difference.

Our research showed that assets protect and empower youth. Best of all, their effect is cumulative. That means the *more* assets you have, the *less* likely you are to struggle, and the *more* likely you are to succeed in life.

There's something else that sets assets apart from the usual answers: They're positive. Upbeat. Optimistic. Hopeful. They don't zero in on what's wrong with kids today; they highlight what's right. If you're sick of hearing only bad news about teens—news about teen pregnancy, crime, violence, school failure, drug use, alcohol use, sexual behavior, suicide, and general craziness—so are we. If you're tired of hearing about programs that are supposed to fix these problems but somehow never do, we are, too.

Each year, governments (national, state, and local) spend millions of dollars to try to make problems go away—or to punish kids for having problems. Asset building is different. Here's how:

13 WAYS ASSET BUILDING IS DIFFERENT

The problem-centered approach:	The asset-building approach:
1. Anticipates the worst in teenagers	Brings out the best in teenagers
2. Sees teens as problems	Sees teens as resources
3. Concentrates on kids at risk or in trouble	Benefits all children and teens
4. Focuses on what's wrong with youth, families, and communities—what needs to be fixed	Focuses on what's right with youth, families, and communities—what they have to offer
5. Isn't clear about what to do	Suggests concrete, specific things to do
6. Reacts to problems after they happen	Builds character, skills, and values that help prevent problems

CONTINUED ON NEXT PAGE...

7. Assumes that only professionals can do it	Assumes that everyone can do it
8. Stresses competition (my way/ program is better than yours)	Stresses cooperation and collaboration (we can all work together)
9. Depends on programs and bureaucracies	Recognizes the power of relationships
10. Relies on public funding	Relies on individuals, families, communities, youth-serving organizations, etc.—anyone who cares about children and teens
11. Takes a short-term, quick-fix view	Takes a long-term, lifetime view
12. Sends a message of despair— problems are too big, widespread, and complex to solve	Sends a message of hope—positive change is possible
13. Emphasizes failures and bad news	Celebrates successes and good news

Look at the Contents again. Notice that assets are called Family Support—not What to Do When Your Parents Don't Care. And Community Values Youth—not Fighting Back When You Feel Useless. And Safety—not Staying Alive in a War Zone. And Self-Esteem—not What to Do When You Feel Bad About Yourself. It matters what words we use. When we focus on the positive, we tend to think positively and act positively.

How this book is organized

What Teens Need to Succeed describes the assets and tells you how to build each one. There are 40 assets, grouped into two main types: External and Internal. The external assets are good things you need in your life; the internal assets are good things you need in yourself. You can build both kinds.

The two main types of assets are divided into eight smaller categories: Support, Empowerment, Boundaries, Constructive Use of Time, Commitment to Learning, Positive Values, Social Competencies, and Positive Identity. Each category has its own title page that explains what those assets are about.

Each asset has its own chapter, divided into sections. You'll find ideas for building assets at home, at school, in your community, in your faith community, and with your friends. You'll also find interesting facts related to the assets, true stories about real people who are building the assets, and resources (books, organizations, Web sites) you can check out if you want to know more. Some of the resources are for your parents, teachers, youth group leaders, and other adults, so be sure to share them.

In Tools and Resources at the end of the book, you'll find pages you can photocopy—including a list of all 40 assets, plus asset-building ideas for adults, families, schools and youth organizations, faith communities and neighborhoods, businesses and government—and a Bibliography.

How to use this book

This is probably not the kind of book you'll read straight through from cover to cover. There isn't a plot and there aren't any characters, and each chapter stands alone. You might think of it as a collection of advice columns on many topics. Some will interest you; some might not. Some will help you get things you want or need; others might describe things you already have.

Start by reading Add Up Your Assets, which follows the Introduction. This chapter includes two checklists you can photocopy. One is for you; the other is for your parents. Read through your checklist and decide how many assets you already have. You might be pleased by how many you have—or concerned because you only seem to have a few. Don't get hung up here; this is not a test. The point of the checklist isn't to make you feel good or bad about yourself, but to head you in the right direction. The assets you *don't* have are the ones you'll probably want to work on first. You might also want to strengthen the assets you *do* have. It's up to you.

Next, take a look at Why You Need Assets. This chapter shows how powerful assets can be and also shows that the more assets you have, the better. The average 6th- to 12th-grader surveyed by Search Institute has only 18 of the 40 assets. Some teens have more; some teens have fewer. If you want, you can develop many more of them. Again, it's up to you.

Choose an asset to start with, then turn to that chapter. Read through it to find ideas you'd like to try. *Tips:*

Be flexible. Don't be limited by the section titles. We wanted to show that you can build assets anywhere—at home, at school, etc. We thought it would be useful to suggest asset-building tips for different parts of your life. But if there's an At Home suggestion you want to try with your friends, feel free.

Come up with your own ideas. Don't assume that you have to use only the ideas on these pages. There are countless ways to build assets. Your own ideas— or those you get from your parents, friends, teachers, youth leaders, and other people you know—might work better for you.

It's okay to start small and slowly. Don't be overwhelmed by the amount of information and number of suggestions in this book. We've tried to offer a wide variety of ideas—from simple things you can do on your own to bigger projects you'll need help with. Some will take a few minutes; others might take days, weeks, or months, depending on how involved you want to get. Pick one thing you want to do, then give it a try. Anything, no matter how small it may seem, has the potential to make a big difference.

You don't have to build every asset today. Start with *one* asset and *one* idea. Once you start building assets and experiencing the benefits, you'll want to keep doing it—maybe for the rest of your life. So there's no big rush.

If you try an idea and it doesn't work—or it doesn't work the way you expected or hoped it would—don't be discouraged. Pick another idea or come up with your own. Or ask an adult for help.

Share these ideas with other people. Share them with your family, friends, teachers, youth group leaders, neighbors, and anyone else who might be interested. Encourage them to be asset builders, too. Whole communities across the country have embraced the asset-building concept—St. Louis Park, Minnesota; Kennebunk, Maine; Albuquerque, New Mexico; Denver, Colorado; and Nampa, Idaho, to name just a few. You'll read some of their stories in this book. *Tip:* These stories—all titled Assets in Action—are other sources of ideas you might want to try. You can also show them to people you know as evidence that teens, adults, and communities everywhere have made a commitment to asset building.

Build assets for and with other people. Throughout this book, you'll find ideas for building assets for your brothers and sisters, friends, younger kids in your neighborhood, classmates, and other people you know and come into contact with. If assets are good for you (which they are), it's reasonable to think they're good for everyone. You have the power to help someone else succeed.

Don't despair if your life isn't perfect—or if it's a long way from being perfect. Building assets can benefit you no matter what your circumstances are. *Examples:*

• If you're under tremendous stress, knowing how to make decisions and having a positive view of your future can help you cope.

• If you spend a lot of time at home alone because of a parent's work schedule, knowing that your parents care—because they've gotten involved with your schooling and set boundaries for your behavior—can make you feel safe and secure.

• If you live in poverty, a supportive family and strong personal values can help you feel confident about your future.

• If you have an alcoholic parent, being part of a caring school, faith community, or youth organization can give you a safe place to go and compensate for some of what your parent doesn't provide.

• If you're in a destructive or abusive family situation, forming positive relationships with other adults and having a sense of purpose can give you hope and show you a way out.

Assets won't make your problems disappear. But they will build the support, skills, and resources that can help you overcome the challenges you face in your life.

A few words about some of the words we use

Throughout this book, we use the words *parents* and *parent* to indicate the adults you live with who take care of you. You might not have two parents or even one parent. You might live with one or more step-parents, foster parents, grandparents, other relatives, or guardians. When we say *parents* and *parent*, we don't mean to exclude teens whose circumstances are different. It's just simpler to say "Talk to your parents . . ." than it is to say "Talk to your biological, adoptive, step-, or foster parent or grandparent, other relative, or guardian. . . ." (Plus doing that would make this book a lot longer than it already is.)

School means the place where you learn—whether it's a public school, private school, urban school, rural school, or whatever. Maybe you're being home schooled. Adapt our ideas to fit your situation, or come up with your own ideas.

We've tried to make this book friendly and accessible to as many teens as possible. If you come across language that doesn't fit you, we invite you to substitute other words that do.

Let us know how these ideas work for you

On page 334, you'll find a form you can photocopy and fill out. Use it to share your own Assets in Action stories—and your asset-building ideas. Or, if you want, you can write us a letter, send us an email, or contact us through our Web site:

What Teens Need
Free Spirit Publishing Inc.
217 Fifth Avenue North, Suite 200
Minneapolis, MN 55401-1299
help4kids@freespirit.com
www.freespirit.com

We hope that you'll choose to start building assets—and that asset building will become part of your life.

Let's get started.

Peter L. Benson, Ph.D.
Judy Galbraith, M.A.
Pamela Espeland

ADD UP YOUR ASSETS

How many assets do you already have? The checklists that follow can help you find out. The one on pages 8–9 is for you; the one on pages 10–11 is for your parents. Both are adaptations of Search Institute's list of 40 assets. *

1. Photocopy the checklists before filling them out. You may want to complete another checklist after trying some of the asset-building ideas. If you write in the book, you won't be able to do this.

2. Fill out your checklist, then add up your assets. How many do you already have? What are your strong areas? What are your weak areas? *Tip:* The numbers of the statements on the checklist are the same as the numbers assigned to the assets.

3. Have your parents fill out their checklist, then compare yours with theirs. Are their results different from yours? Did they give you more or fewer assets than you gave yourself? *Tip:* When you talk with your parents about the checklists, you're building Asset #2: Positive Family Communication.

4. Make a plan. Which asset(s) do you want to start building first? Second? Third? Which one(s) do you want to strengthen? Set goals for yourself. *Tip:* If you're not sure how to do this, see Asset #32: Planning and Decision Making.

5. Think of people who can help you. What about your parents? A teacher? Counselor? Youth leader? Religious leader? A neighbor you've always liked? Are there other adults you trust, respect, and can talk to? Share your plan with them and ask for their support. *Tip:* If you can't think of anyone who might be able to help you, see Asset #3: Other Adult Relationships.

Optional: Form a support group with friends who've completed the checklist. Work together to build assets for yourselves and each other.

---

* *Note:* These checklists don't accurately measure your assets. They're included here to give you a starting point for discussion and awareness. The original survey included many more questions that were grouped together to measure the assets scientifically.

CHECKLIST FOR TEENS

Check each statement that's true for you.

- ❏ 1. I feel loved and supported in my family.
- ❏ 2. I can go to my parents for advice and support. We talk with each other often about many different things, including serious issues.
- ❏ 3. I know at least three adults (besides my parents) I can go to for advice and support.
- ❏ 4. My neighbors give me support and encouragement. They care about me.
- ❏ 5. My school is a caring, encouraging place to be.
- ❏ 6. My parents are actively involved in helping me succeed in school.
- ❏ 7. I feel valued and appreciated by adults in my community.
- ❏ 8. I'm given useful roles and meaningful things to do in my community.
- ❏ 9. I do an hour or more of community service each week.
- ❏ 10. I feel safe at home, at school, and in my neighborhood.
- ❏ 11. My family has both clear rules and consequences for my behavior. They also monitor my whereabouts.
- ❏ 12. My school has clear rules and consequences for behavior.
- ❏ 13. My neighbors take responsibility for monitoring my behavior.
- ❏ 14. My parents and other adults in my life model positive, responsible behavior.
- ❏ 15. My best friends model responsible behavior. They're a good influence on me.
- ❏ 16. My parents and teachers encourage me to do well.
- ❏ 17. I spend three or more hours each week in lessons or practice in music, theater, or other arts.
- ❏ 18. I spend three or more hours each week in school or community sports, clubs, or organizations.
- ❏ 19. I spend one or more hours each week in religious services or spiritual activities.

- [ ] 20. I go out with friends with nothing special to do two or fewer nights each week.
- [ ] 21. I want to do well in school.
- [ ] 22. I like to learn new things.
- [ ] 23. I do an hour or more of homework each school day.
- [ ] 24. I care about my school.
- [ ] 25. I spend three or more hours each week reading for pleasure.
- [ ] 26. I believe that it's really important to help other people.
- [ ] 27. I want to help promote equality and reduce world poverty and hunger.
- [ ] 28. I act on my convictions and stand up for my beliefs.
- [ ] 29. I tell the truth—even when it's not easy.
- [ ] 30. I take personal responsibility for my actions and decisions.
- [ ] 31. I believe that it's important for me not to be sexually active or to use alcohol or other drugs.
- [ ] 32. I'm good at planning ahead and making decisions.
- [ ] 33. I'm good at making and keeping friends.
- [ ] 34. I know and feel comfortable around people of different cultural, racial, and/or ethnic backgrounds.
- [ ] 35. I resist negative peer pressure and avoid dangerous situations.
- [ ] 36. I try to resolve conflicts nonviolently.
- [ ] 37. I feel that I have control over many things that happen to me.
- [ ] 38. I feel good about myself.
- [ ] 39. I believe that my life has a purpose.
- [ ] 40. I feel positive about my future.

CHECKLIST FOR PARENTS

Check each statement that's true for you or your teenager. Mentally fill in the blanks with your teenager's name.

❏ 1. I give _____ a lot of love and support.

❏ 2. _____ can come to me for advice and support. We have frequent, in-depth conversations.

❏ 3. _____ knows at least three other adults he/she can go to for advice and support.

❏ 4. Our neighbors encourage and support _____.

❏ 5. _____'s school provides a caring, encouraging environment.

❏ 6. I'm actively involved in helping _____ succeed in school.

❏ 7. _____ feels valued by adults in our community.

❏ 8. _____ is given useful roles and meaningful things to do in our community.

❏ 9. _____ does an hour or more of community service each week.

❏ 10. _____ feels safe at home, at school, and in our neighborhood.

❏ 11. Our family has both clear rules and consequences for behavior. We also monitor each other's whereabouts.

❏ 12. _____'s school has clear rules and consequences for behavior.

❏ 13. Our neighbors take responsibility for monitoring _____'s behavior.

❏ 14. I model positive, responsible behavior, and so do other adults in _____'s life.

❏ 15. _____'s best friends model responsible behavior. They're a good influence.

❏ 16. I encourage _____ to do well, and so do his/her teachers.

❏ 17. _____ spends three or more hours each week in lessons or practice in music, theater, or other arts.

❑ 18. _____ spends three or more hours each week in school or community sports, clubs, or organizations.

❑ 19. _____ spends one or more hours each week in religious services or spiritual activities.

❑ 20. _____ goes out with friends with nothing special to do two or fewer nights each week.

❑ 21. _____ wants to do well in school.

❑ 22. _____ likes to learn new things.

❑ 23. _____ does an hour or more of homework each school day.

❑ 24. _____ cares about his/her school.

❑ 25. _____ spends three or more hours each week reading for pleasure.

❑ 26. _____ believes that it's really important to help other people.

❑ 27. _____ wants to help promote equality and reduce world poverty and hunger.

❑ 28. _____ acts on his/her convictions and stands up for his/her beliefs.

❑ 29. _____ tells the truth—even when it's not easy.

❑ 30. _____ takes personal responsibility for his/her actions and decisions.

❑ 31. _____ believes that it's important for teenagers not to be sexually active or to use alcohol or other drugs.

❑ 32. _____ is good at planning ahead and making decisions.

❑ 33. _____ is good at making and keeping friends.

❑ 34. _____ knows and feels comfortable around people of different cultural, racial, and/or ethnic backgrounds.

❑ 35. _____ resists negative peer pressure and avoids dangerous situations.

❑ 36. _____ tries to resolve conflicts nonviolently.

❑ 37. _____ feels that he/she has control over many things that happen to him/her.

❑ 38. _____ feels good about himself/herself.

❑ 39. _____ believes that his/her life has a purpose.

❑ 40. _____ feels positive about his/her future.

WHY YOU NEED ASSETS

Assets are good for you

Here are eight reasons why. Once you start building your own assets, you'll probably come up with more reasons of your own.

1. Assets form a strong foundation to build your life on. You know what you stand for, what you won't stand for, what you believe in, who's there for you, and what's important to you.

2. They have a positive influence on the choices you make and the actions you take. Assets guide you in deciding what you will and won't do. They guard you against negative pressure from peers, adults, or the media.

3. They help you become more competent, caring, and responsible. You develop real skills you need to succeed. You reach out to others and make a difference in your home, school, community—and the world. You're accountable for your own choices and actions.

4. They increase in value over time—like financial assets.

5. They provide a sense of security. You know who you are; you know your own strengths. Plus some assets actually make your home, school, and neighborhood safer—as well as more friendly, caring places to be.

6. They are resources you can draw on again and again. When you build assets, you build relationships. You become more competent in many areas of your life.

7. They keep you from getting involved in risky behaviors that can seriously affect you now and in the future. You avoid doing things that could limit your psychological, physical, social, or economic well-being.

8. They make you a better person—someone other people look up to, admire, trust, respect, and count on. A person of character.

Assets give you what you might not be getting

Too many teens today. . .

> . . . don't have positive, ongoing relationships—especially relationships with caring adults
> . . . don't have opportunities to play meaningful roles in their communities and develop leadership skills

. . . aren't involved in youth programs, which can and do make a difference in kids' lives

. . . don't have rules and consequences for their behavior

. . . feel disconnected from their families, schools, and communities

. . . aren't learning important social skills they need to succeed in the world (*examples:* how to make plans and decisions, how to make friends, how to feel comfortable with people who are different from them, how to resolve conflicts nonviolently).

More assets mean fewer problem behaviors

Too many teens today are in trouble with alcohol and other drugs. They're sexually active earlier in life, which may lead to teen pregnancy and sexually transmitted diseases. They're becoming more violent—more likely to get into fights, carry weapons, and get hurt or hurt someone else. They're having more school problems; many can't pass basic competency tests. And they're becoming more depressed. Untreated depression is the #1 cause of suicide—and suicide is the third leading cause of death among teens, after unintentional injury and homicide. See what happens to each of these problem behaviors when teens have assets:

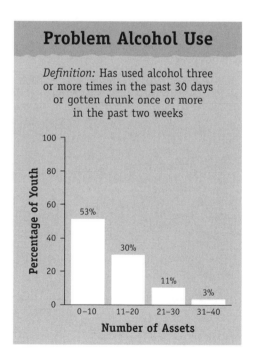

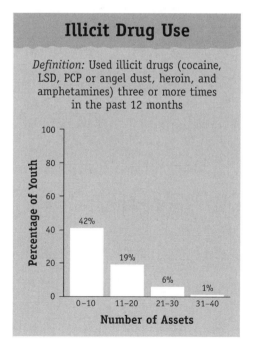

---

* Based on surveys of almost 100,000 6th–12th grade youth in 213 communities across the United States during the 1996–97 school year.

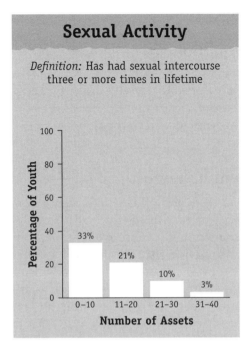

Sexual Activity

Definition: Has had sexual intercourse three or more times in lifetime

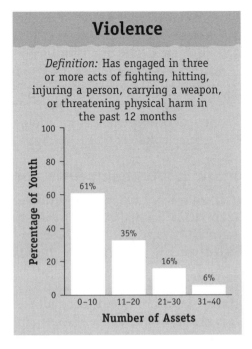

Violence

Definition: Has engaged in three or more acts of fighting, hitting, injuring a person, carrying a weapon, or threatening physical harm in the past 12 months

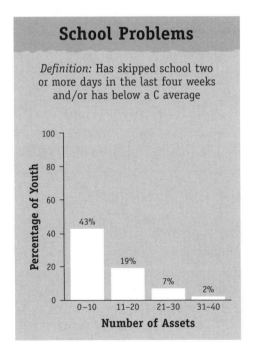

School Problems

Definition: Has skipped school two or more days in the last four weeks and/or has below a C average

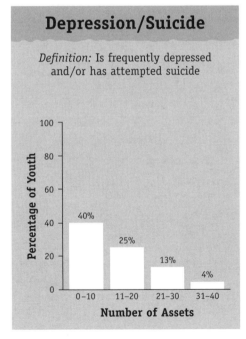

Depression/Suicide

Definition: Is frequently depressed and/or has attempted suicide

More assets mean more positive behaviors

Assets don't just protect you from problems. They also promote positive behaviors—choices and actions that help you to grow and thrive. Here's proof:

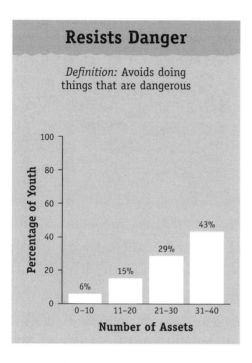

Resists Danger

Definition: Avoids doing things that are dangerous

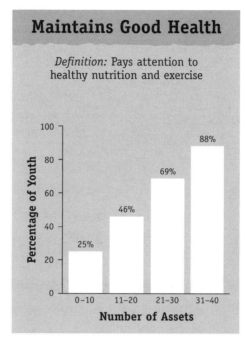

Maintains Good Health

Definition: Pays attention to healthy nutrition and exercise

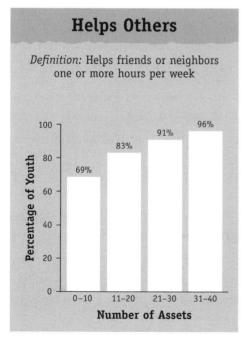

Helps Others

Definition: Helps friends or neighbors one or more hours per week

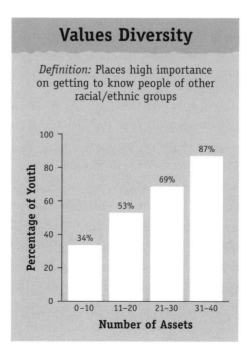

Values Diversity

Definition: Places high importance on getting to know people of other racial/ethnic groups

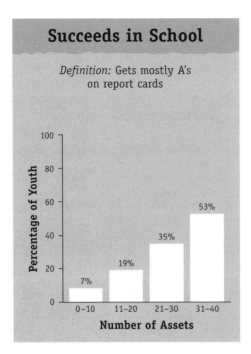

Succeeds in School

Definition: Gets mostly A's on report cards

Percentage of Youth

- 0–10: 7%
- 11–20: 19%
- 21–30: 35%
- 31–40: 53%

Number of Assets

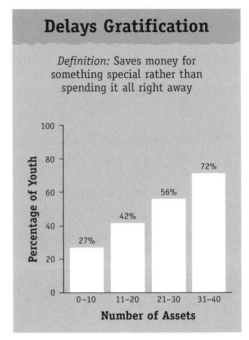

Delays Gratification

Definition: Saves money for something special rather than spending it all right away

Percentage of Youth

- 0–10: 27%
- 11–20: 42%
- 21–30: 56%
- 31–40: 72%

Number of Assets

Why you need to build your own assets

It's possible that your parents, school, and community know it's important to build assets in children and teens. Many communities across the country are already doing this. But there are still too many that aren't involved or haven't heard of the assets. In towns, suburbs, and cities across America, teens are struggling to build their lives without a strong foundation.

Most people realize that caring families, neighborhoods, and schools, high expectations, youth programs, positive role models, reasonable rules and consequences, the ability to make friends, and other assets are good for kids, so why don't more kids have them? Here are some reasons to consider (and maybe talk about with your parents and other people you know):

• Most adults no longer think it's their responsibility to get involved in the lives of children outside their own family.

• Parents are less available for kids because of demands outside the home and cultural norms that undervalue parenting.

• Adults and institutions (schools, organizations, etc.) have become uncomfortable about articulating values or enforcing rules and consequences.

• Society has become more and more age-segregated, providing fewer opportunities for meaningful relationships between people of different ages.

• Socializing systems (families, schools, faith communities, etc.) have become more isolated, competitive, and suspicious of each other.

• The mass media have become influential shapers of kids' attitudes, norms, and values—and let's face it, they don't have your best interests in mind.

• As problems—and solutions—have become more complex, more of the responsibility for young people has been turned over to professionals.

For decades, Americans have invested huge amounts of time, energy, and resources (people, programs, money) to combat the symptoms of these social and cultural changes—to fix the problems. Has it worked? What do you think? If it had, you wouldn't be reading this book. You'd already have the assets you need to succeed in life and shape your future.

Most young people Search Institute surveyed have an average of 18 assets out of 40. Once you add up your assets, you may find that you have more or fewer. The specific number isn't all that important. What's most important is taking time to reflect on how you can gain more—or most—of the assets, since kids with many assets are most likely to be successful in life.

Why you need to build assets for other children and teens

Throughout this book, you'll find suggestions for building assets with—and for—other people you know, including your friends, classmates, younger brothers and sisters, and neighborhood kids. Why should you bother? Because . . .

. . . it's the right thing to do. As human beings, we're responsible for each other—and for giving back to our community. Building assets for others is a great way to do this.

. . . it improves your friendships. If your friends have more assets, they're more likely to influence you positively rather than negatively.

. . . it's your future. Your friends today will be your coworkers, leaders, and neighbors tomorrow. If you help them build assets now, your whole community will benefit later.

. . . it's rewarding and satisfying to help other people. Plus you have a lot to give.

. . . it's a win-win situation. Building assets for others builds assets for you.

FACTS ABOUT ASSET BUILDING

1. Everyone needs assets. Including you. All kids can benefit from more assets than they already have.

2. Everyone can build assets. Including you. All adults, teens, and children can get involved and play a role, large or small. The more people who do, the better it is for you and everyone else you know.

3. Relationships are key. Relationships—between you and your parents, you and other caring adults, you and your friends, and you and younger children—are essential to asset building. That's why so many ideas in this book suggest talking with, working with, and brainstorming with other people. You need them and they need you.

4. Asset building is an ongoing process. Start today; keep it up through high school and college and your life as an adult. While you'll need to really think about assets now, because you're probably not familiar with them, in time asset building will become a habit.

5. Consistent messages are important. You need to receive consistent messages about what's important and what's expected from your family, school, community, the media, and other sources. You also need to send yourself consistent messages—about what's important to you, what you value, why you're building assets, and what you hope to gain from it.

6. Intentional redundancy is important. Continue reinforcing the assets over the years and in all areas of your life. This means, for example, that if you're honest with your friends, you're honest with your family, too.

BUILDING
EXTERNAL ASSETS

20 good things you need in your life and how to get them

SUPPORT

These assets are about having people in your life who love you, care about you, and are there for you in good times and bad (and the times in between). They're about having places in your life where you feel cared for, supported, comfortable, and welcome.

The support assets are:

1. Family Support
2. Positive Family Communication
3. Other Adult Relationships
4. Caring Neighborhood
5. Caring School Climate
6. Parent Involvement in Schooling

64% of the youth
we surveyed have this
asset in their lives.

FAMILY SUPPORT

You feel loved and supported in your family.

At Home

Spend time with your family.

Try to eat at least one meal together every day. Try to set aside one evening a week (or one afternoon a weekend) to spend with your family. Watch a video, go to a movie, take a bike ride, play a game, work on a family project, or whatever you enjoy doing together. You're growing up fast, and it won't be long before you leave home. Most parents feel as if they rank low on their teenager's list of priorities, and they may be right. Your parents will be pleased when you make time for them . . . and you'll benefit, too.

FACT:

Family closeness is good for you!

A study of 133 families found that youth who have close relationships with their parents are more likely than other youth to be emotionally healthy. The study also found that youth develop autonomy within the context of close bonds. To put this in plain English: It's okay to be and stay close to your family. This won't keep you from becoming independent. In fact, you'll be better prepared for life on your own because you'll be emotionally stronger and more together.

Source: *Journal of Early Adolescence* 16 (1996), pages 274–300.

Get physical.

Many teens don't feel comfortable hugging, kissing, or touching their parents or other family members. It's *your* body, and you have the right to decide who can and can't touch you. But physical affection is one way people show love and support for each other. A hug, a goodnight kiss, or a pat on the back feels good and helps keep families close.

If you really don't want your parents to hug or kiss you, tell them how you feel. You're separating from your parents in many ways, and your feelings aren't weird. On the other hand, you might decide that some touching is okay—with a few ground rules. *Examples:* "You can kiss me when I come home from school if you want, but not if I bring a friend home with me." Or "Hugging is okay, but not in front of my softball team."

Get verbal.

When was the last time you said "I love you" to your mom or dad? Or the last time they said it to you? Maybe your family talks freely about feelings, and "I love you" is part of your everyday vocabulary. Or maybe not; many people have a hard time expressing emotions. If your family is the strong, silent type, make a few small moves and see what happens. Toss off a "Later! Love you!" as you race out the door. Or leave a note for your mom or dad signed "XXOO" or "Love." Or when one of your parents does you a favor, say something like "You know, this is one thing I love about you—you're always willing to help me." It's possible that your parents grew up without hearing "I love you" from *their* parents. They may need some training.

Practice random acts of kindness.

Do a chore that isn't your job. Help out when you haven't been asked. Surprise a parent or sibling with a thoughtful word or gesture. You'll be amazed at how powerful these little "random acts" can be—and how good they make you feel. If you're not used to doing things for other people just because, this may take some planning (and practice). Start by writing a short list of simple things you might do for other family members, then work your way down the list. See what happens.

Let family members know when you feel loved and supported.

When family members do a "right" in your eyes, let them know you noticed. Tell them what *words* they said that made a difference to you. Tell them what *actions* they took that helped you feel cared for and loved.

Ask for what you need.

Parents aren't mind readers. Sometimes your parents won't know what you need unless you spell it out for them. Be polite, even if what you need is for them to leave you alone. *(Example:* "I had a bad day, and I don't feel like talking right now. Maybe later, but for now I need to be by myself.") Or maybe what you need is company. *(Example:* "Is it okay if I just sit here for a while?") Or maybe what you need is for them to ease up on their expectations. *(Example:* "When you tell me to ace my math test, it stresses me out. I need you to know that I'll do my best, and to accept the times when I don't do as well as you want me to.")

Do your part to make your home a warm, caring, comfortable, fun place to be.

Try compliments instead of insults, helping instead of teasing, thinking "we" instead of "me." Show some affection, show some interest, listen when other people want to talk, and don't zone out for hours in front of the TV or hole up in your room because it shuts people out. Treat the people in your family the way you wish they would treat you. The effort is worth it.

FUN THINGS TO DO 5 WITH YOUR FAMILY

1. Make a family tree. Gather information about as many family members as you can, going as far back in time as possible, and arrange it on a chart or "tree." Interview family members in person, by phone, by mail and email to get dates and details. Depending on how far you and your family want to go with this project, you might check out the genealogy sections of public libraries; or search town, city, and state historical societies. The National Genealogical Society may also be of help with your research into the past. Write the organization at: National Genealogical Society, 3108 Columbia Pike, Suite 300, Arlington, VA 22204. You may also call or visit them online: 1-800-473-0060; *www.ngsgenealogy.org.*

2. Make a family history scrapbook. Fill it with pictures and other memorabilia—your parents' report cards (and yours), birth announcements, memories. Include a few pages about each family member. Update your scrapbook every few months.

3. Make a family timeline. Note important events and dates in the life of your family.

CONTINUED ON NEXT PAGE...

4. Make a family time capsule. Include information about your family, a special message from each family member (perhaps a secret wish, hope, or dream), a copy of that day's newspaper, current photographs, and whatever else you can think of. Store it in a safe place and plan to open it in a year or two years.

5. Start a new family tradition. *Ideas:* Offer to make dinner one day a month; plant a vegetable garden together in the spring; have an "unbirthday party" once a year; have a family volunteer day; have a video weekend once a month, during which everyone chooses a video and the whole family watches it together.

Adapted from *The Families Book* by Arlene Erlbach. Free Spirit Publishing Inc., 1996, pages 62–89. Used with permission.

At School

Find out what your school is doing to support family closeness and togetherness. Does it schedule open houses, family nights, and other events that welcome families? Does it feature speakers who talk about family life and issues? Are students allowed (and encouraged) to attend school conferences with their parents? Check with your school counselor, social worker, or principal. Offer to help.

In Your Community

● Be polite to your parents, especially in public. Show that you're proud to be with them. Be a role model for your friends and other teens.

● Learn what your community is doing to strengthen families. Are there workshops on positive parenting? Do community education programs include parenting classes? Does your community have at least one family crisis hotline? Check with your community center, mayor's office, or the Community Affairs representative at your local newspaper, radio station, or TV station. Encourage the media to publicize ways in which your community is family-friendly.

Assets in Action

In **St. Louis Park, Minnesota,** the Children First team developed tip sheets suggesting activities for parents and kids to do together. Called "Catch 22," they invited parents to "catch" at least 22 minutes each day with their children. The tip sheets found their way into kids' backpacks, report cards, and school conference material throughout the school year.

In **Moorhead, Minnesota,** *the Moorhead Healthy Community Initiative started a program called Family Meal Time that encourages families to sit down together, turn off the TV, and talk about the events of the day or family history.*

In **Kennebunk, Maine,** *Jane Endres started a parent education program, became a mentor to girls at risk, and launched a foundation. Funding for the foundation came, in part, from money that would have paid for the college education of her daughter, who died tragically at age 17. Her eight-week parent education program, which is free to parents of high school students, teaches ways to build relationships with teenagers.*

In Your Faith Community

Find out what your faith community is doing to encourage family closeness and togetherness. Does the youth program sponsor family nights? What about family dinners, retreats, and other special programs? Ask your youth leader. Offer to help.

Assets in Action

*Beth El Synagogue in **Minneapolis, Minnesota,** has made family support a focal point for its youth programming. The congregation offers workshops and study sessions for parents and sponsors mini-retreats for families.*

With Your Friends

● Support and encourage each other's efforts to build loving, supportive families. If you're making plans and one of you says "Sorry, that's family night for me," resist the urge to tease or groan. Reschedule instead.

● Get to know each other's families. Invite each other to family dinners; bring a friend along on family vacations; arrange group get-togethers that include family members.

● Talk with each other about family problems and possible solutions. Start by agreeing that what's said in the group stays in the group. (*Exception:* If someone reveals a serious problem—abuse, alcoholism, depression—get help right away from an adult you trust.)

● If a friend tells you that his or her family isn't supportive or is going through an especially difficult period, invite him or her to spend more time with your family.

 **IMPORTANT:** *If your family doesn't provide a loving, encouraging, caring, and warm place for you to grow, seek the support you need in other places— your school, neighborhood, community, faith community, or youth organization. Ask your school counselor or social worker, youth group leader, or religious leader for suggestions. Don't give up!*

RESOURCES

For you:

Bringing Up Parents: The Teenager's Handbook by Alex J. Packer, Ph.D. (Minneapolis: Free Spirit Publishing, 1992). Straight talk and specific suggestions on how teens can take the initiative to improve family relationships, resolve conflicts with parents, and help create a healthier, happier home environment.

For your parents:

Get Out Of My Life—but First Could You Drive Me and Cheryl to the Mall? A Parent's Guide to the New Teenager by Anthony E. Wolf (New York: Noonday Press, 1992). A fresh perspective on teenagers, full of insight and humor.

Wonderful Ways to Love a Teen . . . Even When It Seems Impossible by Judy Ford (Berkeley, CA: Conari Press, 1996). Ford is a family therapist who has worked with teens and families for almost 30 years. Her thoughtful, practical advice will help parents build loving bonds with their teenagers and repair rocky relationships.

26% of the youth
we surveyed have this
asset in their lives.

POSITIVE FAMILY COMMUNICATION

**You can go to your parents for advice and support.
You talk with each other often about many different
topics—including serious issues.**

At Home

Just do it.

Talk to your parents every day. Tell them about your day. Make it a point to tell them about *one* interesting, funny, sad, frustrating, silly, or strange thing that happened to you. Then ask them about *their* day.

Even if you don't feel like it, come out of your room and have a ten-minute conversation with your parents each night. Try this for a week and see if it makes a difference.

Talk about their favorite subject.

Most people love talking about themselves. Talk with your parents about their growing-up years. Ask a lot of questions. *Examples:* "What did you think of your parents when you were a teenager?" "What are some of your best memories of your parents?" "What did you talk about in your family?" "What do you wish you had talked about?" "What did you like best about your family? Least?" "What do you think of the way your parents raised you?" Afterward, think about your experience. How did it feel to ask your parents these questions? Did you learn anything that surprised you? Do you understand your parents a little better now?

FACT:

If you want your parents to listen to you, you're not alone!

The Colorado Psychiatric Society came up with this essay topic for a statewide contest for high school students:

> *Teenagers today continue to be the victims of psychiatric crises—suicide, depression, eating disorders and drug addiction, to name a few. What are the issues behind this that adults need to understand in order to be of more help?*

The Society expected to hear about the dangers of peer pressure, or about how parents interfere in the lives of their kids. Instead, the nearly universal response was "We want our parents to listen to us." As one student wrote, "Just talk to me . . . . Make time in your busy schedule to learn more about me."

Source: Scripps Howard News Service, *Minneapolis Star/Tribune,* July 21, 1997.

Talk about the assets.

Make a copy of the list of 40 assets (see pages 335–336) and post it on the refrigerator. Talk about the assets with your parents and within your family as a whole. Which assets do family members think are the strongest in your family? Which assets does your family need to work on?

Write it down.

Write a letter to your parents about a topic you really want to talk about but don't feel comfortable bringing up. You can decide later if you want to give your parents the letter; for now, just write it. Afterward, think about how it felt to write your letter. What do you think would happen if you actually gave it to your parents? What's the worst thing that could happen? The best?

Accept their limitations.

Some parents simply can't discuss certain things with their children. They'd rather be boiled in oil than talk about s-e-x, or they're too uptight to talk about feelings, alcohol and other drugs, HIV/AIDS, violence, gangs, depression, teen suicide, and other issues you really need to talk about with *someone*. If this describes your parents, find other adults to talk to. See Asset #3: Other Adult Relationships.

Be there for siblings who want to talk.

Build assets on the home front by making yourself available to your pesky sister and bratty brother. (*Tip:* Watch for hints. A child who hangs around usually wants to talk.) What if you're in the middle of something? Arrange a time when you can talk—soon. Then really *listen.* Never label a child's opinions, beliefs, feelings, or experiences silly, stupid, babyish, lame, or wrong; it's demoralizing and hurtful.

Learn what positive communication is all about.

Read books about communication skills (your librarian can help you find some). Take a class on communication, or suggest that your family take a class together. Remember that developing effective communication skills takes time and practice.

TIPS FOR TALKING TO PARENTS

1. Choose your time wisely. Don't try to start a serious conversation when your parents are obviously 1) cranky, 2) stressed out, 3) busy doing something else, or 4) asleep.

2. Be respectful. Your parents will be much more willing to hear you out if they don't feel like they're being attacked or ridiculed.

3. Speak precisely and concisely. Say what you mean and don't take forever to say it.

4. When you approach your parents with a problem, come prepared with suggestions for solving it. Why should they do all the work? (Make sure that you present these as suggestions, not demands.)

5. Make a genuine effort to see their point of view. Put yourself in their shoes. Try to empathize with them. You're not the only person with an opinion, a brain, or feelings.

6. Watch your body language. Glaring, turning your back, slouching, shaking a fist, pointing a finger, sneering, gagging, and rolling your eyes are not recommended.

7. Keep your voice down, please. Nobody likes to be yelled at.

8. Avoid "you statements." "You don't understand me" or "You never let me do what I want" don't help to get your point across. Instead, use "I statements"—like "I guess I haven't done a very good job of explaining myself to you" or "I feel like you don't trust me to make decisions."

CONTINUED ON NEXT PAGE...

9. Pay attention. You'll be more effective if you look at your parents (not at the wall or out the window) while they're speaking.

10. Be willing to compromise. Give a little and you might get a lot.

Adapted from *The Gifted Kids' Survival Guide: A Teen Handbook* by Judy Galbraith, M.A., and Jim Delisle, Ph.D. Free Spirit Publishing Inc., 1996, page 235. Used with permission.

At School

● Pull your parents into your homework assignments. If you're doing a report on the '80s, ask them what life was like back then. Or tape an interview with them as part of an oral history project.

● Find out what your school is doing to promote family communication. Do they have brochures and other printed materials available on alcohol and other drugs, HIV/AIDS, teen pregnancy, sexual behavior, and similarly touchy topics? Many parents really *do* want to talk with their teens about these subjects, but they don't know where to start or what to say. They may even be ill-informed.

● Bring home the skills you learn in your composition, speech, and communication classes. Try them out on your family.

Assets in Action

One family in **Minneapolis, Minnesota,** *holds a family meeting every Sunday. They discuss how their assigned chores went during that week, make choices for chores the next week, and talk about how upcoming events that week might affect the family schedule. Leadership rotates weekly so everyone has an opportunity to feel he or she has some power and control in the family. Even the eight-year-old has learned to conduct a meeting, using a simple agenda (the list of chores) and minutes (a notebook to record decisions and ideas). Issues that need a hard look, like episodes of treating each other disrespectfully, are talked about at the family meeting, when tempers have cooled. The teenagers often use the setting to renegotiate boundaries or rules they feel are too restrictive.*

In Your Community

● Talk to your parents when you're out with them—at a restaurant, the mall, or wherever. Ask their opinions of the menu, the clerk, or the movies at the multiplex. Form the habit of chitchat in public and it might get easier to talk about serious stuff at home.

● See if your community offers classes or workshops on communication skills—at local schools, community centers, libraries, or other places. If not, suggest that classes be made available. Offer to help.

● Ask the people at your community center to sponsor discussion nights for parents and teens. Work with them to publicize the topics in advance. Encourage them to build in time for conversation during activities and special events that bring youth and parents together.

In Your Faith Community

● As you plan your youth program's upcoming events, include parent-teen get-togethers that encourage conversation—dinners, retreats, discussion groups.

● Poll the youth in your faith community to learn what they'd like to talk about with their parents and other adults. Publish a "Hot Teen Topics" list in the worship bulletin, with the suggestion that parents talk with their teens about these issues.

● Within your youth group, talk with each other about communication in your families. What seems to work? What doesn't? Share insights and advice.

With Your Friends

● Talk with each other about communication in your families. What seems to work? What doesn't? Share insights and advice.

● Plan events that include each other's families. *Example:* Try a progressive dinner (salad at your house, the main course at another friend's house, dessert at a third friend's house). Pick conversation topics for each course.

RESOURCES

For your parents:

You and Your Adolescent: A Parent's Guide for Ages 10 to 20 by Laurence Steinberg and Ann Levine (New York: HarperCollins, 1997). The revised and updated edition of a standard reference on adolescent development. Check out the chapter on family communication and problem solving.

Grounded for Life?! Stop Blowing Your Fuse and Start Communicating with Your Teenager by Louise Felton Tracy (Seattle, WA: Parenting Press, 1994). Practical advice from a middle-school counselor and mother of six.

OTHER ADULT RELATIONSHIPS

**You know at least three adults (besides your parents)
you can go to for advice and support. You talk with each other
often about many different topics—including serious issues.**

At Home

Take stock and take action.

Do you already know three or more adults besides your parents you can go to for advice and support? If you do, take good care of those relationships. (Pick up the phone and say hi, or write a note to each person saying how much you appreciate him or her.) If you don't, take action. There are adults around you who would be flattered by your interest.

Make a list.

Make a list of adults you respect, admire, and trust—or might if you knew them better. What about a teacher? The school counselor? The youth leader in your club or faith community? A neighbor? A friend's parent? An aunt, uncle, grandparent, or cousin? If you can't think of anyone, you need to meet new people. A good place to start is with a youth program—an adult-led team, club, or organization. See Asset #18: Youth Programs.

Reach out.

Once you've made your list, circle *one* name. During the next two weeks, do *one* thing to let that person know he or she is important to you. Call, visit, or send a note or email. Keep it simple. Say thanks for something nice the person said or did, give a compliment, or ask for help or advice. (*Examples:* "I like that book we just read. Can you recommend more like it?" "I'm thinking about trying out for the swim team. Got any suggestions?" "Those cookies you made last week were great. I'd love the recipe.") Choose a different adult to reach out to each month. You can always go back and add new names to your list.

FACT:

Other adults won't replace your parents!

Some parents feel threatened when their teenagers go outside the family for friendship, conversation, and advice. If you think your parents might feel this way, offer reassurance: According to experts, strong relationships with nonfamily adults typically *don't* compete with strong relationships with parents. Some research suggests that the two go together.

Source: *Journal of Early Adolescence* 16 (1996), pages 365–389.

Get a mentor.

What's a mentor? Here's a definition from the Points of Light Institute:*

A mentor is any caring adult who makes an active, positive contribution to the life of a child who is not his or her own. It's someone who has found ways to succeed in life—and cares enough to pass those lessons along. A friend, a guide, a coach.

Why get a mentor? Because it's one of the best things you can do for yourself.

● A 1995 study for Big Brothers Big Sisters of America found that young people with mentors are 46 percent less likely to start using illegal drugs, 27 percent less likely to start using alcohol, 53 percent less likely to skip school, more confident of their school performance, and less likely to hit someone. Plus they get along better with their families.

● According to a 1989 Louis Harris Poll, 59 percent of mentored teens get better grades and 73 percent raise their goals.

● A 1994 study from the Center for Intergenerational Learning at Temple University showed that young people with older mentors (average age: 65) have more self-confidence and personal skills.

---

* For more about the Points of Light Institute, see page 84.

HOW TO FIND A MENTOR

TIPS FROM THE NATIONAL MENTORING PARTNERSHIP

1. Think about what you want help with. A mentor can:

- Listen to you and help you stay motivated to succeed
- Help you with your studies
- Help you plan for your education
- Help you find a job
- Help you learn a particular skill, like how to fix a car

2. Make a list of all the people you know who might be able to be your mentor or help you find a mentor. Family members, neighbors, teachers, coaches, ministers or recreation center staff are all options to ask for advice. Here is what to look for:

- Someone who believes in you and will go to bat for you
- Someone who will tell you the truth
- Someone who is not afraid of hard work
- Someone who cares about doing the right thing
- Someone you can trust

3. Here is where to look for adults who might agree to be your mentor:

- In your neighborhood
- Where your parents, relatives or neighbors work
- At school
- At recreation centers
- In your faith community
- Through youth service organizations such as Big Brothers Big Sisters; Boys Clubs; Girls, Inc.; Cities in Schools; Camp Fire Boys and Girls; 4-H; YMCA/YWCA; Boy Scouts; Girl Scouts; Junior Achievement

4. Do it! Ask someone to be your mentor!

- Tell them what you want from a mentor
- Tell them why you think they would be a good mentor
- Ask if they would be willing to be your mentor, or to help you find one
- Suggest a trial period—one month, for instance—for both of you to see if it works
- If at first you don't succeed, try again. Don't give up and don't get discouraged. You may hear a "no" from four different people before you hear that "yes" from person number five!

© 1996 The One to One Partnership, Inc. All rights reserved. Reprinted with permission.

At School

- Join a group or club that interests you. Get to know the adult leaders or sponsors.

- Get to know a teacher, a counselor, or another adult who seems friendly and interested.

- Start noticing the adults you see every day—secretaries, other teachers, cafeteria workers, custodians, parent volunteers. Take time to talk with them.

Assets in Action

*Through the Listening Post program in **Denver, Colorado,** senior citizens visit local schools weekly during the lunch hour, and kids can talk to them about anything they want. Many friendships have formed over the years.*

In Your Community

- With one of your parents, visit three households in your neighborhood and say hello. Learn your neighbors' names and favorite activities. Ask when their birthdays are, then hand-deliver cards on those days.

- Invite an adult to one of your sporting or musical events. Afterward, go out for a treat.

- Read one of your favorite short stories to an adult. Or arrange for you and an adult to read one chapter a week from a novel, then get together to discuss it.

- Make a friend in a nursing home. Visit weekly (or write a note when you can't make it). Read newspapers aloud or just chat.

- Do some of your neighbors have dogs? Choose one you'd like to get to know better (the neighbor or the dog), then ask if you can go dog walking together once a week.

- Teach a computer-phobic adult how to play a computer game or use email.

- Befriend an adult who likes to work on cars. Offer to wash his or her car and help with maintenance. Learn about car care and repair.

- Get involved in service projects in your neighborhood. See assets #9: Service to Others and #26: Caring.

Assets in Action

In **LaCrosse, Wisconsin,** *youth and adults cochair committees that are developing asset-building plans. They spend time together and form relationships. Members created sweatshirts to wear in support of the effort.*

Paul Miller of **Minneapolis, Minnesota,** *learned to be a mentor when his 12-year-old neighbor Anna Navarro asked for help with a science fair project. Together they embarked on a six-year journey that brought Navarro to international competition and presentations before Nobel Laureates. By the time Navarro's six award-winning projects were completed, Miller and his wife Felicia had converted their basement into a science lab and their kitchen into a strategy room. Navarro won dozens of state, national, and international awards for her projects; Paul Miller contributed up to 20 hours a week for six months of each year they worked together. "If I had known up front what I was getting into," he says, "I might have been afraid of doing it. But when you see what a child can do, it's worth it."*

In Your Faith Community

● Reach out to other adults in your faith community. Get to know three or more.

● Suggest that everyone wear name tags every week—children, teens, and adults.

● Learn what your faith community does to build relationships between adults and teens. Maybe programs and opportunities already exist. If so, get involved. If not, talk with an adult leader about starting one or more of these:

— intergenerational programs (*examples:* educational events, choir, plays)
— intergenerational social activities (*examples:* softball games, picnics, festivals)
— worship services that involve people of all ages
— mentoring programs
— opportunities for youth, parents, and other adults to spend time together (*examples:* classes, retreats, discussion groups).

Assets in Action

At St. Luke Presbyterian Church in **Minnetonka, Minnesota,** *a program called Faith Partners pairs children and youths with adults outside their families to build relationships, create support through prayer and faith sharing, and have fun. Participants fill out a form with their name, age, prayer requests, hobbies and interests. The forms are collected and reviewed by the adult cofounders of the program, and a match is made. Information about each, along with a list of 30 ideas for being a Faith Partner, is mailed out shortly after—then it's up to the partners to make the next move. The commitment runs from October through May. As 15-year-old Katie says, "It's been nice to get to know some older people in our church and make connections."*

Each year, Mayflower Congregational Church in **Minneapolis, Minnesota,** *has a Senior Friend program in which an older member or couple "adopts" a Sunday school class and stays with it until it graduates. The seniors bring treats to the classes or read stories. On special days, kids sit with their "grandparents" during worship service. If a Senior Friend becomes hospitalized or moves to a nursing home, the children send cards or visit.*

With Your Friends

● Spend time in your friends' homes. Talk with their parents. Ask them about their interests; tell them about yours.

● Ask your parents if you can invite a friend and his or her family to your home for dinner. Offer to help cook and clean up.

● Together with a friend, "adopt" a senior citizen you can visit on a regular basis.

● Play "Who would you talk to if. . .?" Name issues or situations like the ones listed below. Decide who you'd talk to in each case. If you can't think of anyone, maybe someone else will have a suggestion.

Who would you talk to if . . .

. . . you just wanted to talk?
. . . you wanted to talk about dating and relationships?
. . . you wanted to talk about what to do after graduation?
. . . you needed to talk about getting in trouble with the police?
. . . you or a friend got pregnant or got someone pregnant?
. . . you just wanted to hang out with someone?
. . . you needed to borrow money?
. . . you had questions about alcohol or other drugs?
. . . you just got your report card and it's b-a-d?
. . . you needed to figure out where you stand on an issue?
. . . you were feeling pressured to do something you don't want to do?

RESOURCES

For everyone:

Creating Intergenerational Community by Jolene L. Roehlkepartain (Minneapolis: Search Institute, 1996). Includes 75 ideas for ways individuals and groups can build relationships between people of different ages.

Together for Tomorrow: Building Community Through Intergenerational Dialogue by James V. Gambone (Crystal Bay, MN: Elder Eye Press, 1997). Describes a creative process to help all generations learn to understand and respect each other.

Mentor/National Mentoring Partnership
1680 Duke Street, 2nd Floor
Alexandria, VA 22314
(703) 224-2200
www.mentoring.org
A resource for mentors and mentoring initiatives nationwide, the National Mentoring Partnership forges partnerships with communities and organizations to promote mentoring. It also educates youth and adults about how to find and become mentors.

For grandparents:

Wonderful Ways to Love a Grandchild by Judy Ford (Berkeley, CA: Conari Press, 1997). More than 60 inspiring suggestions for how grandparents can actively participate in their grandchildren's lives, whether they live down the block or across the country.

For teachers, counselors, and youth group leaders:

The Essential Guide to Talking with Teens by Jean Sunde Peterson, Ph.D. (Minneapolis: Free Spirit Publishing, 2007). These ready-to-use guided discussions are proven ways to reach out to youth.

Asset #4

40% of the youth
we surveyed have this
asset in their lives.

CARING NEIGHBORHOOD

**You have neighbors who support you,
encourage you, and care about you.**

At Home

Make a neighborhood map.

With your family, make a map of your neighborhood. If you live in a house,
draw the houses on your block; if you live in an apartment building, draw the
apartments on your floor or in your building. Make a box to represent each
household. In each box, write the names of the people and pets who live there.
If you're not sure of their names, describe what you know about the occupants.
Example: "Apartment 12A: man, woman, teenage boy, little girl, big white dog."

Afterward, talk about your map. How many neighbors do you know? What do
your neighbors know about you and your family? How do you feel about your
neighbors? Which seem friendly? Which don't?

Make a family plan.

Brainstorm specific things you can do as a family to get to know your neighbors,
then make a plan to do them. Following are 10 ideas to start with; try them or
come up with your own.

41

WAYS TO GET TO KNOW YOUR NEIGHBORS

IDEAS TO TRY WITH YOUR FAMILY

1. Introduce yourselves to neighbors you meet on the street, in the park, at neighborhood stores, in the hallways or entryway of your apartment building. Learn their names. Then, whenever you see them, smile at them and greet them by name. *Tip:* Be sure to ask permission before calling adults by their first names.

2. Revive the tradition of welcoming new neighbors with a plate of cookies or a cake. Or bring some cookies to any neighbor you'd like to know better.

3. Each month, choose one neighbor you'd like to visit. Prepare a few questions to use as conversation starters. (*Examples:* "What do you like best about our neighborhood?" "What do you like to do in your spare time?") You might also ask questions based on what you already know about that person. (*Examples:* "It seems like you're always building something. What are you building now?" "You ride your bike a lot. Where do you like to ride?")

4. Invite a different neighbor for dinner once a month. Or take a day trip together. *Examples:* Go to the zoo, a museum, a nature center, an auto show, or an antiques mall.

5. Work with your neighbors to plan an event that will bring people together. *Examples:* a block party or neighborhood cleanup; a potluck picnic or cookout; a Fourth of July parade or fall festival; a neighborhood yard sale; a safe Halloween party for kids.

6. Start a new neighborhood group or club. Be creative. What about an art group or music group? A bartering club? (*Example:* Neighbors exchange an hour of baby-sitting for an hour of lawn mowing.) A talent swap? (*Examples:* A neighbor offers a bread-making class; a Spanish-speaking teen teaches words and phrases to interested neighbors; computer-savvy kids teach adults how to surf the Internet.) Or join an existing group, club, or association.

7. Find ways to serve in your neighborhood as a family. Start by thinking about individual neighbors or families who could use a hand, and offer to help. (Don't forget seniors and singles.) Then broaden your thinking to include your whole neighborhood. Is there a park that needs tending? Graffiti that needs painting over? A vacant lot that could be turned into a neighborhood garden?

8. Start a neighborhood newsletter. Work with other families to gather information about the events and people in your neighborhood; invite neighbors (kids included) to contribute articles, stories, and drawings. Have kids or teen do the desktop publishing; form a group of neighborhood youth to distribute the newsletter door-to-door.

CONTINUED ON NEXT PAGE...

9. Become a "mentor family" to provide support and role modeling for a family that's struggling.

10. Work with your neighbors to draw up a neighborhood contract committing all adults to look out for kids. Your contract might include simple statements like "I commit to being a good role model for kids on my block," "I commit to setting good boundaries with youth," and "I commit to being a good partner with parents of kids in my neighborhood."

Assets in Action

In **Minneapolis, Minnesota,** *Mayor Sharon Sayles Belton makes it a priority to spend time with young people in her neighborhood. "Every other weekend or so, I make time in my schedule just to be home with my kids. They invite their friends from the neighborhood over, and pretty soon I've got a whole bunch of kids in my living room. I play LEGOs with them or watch a movie. But most of all, I talk to them and I listen to what they say. And that day, I'm not the mayor; I'm just a mother. I can't tell you how good I feel when I drive down the street in my neighborhood and see the kids waiting for the bus and they wave and say hi."*

In **St. Louis Park, Minnesota,** *neighbors involved in the Children First initiative invite young people into their homes to bake cookies together, play basketball in the driveway, and do other activities.*

At School

● Ask your teachers to assign projects that encourage students to get to know their neighbors. *Examples:* Interview a neighbor, then give an oral report to the class about what you learned. Or create a photo essay about the people in your neighborhood.

● As a class, brainstorm ways to promote caring in your neighborhoods. Choose ideas to try, then report on the results.

● Encourage your neighbors to volunteer in the schools. (*Examples:* Seniors might visit as lunchtime listeners, sitting at the cafeteria tables and talking with students.) Or invite them to concerts, plays, and other special events at your school.

● Find ways for student groups or clubs to serve your school neighborhood— even if many or most students come from other neighborhoods. Contact a neighborhood group or association and ask how you can help.

Assets in Action

In **Los Angeles, California,** *neighbors living near the University of Southern California's University Park campus keep their eyes on children as they walk to and from school. Volunteers in the Kids Watch program spend time outdoors from 8 A.M. to 9 A.M. and from 3 P.M. to 4 P.M.*

In Your Community

● Be friendly toward your neighbors. Smile and say hi when you see them; spend time talking with them; offer to help a neighbor who needs help (carrying groceries, shoveling snow, weeding a garden, painting a fence). Hold the elevator for a neighbor you see coming down the hall.

● Get to know the kids on your block or in your building. See "55 Ways to Show Kids You Care" on page 66.

● Introduce kids in your neighborhood to adults you know in your neighborhood.

● Be aware that some adults are intimidated by groups of kids, especially teenagers. If you and several friends are walking down the street and you see a neighbor you know, stop and say hi. If you're walking toward each other, don't make your neighbor walk around you. Move out of the way so he or she can pass.

FACT:

Caring neighborhoods are safer neighborhoods!

A study of 343 neighborhoods in Chicago found lower rates of violence in urban neighborhoods where there's a strong sense of community and values, and where most adults are willing to intervene in the lives of children—to stop acts like truancy, graffiti painting, and street-corner "hanging" by teenagers.

Source: R. Sampson, S. Raudenbush, and F. Earls, "Neighborhood and violent crime," *Science* 277 (August 15, 1997).

● Survey your neighbors about an issue important to the neighborhood. This is a great opportunity to meet people face-to-face. *Important:* Go with a parent or friend.

● Attend neighborhood meetings so adults know that you care about your neighborhood as much as they do. Participate in activities sponsored by the neighborhood association. Your presence will encourage adults to keep youth in mind when making neighborhood policy decisions.

● Organize informal activities (such as pick-up basketball) for neighborhood youth.

● Start a New Games group in your neighborhood or building. Once a month, adults and youth get together to play noncompetitive, cooperative games. If you don't know any, ask a librarian for help. Several books were published in the 1970s and 1980s; while some are out of print, you can probably find them in libraries. Look for *New Games for the Whole Family* by Dale Lefevre, *Playfair: Everybody's Guide to Noncompetitive Play* by Matt Weinstein and Joel Goodman, *The Cooperative Sports and Games Book* by Terry Orlick, and other books with "cooperative," "noncompetitive," and "New Games" in their titles.

● Organize a group of youth and adults to decorate a yard, several yards, a whole block, or an apartment building or hallway for Valentine's Day or Independence Day. Then have a party.

Assets in Action

In **Bemidji, Minnesota,** *adults made a pact to start smiling at teenagers when they see them on the street. It's a first step in breaking down suspicions and rebuilding trust.*

In **Moorhead, Minnesota,** *the Moorhead Healthy Community Initiative (MHCI) is working to mobilize everyone around asset building. Some 30 block clubs are learning the names of children in their neighborhoods and creating social situations that bring youth and seniors together.*

In Your Faith Community

● Find out what your faith community is doing to encourage caring neighborhoods. Are there any special events—dinners, pancake breakfasts, plays—to which youth may invite their neighbors? Volunteer to help start something.

● Work with your youth group and adult members to be a positive presence in your faith community's neighborhood. *Examples:* Help plan a social for adults and youth in the neighborhood; help start and run a drop-in day-care center or an after-school program for neighborhood kids.

With Your Friends

● Start a baby-sitting coop in your neighborhood. Find out which friends are interested in baby-sitting. Take a baby-sitting class together (contact your local Red Cross chapter for information). Print up flyers with your names, telephone numbers, and rates.

● Prepare a "Know Your Neighbors" directory. List the names, addresses, phone numbers, hobbies, occupations, and special interests of neighbors who want to be included in your directory. Make copies for all neighbors who participate.

● Work together to create a neighborhood banner, logo, or name.

● Be nice to younger kids you see on the street, in the park, in stores, or wherever. Don't tolerate bullying.

● Have a neighborhood pet show. Award prizes for Hairiest Dog, Fattest Cat, Cutest Gerbil, or whatever else sounds like fun.

● Plan a neighborhood art show. Display children's and adults' artwork, crafts, and hobbies in your community center or a neighbor's garage.

● Start a walking, hiking, or biking club for youth and adults in your neighborhood.

● If you and your friends are mechanically inclined, help adult neighbors repair lawn mowers, snowblowers, bicycles, and other broken items. Or volunteer to help fix playground equipment and park benches.

RESOURCES

For your parents and neighbors:

101 Things You Can Do for Our Children's Future by Richard Louv (New York: Anchor, 1994). A primer for parents (and every adult) on how to create a better life for children. See especially Chapter 3, What You Can Do in Your Neighborhood.

National Crime Prevention Council
www.ncpc.org
With the goal of creating safe and supportive communities for all residents, this organization has many ideas and action plans for raising community awareness.

24% of the youth we surveyed have this asset in their lives.

CARING SCHOOL CLIMATE

Your school is a caring, encouraging place to be.

At Home

● Discuss school issues and events with your family. Talk about the positives and the negatives, about adults (teachers, administrators, staff) who seem to care and those who don't, about students who contribute and those who cause problems. Ask your parents' advice about things you'd like to see changed at your school.

● Encourage your parents to volunteer in your school—on a regular basis, for special events, with a parent-teacher organization, or whatever their schedule allows. Schools become stronger and more caring when parents are active and informed. See Asset #6: Parent Involvement in Schooling.

At School

Do your part.

Help others at school feel cared about and supported—*by you.* Following are ten ideas to try.

10 WAYS TO BE MORE CARING AT SCHOOL

1. Learn the names of as many students as you can. Smile at them and greet them by name when you see them in the halls, at extracurricular events, and in your community.

2. Reach out to kids who seem isolated or lonely and aren't included in cliques or groups. Be a friend to them.

3. When you're picking teams for gym class activities or after-school sports, don't just choose your friends.

4. Don't tolerate bullying, and stick up for kids who are bullied by others.

5. Respect school property and encourage other students to do the same.

6. Make an effort to get to know your teachers.

7. Treat everyone—students, faculty, staff, administrators, visitors—with courtesy and respect.

8. Thank teachers, support staff, and others for the work they do.

9. Get involved in programs (such as peer helping) that build assets.

10. Get involved in student leadership. Work to create a warm, caring, supportive school climate for everyone.

Be a joiner.

When you're involved in school activities, you're more likely to feel cared about and supported than if you're on the outside looking in. Try out for a team, write for the school paper, join (or start) a club or service group. If you're not sure what opportunities exist in your school, ask a teacher or administrator.

Do something.

If you're unhappy with your school's environment, don't just complain about it. Do something to make it better. Run for student council or join another leadership organization committed to student representation. Start a campaign to determine what things in your school need improving. You might take a survey (see pages 49–50) or hold forums to gather student input. Then develop a plan for making improvements. Include teachers, administrators, and community leaders so you're sure to take appropriate (meaning legal and allowable) action.

If taking on the whole school environment is too much of a challenge or time commitment for you, start smaller. Work on changing just one thing about your school. *Examples:* a specific school rule, the food served in the cafeteria, not enough challenging classes, too much litter.

FACT:

If you think your school needs improving, you're not alone!

According to a recent survey of over 1,300 high school students, only 13 percent of public school teens say their classmates are "very respectful" of teachers. Just 30 percent say most of their teachers care personally about them. Nearly 78 percent say kids in their schools pay "too much attention to what they are wearing and what they look like."

Source: *Getting By: What American Teenagers Really Think About Their Schools* (New York: Public Agenda, 1997).

Make a wish list.

Work with your class, club, team, or group to brainstorm ways to make your school more caring. Start with these categories:

• Relationships among students
• Student-teacher relationships
• Administration
• Extracurricular activities
• School environment/building
• Student government/student council
• School social functions
• What else?

Share your ideas with teachers, administrators, and other students. Gather input from them. Make a plan to put your ideas into action.

Take a survey.

Survey the students in your school to learn what they think about the school climate. Work with your class, club, student council, or school newspaper staff to come up with a series of multiple choice questions. Organize them into a survey, make enough copies for everyone, distribute them, and arrange for one or more collection points around the school. See page 50 for sample questions.

1. How caring and encouraging do you think our school is?
   ❏ Very caring   ❏ Somewhat caring   ❏ Not caring at all

2. What do you like BEST about our school?
   ❏ Open lunches   ❏ State basketball champions
   ❏ Most students graduate   ❏ Study hall
   ❏ Other: _____

3. What do you like LEAST about our school?
   ❏ Too many suspensions   ❏ Graffiti on the walls
   ❏ Not enough class choices   ❏ Poor selection in vending machines
   ❏ Other: _____

4. Who tends to show a lot of care toward students? Check all that apply:
   ❏ Teachers   ❏ Coaches   ❏ Administrators
   ❏ Aides and volunteers   ❏ Extracurricular adult leaders
   ❏ Advisors and counselors   ❏ Other students
   ❏ Custodians   ❏ Secretaries and their support staff
   ❏ Other: _____

Tips: Keep your survey short—20 questions at the most. Make it anonymous (students don't have to sign their names). Include a date by which surveys must be returned to be counted.

When your surveys are in, tabulate the results. Calculate totals and percentages for each question. Make your findings public; you might publish them in the school newsletter, print them on a flyer to hand out to everyone, or report them in the morning announcements. Work with your school's staff, administration, and student groups to come up with a plan to make your school more caring— a place where *all* students feel challenged and supported to succeed.

Assets in Action

At one school in **Minneapolis, Minnesota,** *people could count on the school secretary. She always had a smile on her face and knew everyone by name. Students often stopped by to see her because she helped them feel valued and cared for. When she retired, she received more than 1,000 flowers—one from each student.*

In **Nampa, Idaho,** *a teen parent program, an extension of Nampa High School, helps teens who are pregnant or parenting to stay in school. Students study parenting and child care along with regular high school courses. An in-school nursery helps care for their babies.*

In Your Community

● Encourage your parents, neighbors, and other adults to support your local schools. Ask them to vote yes for referendums that lower class sizes and improve facilities.

● Encourage local media (newspapers, TV stations, radio stations) to spotlight and feature caring schools, teachers, and administrators.

Assets in Action

*Two **Tucson, Arizona,** middle schools have become more welcoming places for students and parents, thanks to the Imagine Project sponsored by the Arizona Department of Health Services. Students planned a year of events and activities to foster a warm, caring school environment; to strengthen relationships between students and adults; and to encourage parents to participate in school activities. Before the school year started, parents and students gathered for a celebration and a scavenger hunt. Recently, many participated in a dialogue designed to strengthen relationships among students and parents from differing communities.*

*In **St. Paul, Minnesota,** the Company for Breakfast program is bringing students and caring adults together. Community members take turns eating breakfast with students each morning, providing them with one more connection to the community.*

In Your Faith Community

● With your youth group, sponsor roundtable discussions on the topic of caring schools. Invite parents and kids to share their ideas and concerns. Summarize the comments and communicate them to area schools.

● Identify the teachers, school administrators, and other educators in your faith community. Find ways to acknowledge and honor their efforts.

● When your youth group looks for service projects, don't forget nearby schools. *Examples:* You might volunteer to paint, work on the grounds, make repairs, or help out in other ways. See Asset #9: Service to Others.

With Your Friends

As a group, agree to practice the "10 Ways to Be More Caring at School" on page 48—or other ideas you come up with for helping other students feel cared about and supported. Be role models for everyone in your school.

RESOURCES

For educators:

The Challenge to Care in Schools: An Alternative Approach to Education by Nel Noddings (New York: Teacher's College Press, 1992). Noddings emphasizes that caring and being cared for are fundamental human needs, then calls on schools to address these needs and nourish students' growth.

Getting By: What American Teenagers Really Think About Their Schools (New York: Public Agenda, 1997). The eye-opening results of a national survey. Write or call: Public Agenda, 6 East 39th Street, 9th Floor, New York, NY 10016; (212) 686-6610. On the Web, go to: *www.publicagenda.org*

Learning and Living: How Asset Building for Youth Can Unify a School's Mission by Donald Draayer and Eugene C. Roehlkepartain, rev. ed. (Minneapolis: Search Institute, 1998). This booklet helps schools build assets for students.

Asset #6

29% of the youth
we surveyed have this
asset in their lives.

PARENT INVOLVEMENT IN SCHOOLING

Your parents are actively involved in helping you succeed in school. They talk with you about school, sometimes help with your schoolwork, and attend school events.

At Home

Talk with your parents about school.

Tell them about your day, your successes, your frustrations and failures. Share funny stories. Describe an argument someone had with a teacher, the movie you saw in history class, the kid with the scary new spider tattoo (oops, maybe that's you). School is a big part of *your* life; make sure it's part of *their* life, too.

Keep them informed.

When your teachers send notes, schedules, and announcements home with you, be sure to pass them along to your parents. Don't let them pile up in your locker or line the bottom of your backpack. Bring home extra copies of your class newsletter or school paper for your parents to read.

Tell your parents about upcoming school events as soon as you hear about them. Offer to write them on the family calendar. Try a gentle reminder now and then. *Examples:* "Mom, Dad, remember—school conferences on Tuesday night." "Can you make it to the musical on Friday? I'm only in the chorus, but I'd like you to be there."

If your parents are booked or not interested, see if another adult can accompany you. What about a grandparent? An aunt? A cousin? A neighbor? Don't be embarrassed to attend a school function without an official "parent." Almost any adult will do. (If it's something specific, like a mother-daughter get-together, ask a teacher first.)

FACT:

Dads make a difference!

According to a new national study, children and teens do better in school when their fathers are involved in their schools. They're more likely to get mostly A's and enjoy school more, less likely to repeat a grade. This is true whether their fathers live with them or not, and it's true even if their mothers are also involved.

Source: *Fathers' Involvement in Their Children's Schools* (Washington, DC: National Center for Education Statistics, 1997).

Tell them you really *want* them to be involved.

Trust us; you *do* want this. The more your parents are involved in your schooling—and the longer they stay involved—the better it is for you.

Parent involvement in schooling tends to decrease as kids get older. Most parents are very active when their children are in kindergarten and grade school, then slack off during middle school and high school. According to the National Center for Education Statistics, 73 percent of parents of students in grades 3–5 are involved with their children's schools. Of the youth we surveyed, 44 percent of 6th graders have this asset—but only 17 percent of 12th graders do. (The 29 percent cited at the start of this chapter is an average of all 6th–12th graders surveyed.)

If your parents *aren't* involved, maybe they think you prefer it that way. Maybe they're respecting your space and your independence. Or maybe they have other reasons. If you want to know, ask. Then tell them you really *want* them to be involved (and give them a few moments to get over their shock).

If your parents *are* involved, thank them . . . because a lot of parents couldn't care less. According to Temple University psychology professor Laurence Steinberg, 25 percent of parents ignore or pay little attention to how their children are doing in school.

12 REASONS WHY PARENT INVOLVEMENT IS A PLUS

FACTS TO SHARE WITH MOM AND DAD

Students whose parents are involved in their schools are:

1. *less* likely to have learning problems
2. *less* likely to have behavior problems
3. *less* likely to repeat a grade
4. *less* likely to be suspended or expelled
5. *more* likely to get higher grades and test scores
6. *more* likely to participate in extracurricular activities at school and organized youth activities outside of school
7. *more* likely to resist negative peer pressure
8. *more* likely to graduate
9. *more* likely to go on to college.

They also:

10. have better school attendance
11. do more homework
12. demonstrate more positive attitudes.

Parent involvement in schooling is so important that the Governors and the Congress of the United States made it one of the eight National Education Goals. They consider it vital to improving learning and teaching in our nation's education system.

Sources: National Center for Education Statistics, National Committee for Citizens in Education, National Education Goals Panel, National Institute of Education.

Give them ideas.

Talk with your parents about different ways they can get involved in your schooling. Share these ideas from the American Association of School Administrators and other experts.

Parents can . . .

. . . ask you what happened in school each day
. . . help you with your homework
. . . read a book along with you, then talk about it afterward
. . . call your teacher(s) now and then to check on how you're doing in school
. . . attend parent-teacher conferences
. . . join the school's parent-teacher association (PTA) or organization (PTO)
. . . volunteer in the classroom

. . . help out with projects as needed (setting up a computer, building a bookshelf, organizing a book fair)

. . . chaperon a field trip

. . . attend a school open house, play, performance, or athletic event

. . . attend a school board meeting

. . . visit a class to talk about their career

. . . invite a class to visit their workplace

. . . serve on a building- or district-based committee, advisory group, or task force.

What would *you* like your parents to do? What would mean the most to you? Be specific. (Wishing is okay, but asking is faster.) *Tips:* Be sensitive to your parents' schedules and the other demands on their time. Never volunteer them for anything without getting their permission first.

At School

Find out what your school is doing to encourage parent involvement.

Ask your teachers, the principal, and parents (yours and your friends'). Following are 12 ideas from other schools and education experts. See which ones your school already uses; suggest that they try some others. Offer to help.

1. Have teachers personally contact each student's family at least once during the school year.

2. Have teachers send notes home to parents frequently about what students are working on and learning in class. (Families who are consistently informed about their children's progress at school have higher-achieving children.)

3. Encourage parents to get involved through calls, letters, and visits by school staff and other parents.

4. Hold meetings (PTA/PTO, school conferences, committee meetings, etc.) at hours that are convenient for working parents.

5. Print extra copies of class newsletters and school papers to send home to parents.

6. Establish a family resource center—a place where parents can come for information, reading materials, and support.

7. Offer free transportation to and from school for special events, school functions, and conferences.

8. Offer free child care during school functions and PTA/PTO meetings. (Your school group or club can step in here.)

9. Have interpreters and native speakers of languages other than English present at school functions; make materials and handouts available in other languages. (A project for your Spanish class?)

10. Create ways to communicate with families and students after school hours. *Examples:* voicemail; a school Web site; a homework hotline.

11. Form a parent advisory committee to give input into school policy decisions.

12. Schedule special events—breakfasts, dinners, celebrations—to honor parent volunteers.

Assets in Action

In 1997, Decatur High School in **Decatur, Georgia,** *created three new ways for parents to get involved in school affairs: the Academic Boosters (a group to help publicize students' academic efforts and successes and raise funds to recognize student achievement); the Activity Boosters (a group to provide transportation, chaperons, contacts, and ideas for out-of-class activities); and Policy Support Groups (where parents work with school personnel to provide input that affects school operation decisions). The school announced the groups in a letter sent out with student schedules in August.*

Work to make your school more family-friendly.

High schools in particular have a reputation for being *un*friendly. Many don't require parent participation in school activities, and some don't encourage it. Here are five ways to make your school more family-friendly:

● Create a school climate where parent participation is expected and welcomed.

● Be polite to parents who visit or volunteer at your school. Offer to show them around if they're unfamiliar with the building.

● Come up with easy ways for parents to help in your school. Hold a contest to see which homeroom or class can get the most parents to sign up.

● Form a student-faculty committee to review written materials given to parents. Make sure they're clear, straightforward, easy to read, and jargon-free.

● Create a school climate where teachers and students respect each other, and where classroom and school discipline are maintained. *Everyone* feels more welcome in this type of school. See Asset #12: School Boundaries.

Assets in Action

In the largely Hispanic community of **McAllen, Texas,** *schools throughout the district encourage parent involvement with education programs, school-to-home communications, volunteer opportunities, and active parent-teacher organizations. Parent training specialists, social workers, and other staff reach out to parents; families and teachers at each school tailor plans to that school's needs. Almost all parents in McAllen have some productive contact with their child's school.*

*When new children are registered at schools in **Hackettstown, New Jersey,** the First Contact program makes a good first impression. Parents are given a packet including bus and train schedules, lists of social and sports organizations, a school handbook and fact sheet, town directory, physicians' directory, list of child care providers, and other materials. Parents trained as First Contact volunteers are available to answer questions about the school and the community and meet with the new family.*

In Your Community

● Invite your neighbors to get involved in your school—even if they don't have children in the school. Everyone has something to contribute, whether it's time, expertise, or listening skills. You might ask them to help with a special event, chaperon a field trip, or attend school events (*examples:* an open house, concert, or play).

● Encourage the media to notice schools' efforts to involve parents. *Example:* A newspaper might publish announcements of open houses, list names and telephone numbers of parent volunteer coordinators, or feature articles on family-friendly schools. A radio station might set aside a few minutes in the middle of the day for school news. Offer to help by writing news releases or public service announcements.

● Volunteer to baby-sit for neighbors on nights when they have PTA/PTO meetings.

Assets in Action

*Hourly employees at Owens Corning's **Newark, Ohio,** plant can take a paid hour off each week to mentor at a nearby school or volunteer at school events. They drive to school, spend an hour with their student, and drive back to the plant, all without clocking out.*

In Your Faith Community

● As much as possible, coordinate with schools so youth activities don't conflict with school activities.

● Within your youth group, brainstorm ways to encourage your parents to get involved and stay involved with the schools.

With Your Friends

- Set a good example for other students by treating visiting parents with respect.

- Notice and welcome each other's parents when they visit your school. Thank them for being there.

- Invite a friend's parents to a special event at your school.

RESOURCES

For everyone:

EduGuide
321 North Pine Street
Lansing, MI 48933
(517) 374-4083
www.eduguide.org
Dedicated to maximizing learning in the home and in the community, this nonprofit organization aids schools in partnering with families and community leaders on education opportunities outside of the classroom.

National Coalition for Parent Involvement in Education
1400 L Street NW, Suite 300
Washington, DC 20005
(202) 289-6790
www.ncpie.org
Provides resources on family involvement in children's education for parents, educators, and administrators. Visit the Web site for a listing of publications and tips for connecting education to the home and community.

U.S. Department of Education
www.ed.gov
Check out this Web site for free publications on family involvement in learning.

EMPOWERMENT

These assets are about being valued and appreciated—knowing that you matter to other people. They're about having chances to contribute and serve, make a difference and get noticed for your efforts. They're about being safe, because it's hard to feel strong and capable when you're scared.

The empowerment assets are:

7. Community Values Youth
8. Youth as Resources
9. Service to Others
10. Safety

Asset #7

20% of the youth we surveyed have this asset in their lives.

COMMUNITY VALUES YOUTH

You feel that the adults in your community value and appreciate young people.

At Home

● Talk with your parents about the adults in your life who help you feel valued and appreciated. *Hints:* You feel valued when adults take time to be with you, listen to you, take you seriously, seek you out, and ask your opinions and advice. Who does these things for you? Your parents? Other relatives? A neighbor? A teacher? A coach or youth group leader? Try to identify at least three people. If you can't, see Asset #3: Other Adult Relationships.

● Tell your parents about the adults in your life who are rude to you, ignore you, or try to make you feel stupid or worthless. What can you do to improve those relationships? *Tip:* Sometimes there's nothing you can do. Avoid those people whenever possible. If you can't avoid them, tell yourself: *It doesn't matter what they think of me. It matters what I think of me. I refuse to let them get to me. I refuse to accept what they say.*

● Role-play with your family positive, appropriate ways to respond when people treat you disrespectfully.

● When your parents attend community meetings and events, go with them. This will give other adults a more positive perception of you—and vice versa.

Assets in Action

In **Manchester, New Hampshire,** *the Makin' It Happen Coalition for Resilient Youth created a coupon book with a twist. Along with the usual coupons for restaurants, movie theaters, and other places of entertainment, the book includes asset-building coupons youth can redeem from their parents. One coupon offers a supervised party at home; another offers two hours of homework help.*

At School

Work with your school to make a good impression on your community. Ideas to try:

● Invite community members to an open house hosted by students.

● Invite people from your school neighborhood to events that showcase students' achievements and creativity. *Examples:* school plays, science fairs, athletic events.

● Find ways for students to get involved in community service. See Asset #9: Service to Others.

● Wear school jackets, caps, and T-shirts when you're out and about. Model respectful, responsible behavior.

● If you spend time in your school neighborhood—before and after school, during lunch or breaks in your day—be polite and respectful to the people you meet.

● Keep your school grounds clean. Pick up litter and paint over graffiti. Respect the neighbors' property.

In Your Community

Learn what your community is doing for youth.

Some excellent programs for youth aren't well-publicized, if they're publicized at all. So stroll around, get on your bike, or drive around and find out what's available. Let your fingers do the walking through your telephone book. Does your community have plenty of after-school programs? Recreation programs? Youth organizations? Contact your mayor's office and ask what your community offers children and teens. Call schools, parks, community centers, and religious organizations to learn what they're doing. Visit a few programs that come highly recommended (by adults *and* kids). When you see adults working on behalf of youth, you'll feel that youth are valued and appreciated.

Check out the hangouts.

With your youth group, class, or family, tour your community and check out the hangouts—places that attract kids and teens. What about parks? Recreation centers? Restaurants? Street corners? Convenience stores? School playgrounds? List them, describe them, and give each one a rating from 1 (unhealthy/unsafe) to 10 (great). Decide what you'll base your ratings on. *Tips:* Is it clean? Safe? Is there adult supervision? Are there activities and fun things to do? Do the kids and teens seem happy or bored?

Afterward, try to answer questions like these:

• Does our community have enough great places for kids and teens to hang out?
• Are there more great places for children than for teens?
• What could be done to move kids away from the unhealthy/unsafe places to better places?

Write up your findings and present them to your mayor or other elected official. Volunteer to help make hangouts better for kids and teens in your community.

Assets in Action

The Communities in Collaboration Council, a network of 21 asset-building communities in the western suburbs of **Minneapolis, Minnesota,** sponsors a month-long "We Love Our Kids!" celebration in February.

Housing developer Gary Walker wants Las Sendas, the planned community he's building in **Mesa, Arizona,** to be a place where children are valued. His company, United Development, Inc., is integrating asset building into its plans. They've published a brochure called "A Community Designed with Kids in Mind" and are training people to talk knowledgeably about the assets. Eventually there will be 2,000 or more families living in Las Sendas, which will include a community center, other safe gathering places, and programs for youth.

Fight back against teen bashing and trashing.

Some adults have negative, ill-informed perceptions about teens. Without even knowing you, they may assume you're a slacker, a punk, or a thug—someone to be ignored, avoided, or feared. The more you can do to prove them wrong, the better life will be for you and all young people.

You might think *Hey, they're the grownups—how come I have to educate THEM?* You're right; it's sad (and maddening) that more adults aren't positive toward teens. You can't change everyone's mind, but you can set things straight with the people in your neighborhood and community. You can let them know how you (and many other teens) really are. Ideas to try:

● Be polite and respectful toward adults you meet—even when they're rude to you. Don't let *them* control *your* behavior.

● Do good works. Be thoughtful, helpful, courteous, and kind whenever you get the chance.

● When adults say or do things that make you feel valued, thank them. When they show their bias or prejudice toward teens, challenge them. *Example:* "You know, it's simply not true that we teenagers want everything handed to us. I have a part-time job, and so do most of my friends."

● When the media bash and trash teens with stories about kids in trouble, committing crimes, acting out, or taking foolish risks, speak up. Write a letter to the editor or call TV or radio stations. Ask them to feature more positive stories about teens. (They know those stories are out there.)

FACT:

If you think adults don't value teens, you're right!

According to a recent survey of 2,600 adults and parents, only 37 percent of Americans believe that today's children, once grown, will make this country a better place. Sixty-five percent who say they have a lot of contact with teenagers describe them as "rude," "irresponsible," or "wild." Only 12 percent say that it's common for teens to be friendly or helpful toward neighbors.

Source: *Kids These Days: What Americans Really Think About the Next Generation* (New York: Public Agenda, 1997).

Be valuable.

The best way to get respect is to earn it. And the best way to be valued is by being valuable—to your family, friends, neighbors, school, community, and the world. Get involved in a neighborhood service project. Be a leader in your school or youth group. Do your part to make your community a better place. And don't be too shy to speak out about the good things you're doing. (If you really don't want to talk about yourself, speak proudly about your friends.)

Value others.

● Show that you value people who work with children and youth—teachers, group leaders, social service providers, faith community leaders, coaches, volunteers, and others. Thank them for their time and commitment.

● Help younger children in your community feel valued—by you. Build relationships with them through volunteering, tutoring, baby-sitting, and just being friendly. Following are simple, practical tips you can try.

WAYS TO SHOW **55** KIDS YOU CARE

1. Notice them.
2. Smile at them.
3. Learn their names.
4. Look them in the eye when you talk to them.
5. Ask them about themselves.
6. Let them tell you how they feel.
7. Listen to their stories.
8. Laugh at their jokes.
9. Answer their questions.
10. Ask their opinions.
11. Give them your undivided attention.
12. Believe what they say.
13. Tell them what you like about them.
14. Delight in their discoveries.
15. Applaud their successes.
16. Tolerate their interruptions.
17. Let them act their age.
18. Accept them as they are.
19. Tell them how much you like being with them.
20. Tell them about yourself.
21. Be nice to them.
22. Be honest with them.
23. Keep the promises you make to them.
24. Tell them what you expect of them.
25. Respect them.
26. Believe in them.
27. Make time to be with them.
28. Be excited when you see them.
29. Notice when they grow.
30. Remember their birthdays.
31. Introduce them to your friends and family.
32. Meet their friends and family.
33. Include them in conversations.
34. Call them on the phone just to say hi.
35. Give them your phone number.
36. Send them a letter, postcard, or email.
37. Find a common interest.
38. Do what they like to do.
39. Listen to their favorite music with them.
40. Contribute to their collections.
41. Show up at their games, concerts, and special events.
42. Read aloud together.
43. Share a meal together.
44. Go places together.
45. Build something together.
46. Make decisions together.
47. Help them learn something new.
48. Ask them to help you with something.
49. Encourage them to help others.
50. Let them make mistakes.
51. Admit when you make a mistake.
52. Suggest better behaviors when they act up or act out.
53. Help them take a stand, then stand with them.
54. Tell them how proud you are of them.
55. Encourage them to think big.

Adapted from "150 Ways to Show Kids You Care" by Jolene L. Roehlkepartain. Search Institute, 1996. Used with permission.

In Your Faith Community

● Within your youth group, talk about people who help you feel valued and appreciated. Talk about people who don't. What can you do as a group to improve adults' perceptions of youth? How do you think you're perceived by the adults in your faith community?

● Work to educate your faith community about negative stereotypes of youth. Have an intergenerational discussion group to talk about them and brainstorm solutions.

● Be nice to the younger kids in your faith community. Try some of the "55 Ways to Show Kids You Care" on page 66.

Assets in Action

In **St. Louis Park, Minnesota,** *two high school girls started a Tuesday-night baby-sitting service at the Reformation Lutheran Church. Parents can drop off their kids for three hours and pay just $1 per child.*

With Your Friends

Think about places in your community where you feel valued—and places where you don't. Try to spend most of your time in places where you feel valued.

When you're out in public, be aware of your behavior and how others might perceive it. This doesn't mean you can't be yourself and have fun. Small gestures can make a big difference—like saying hi to neighbors you see on the street, turning down the volume on your boombox or car stereo, picking up your burger bags and soda cans when you leave the park. What else can you think of? As a group, can you agree on some things to try?

RESOURCES

For everyone:

Creating Community Anywhere: Finding Support and Connection in a Fragmented World by Carolyn R. Shaffer and Kristin Anundsen (New York: Jeremy P. Tarcher, 1993). The authors define community as "groups of people who play, work, learn, and celebrate together," then describe specific ways to organize, manage, and enjoy such groups across geographic, age, and other boundaries.

America's Promise Alliance
1110 Vermont Avenue, NW, Suite 900
Washington, DC 20005
(202) 657-0600
www.americaspromise.org
A multi-year national campaign launched at the Presidents' Summit for America's Future in April, 1997, led by General Colin Powell, America's Promise is mobilizing corporate America and a vast volunteer army on behalf of young people at risk. The goal is to make sure that all young people have access to five fundamental resources: mentors, safe places, a healthy start, marketable skills, and opportunities to serve in their communities.

For community leaders:

Healthy Communities, Healthy Youth Tool Kit (Minneapolis: Search Institute, 1998). Ideas, strategies, and more than 300 examples for mobilizing your community or organization to build assets, plus dozens of ready-to-use worksheets and handouts, all in a three-ring binder.

Asset #8

24% of the youth
we surveyed have this
asset in their lives.

YOUTH AS RESOURCES

**You and other young people are given useful roles
and meaningful things to do in your community.**

At Home

● Hold a family meeting to talk about and identify each other's talents and abilities. What do individual family members like to do? Who's really good at what? Review everyone's current chores and responsibilities around the house. Make changes based on people's talents, abilities, and interests.

● Instead of always buying gifts for birthdays and holidays, make some. Or think of useful, meaningful things you can do for other people, then present them with gift certificates describing what you'll do and when.

● Use some of your chores and projects as teaching opportunities. *Examples:* Enlist your little sister to help you repair your bike. Ask your younger brother to help you prepare a meal. Give them useful, meaningful things to do—not just the grunt work.

● Ask a sibling to teach you something—the latest slang at school, a hobby, a song, a skill, a game.

● Spend *less* time in front of the TV, surfing the Net, or hanging out so you have *more* time for other things—helping around the house, working on the school newspaper, serving in your community, visiting with a neighbor. *Tip:* This doesn't mean you should give up having fun or relaxing. Doing nothing is a great way to recharge your batteries. On the other hand, doing something that matters is a great way to build your sense of self-worth and self-esteem. Try to find a balance.

At School

● Get involved in decision making at your school. *Examples:* You might run for student council, sit on a planning committee, form a team to revise the school handbook, or prepare the agenda for your school's annual open house.

● With your class or club, develop a proposal for an activity or class you'd like to see available in your school. This might be a new option or a way to make an existing option more worthwhile and meaningful. Think through the details—the benefits, timing, number of youth involved, sponsors, funds needed, and so on. Describe what you hope to accomplish with the activity or class and how it will benefit the students and the school. Once your proposal is fleshed out, present it to your principal or student council.

● Many students serve on parent-teacher association (PTA) or organization (PTO) boards. Some schools have formed PTSAs (parent-teacher-student associations). Find out if your school lets students serve on adult boards or has a PTSA. If so, get involved. If not, suggest that your school start involving students.

Assets in Action

Sixteen-year-old Ben Smilowitz of **West Hartford, Connecticut,** *wasn't content with serving on a student advisory committee to his state board of education. He's been lobbying in his state to create two student seats on the state board. Ten states and the District of Columbia currently have student members—and four of those states allow student members to vote.*

In **Ruidoso, New Mexico,** *high school students have developed a speakers' bureau to share the asset-building story with civic, parent, student, religious, and other community groups.*

In Your Community

Look around your community.

Learn about the many opportunities available to give something back. Where can you contribute? Where can you lead? Can you be an officer in your youth organization? Are there neighborhood, town, or city councils, committees, or boards that welcome youth involvement? (If they don't welcome it yet, they might with a little encouragement.) Are teens involved in planning and running community programs? (If they aren't, they should be—from the start. Especially if those programs serve children and youth.)

6 TIPS FOR GAINING REPRESENTATION

1. Find the right agency or council. What kinds of things are you interested in? Follow one of your interests. Call your chamber of commerce or city offices (the mayor, the city council) to ask if there are any committees serving on that subject. *Examples:*

If you're interested in . . .	you might try . . .
animals	the Humane Society
environmental issues	the Sierra Club national wildlife groups
health issues	state health agencies the Red Cross

Most communities have neighborhood councils you could attend. While you're there, ask for more suggestions of groups you might join. Or try your board of education. Why not?

2. Campaign for yourself. You might pass a petition, collecting other people's signatures, to ask for representation on a particular board or council. Let newspaper and TV reporters know that you're seeking representation and tell them why. Making the public aware of you increases your chances of being accepted.

3. Be realistic. It's often easier for you to sit on a board or council as a student advisor than to become a voting member. But you can have power to influence decisions as an advisor.

4. Ask questions. Meetings can be boring, but they're a lot *less* boring if you assert yourself and *ask questions*. Ask the other members to repeat or explain anything you don't understand. If you get involved in the discussions, meetings will be much more exciting for you. And you just might teach the committee a thing or two about how to get things done faster. (Teens seem to know how to cut through red tape.)

5. Stick up for yourself. Don't allow other people to put you down. Most will appreciate your ideas. And most will answer your questions respectfully and explain things to you. You have a right to know what's going on and to understand it.

CONTINUED ON NEXT PAGE...

6. Always be polite, even if you sometimes get discouraged or angry. As the old saying goes, you can catch more flies with honey than with vinegar. People are more willing to listen, keep an open mind, and even change their mind when they're not under attack or on the defensive.

Adapted from *The Kid's Guide to Social Action* by Barbara A. Lewis, rev. ed. Free Spirit Publishing Inc., 1998, page 89. Used with permission.

Assets in Action

When **Bridgeport, Connecticut,** *kicked off its Just Assets initiative, some of its early adult-led efforts flopped. So the community decided to get youth involved. Today kids sit on the board and executive committees, making decisions as full partners with the adults.*

In **Hudson, Wisconsin,** *the Rotary Clubs conducted focus groups with 120 students in grades 4–12, then created a youth-designed, youth-governed 22,500-square-feet outdoor park. In the summer, kids can go there for inline skating and skateboarding; in the winter, for ice skating. More than two dozen teenagers (and a few adults) worked together to plan the park. The Rotary Clubs are raising the money for the $105,000 construction cost from local groups and fund-raising events, and YMCA staff will be on hand to teach safety and skating skills and provide supervision. Once the park opens, youth will serve on a policy board.*

Don't wait to be given a useful role.

Create one for yourself. Stand up, speak out, and stay informed. Most people agree that being out in the world makes life more interesting and meaningful. Don't wait to be asked to be part of your community; jump in by volunteering your time, talents, and abilities. Here are 10 ideas to try:

1. Identify something that needs changing, then work to change it.

2. Write letters to the editor of your local newspaper on issues that concern you.

3. Lobby for (or against) ordinances or laws.

4. Give a speech on a topic you care about—children's rights, homelessness, domestic violence, education, senior citizens, health care.

5. Create and/or update a community Web page.

6. Join a group that builds or renovates housing for low-income or homeless families.

7. Develop a skill you can share and teach others.

8. Become an expert on a topic that's important to you—computers, cats, clean air, recycling—and educate others.

9. Campaign for someone who's running for office in your school, city, or state.

10. Alert your local media (newspapers, TV and radio stations) when you see your peers contributing to the community.

It's your community, too, and you have the right to be an active, important part of it. You'll also be helping to change (some) people's negative perceptions of teens.

FACT:

Everyone benefits when youth get involved!

Communities benefit from developing a pool of future leaders who are skilled, experienced, and committed. They gain new energy from young people that builds positive community spirit.

Organizations benefit from fresh ideas that aren't bound by "the-way-things-have-always-been-done" thinking. They learn what young people really want and need.

Adults benefit because they no longer have to do everything—they have help! They gain appreciation for the creative energy young people contribute to make programs successful.

Youth benefit by developing new skills and gaining leadership experience. Involvement boosts their self-esteem and broadens their future career choices.

Source: *A Guide to Resources on Youth as Leaders and Partners: Strategies, Programs, and Information* by Xuan Ma (1995); Indiana Youth Institute.

Offer useful roles to others.

Get other kids involved in your efforts and offer them meaningful things to do. *Example:* If you're campaigning for a candidate, they can help you hand out flyers. Younger kids love it when older, wiser kids take them seriously and make them feel wanted and needed.

Make your work meaningful.

If you don't have time to volunteer because you must hold a part-time job, try to work someplace that's meaningful to you—and useful to your community. Is there a company you respect that emphasizes service? A nonprofit organization that's contributing to your community? Even if your choices are limited, give your job your best shot. Being a responsible, committed worker makes your community stronger.

In Your Faith Community

● Take advantage of opportunities to lead and serve in your faith community. Can you get involved with a council, committee, or board? Can you help teach and care for younger children? Can you help lead a worship service or other intergenerational event?

● Within your youth group, brainstorm useful roles for children and teens in your faith community. What can you do? What would you like to do? How would each role help your faith community? Your community? Make a list of your Top 5 choices and present them to adult leaders. Ask which one they'd like you to do—and how soon you can start.

Assets in Action

When First Presbyterian Church of Crafton Heights in **Pittsburgh, Pennsylvania,** *decided to convert an old movie theater into a community recreation center, one of their main goals was to get kids involved. Youth sponsored fund-raisers and went along when adults sought grant money. They helped with the renovation by hauling cement and busting down old walls. All told, they spent 18 months on the project.*

With Your Friends

Take an informal survey of your friends to find out how many are willing to volunteer in your community. Have a meeting for everyone who's interested, and give each person an assignment: to learn about one organization, group, or program that welcomes teen volunteers. Have another meeting to share the information you've collected. Take a vote to decide which organization(s) you'd like to help.

Like starting a regular exercise program, volunteering is easier and more fun when you can share the experience with people you know.

RESOURCES

For everyone:

Younger Voices, Stronger Choices: Promise Project's Guide to Forming Youth/Adult Partnerships by Loring Leifer and Michael McLarney (Kansas City, MO: Kansas City Consensus, 1997). Direction, resources, and examples for organizations interested in creating youth/adult partnerships. Written by a high school senior and an adult, with their email communications woven throughout the chapters.

For you:

The Kid's Guide to Social Action by Barbara A. Lewis, rev. ed. (Minneapolis: Free Spirit Publishing, 1998). This award-winning guide includes step-by-step instructions for building social action skills, true stories about youth who are doing great things, reproducible forms, and extensive resources.

Do Something!
www.dosomething.org
This national program trains, funds, and mobilizes youth to be leaders who measurably strengthen their communities.

For community leaders:

Community Partnership for Youth
PO Box 42
Monterey, CA 93942
(831) 394-4279
www.cpy.org
Provides resources, training, and technical assistance on effective ways to involve youth in decision-making and leadership roles.

Youth on Board
58 Day Street
Somerville, MA 02144
(617) 741-1242
www.youthonboard.org
Works to ensure that young people's voices are heard and heeded in all nonprofit organizations involving youth; publishes the booklet "Youth Governance: 14 Points to Successfully Involving Youth in Organizational Decision Making."

Asset #9

50% of the youth
we surveyed have this
asset in their lives.

SERVICE TO OTHERS

You do an hour or more of community service each week.

At Home

Make service a family affair.

You don't have to commit to a large project. Service can be as simple as visiting someone who's homebound, picking up litter in a park, shoveling snow for an elderly neighbor, or baking cookies for the family across the hall.

When you're ready for a bigger commitment, try these suggestions from Susan J. Ellis, president of Energize, Inc., an international training, consulting, and publishing firm specializing in volunteerism:*

1. Have a family meeting to consider this whole idea. Make sure everyone, no matter how young, participates in the discussion.

2. Make a list of all the volunteering each member of the family is doing now. Would the others like to help with any of these activities?

3. What causes interest you? Allow everyone to suggest a community problem of concern to him or her. If some of the ideas intrigue the whole family, start exploring what organizations in your community are already working on these. Use the Yellow Pages, go to the library, visit the Volunteer Center, or search the Internet.

---

* Adapted from *Children as Volunteers* by Susan J. Ellis, *et al.*, © 1991, Energize, Inc. Used with permission.

4. Consider what types of work everyone wants to do. Make two lists: one for Things We Know How to Do and one for Things We Would Like to Learn How to Do. Make sure something is listed for each member of the family. (This is a great opportunity to acknowledge each other's talents. The lists will also prove helpful when you interview with an agency.)

5. Call several organizations for appointments and screen your options. See whether the agency representatives are comfortable talking to children and teens as well as to adults. Ask if the agency has something meaningful for you to do as a group.

6. You may want to begin with a one-time activity. This will test the water to see how everyone likes volunteering together.

7. Once you commit to a volunteer project, take it seriously. Talk about it during the week and plan ahead to do it, even when things get hectic.

8. Enjoy the many benefits of volunteering as a family: spending quality time together, getting to know each other in new ways, demonstrating skills and learning new ones (which builds mutual respect), working together toward the same goals—and having something to talk about all week!

Bonus: Serving as a family builds several assets at the same time. As a family, you might review the list of assets on pages 335–336 and guess which ones.

FACT:

Serving others is good for you!

When Independent Sector surveyed youth who serve, the teenagers reported 18 benefits of their volunteer experience. Here are the Top 10:

1. They learned to respect others.
2. They learned to be helpful and kind.
3. They learned how to get along with and relate to others.
4. They gained satisfaction from helping others.
5. They learned to understand people who are different from them.
6. They learned how to relate to younger children.
7. They became better people.
8. They learned new skills.
9. They developed leadership skills.
10. They became more patient with others.

Source: *Volunteering and Giving Among American Teenagers 12 to 17 Years of Age* (Washington, DC: Independent Sector, 1996).

Take out your wallet.

Choose an organization or cause you'd like to support, then commit to donating a certain amount of *your own money* each month. According to estimates by Market Facts Inc., American youth ages 8–17 have an annual income of $120 billion, much of it discretionary (meaning they can spend it however they like). Surveys by Independent Sector found that 12- to 17-year-olds give an average contribution of $56 per year. If you can afford that much (or more), great. If you can't, give what you can. *Tip:* Make sure that your money will be put to good use. Check into the organization *before* you donate by calling your state's Attorney General or local Better Business Bureau.

At School

Join or start a service club.

Many schools host one or more service clubs for students. Find out if your school does. *Examples:* Interact Club (sponsored by Rotary International), Key Club (Kiwanis International), Leo Club (Lions Clubs International). If there are no service clubs at your school, work with other students, faculty, staff, and community organizations to start one.

Assets in Action

Here's just a sampling of what Interact Club members are doing across the U.S.: At Claremont High School in **Claremont, California,** *students raise money to buy shoes, toys, and clothing for needy children and visit with residents at a nursing home. At Bozeman High School in* **Bozeman, Montana,** *students help support a local chapter of Big Brothers Big Sisters of America. At River Oaks High School in* **River Oaks, Texas,** *students volunteer their time at the Salvation Army soup kitchen.*

Honor youth who serve.

Your school probably recognizes its star athletes and academic achievers. But does it honor volunteers? If not, suggest that they start. You might campaign for a Service Letter for students who excel in volunteerism. Or come up with other ideas. *Examples:* Hold awards ceremonies for students who serve; publish articles about them in the school newsletter; give scholarships for service.

Promote and support service learning at your school.

Service learning is not the same as volunteerism or community service. Here's how the Maryland Student Service Alliance defines it:

Service-learning education develops responsible citizens by engaging students in service (action) beneficial to their communities that includes academic preparation and structured reflection.

Student service learning is a new way to get back to basics. It's a learn-by-doing approach to the curriculum. Students get real-life experience in the subjects they study by meeting community needs.

In 1992, Maryland became the first state in the country to mandate volunteer service for all high school students. It became a graduation requirement starting with the class of 1997.

If your school offers service learning as part of the curriculum, get involved. If it doesn't, talk to a teacher, a counselor, or your principal. You might even give a speech to your school board about the need for service learning in your community's schools. Or go straight to the top and contact your state board of education. For more information about Maryland's efforts (and ammunition for your own campaign to bring service learning to your school), contact:

Service-Learning in Maryland
c/o Maryland State Department of Education
200 West Baltimore Street
Baltimore, MD 21201
(410) 767-0358
www.mdservice-learning.org

 FACT:

Most teens believe that youth should serve . . .

A national survey of young people conducted in 1995 revealed that youth want to be involved in their communities. Ninety-five percent thought students should be required to serve as part of their schooling.

. . . and most do!

An estimated 13.3 *million* 12- to 17-year-olds volunteered during 1995—that's 59 percent of all teenagers. The average teen volunteer gives 3.5 hours per week, or 182 hours per year.

Sources: Margaret A. O'Neill, "All Students Can Serve," *Education Week* (May 1, 1996); *Volunteering and Giving Among Teenagers 12 to 17 Years of Age* (Washington, DC: Independent Sector, 1997).

In Your Community

Get started.

Serving in your community is a great way to meet people and find new meaning in life. There are countless ways to serve. Think about your neighbors, homeless people, elderly people, animals, children, people with disabilities, the environment, poverty, crime . . . what else? Figure out what you'd like to do, then find out where you can do the most good. One hour per week is almost no time at all; you probably spend at least that long channel surfing or just hanging out.

If you want to know how it feels to serve but you're not quite ready to commit, try doing a "secret service" for someone. Set the table when it's your brother's turn. Leave a treat in a friend's locker or a potted plant on a neighbor's porch. Or talk to other people who are active in community service. Ask them what they give—and what they get in return.

If you're not sure where to start serving, check with people in your school or faith community about opportunities. Or check your phone book to see if any of these organizations have chapters near you:

- Boys & Girls Clubs of America
- Boy Scouts of America
- Girls, Inc.
- Girl Scouts of the U.S.A.
- Habitat for Humanity International
- United Way of America

Or contact one or more of these national programs that promote youth service:

**Corporation for National
& Community Service**
1201 New York Avenue, NW
Washington, DC 20525
(202) 606-5000
www.nationalservice.gov

National Youth Leadership Council
1667 Snelling Avenue North
Suite D300
St. Paul, MN 55108
(651) 631-3672
www.nylc.org

National Collaboration for Youth
1319 F Street, NW, Suite 402
Washington, DC 20004
(202) 347-2080
www.collab4youth.org

Youth Service America
1101 15th Street, NW, Suite 200
Washington, DC 20005
(202) 296-2992
www.ysa.org

Or maybe your service doesn't have to be "organized." You can quietly spend an hour or more each week picking up trash, helping out at school, reading aloud to a neighbor, or . . . what else?

Take part in a national day of service.

It's a thrill to be part of a huge national effort—a day when millions of people across the country are joining forces to help others. Two big national service days are:

● **National Youth Service Day.** *Date:* The third Tuesday of April. A project of Youth Service America, NYSD celebrates and recognizes the volunteer work that youth are doing in their communities. It's the largest volunteer event in the world, generating 10 *million* hours of volunteer service. In 1997, more than 2 million young people in 1,000 cities around the country took part in the ninth annual NYSD. For more information, contact Youth Service America or visit the Web site (see page 80).

● **Make a Difference Day.** *Date:* The fourth Saturday of October. Created by *USA Weekend* in partnership with the Points of Light Institute, Make a Difference Day is a celebration of neighbors helping neighbors. In 1996, more than 1 million people accomplished thousands of projects in hundreds of towns and helped millions. Each year in April, $120,000 in charitable awards are made to projects that capture the Make a Difference Day spirit. Ten national honorees are selected by a panel of judges, and each receives $2,000 from *USA Weekend* to be directed to a local charity of his or her choice. For more information, call the Make a Difference Day Hotline at 1-800-416-3824. On the Web, go to: *www.usaweekend.com/section/MDDAY*

Assets in Action

At Richmond High School in **Richmond, Indiana,** *more than 1,400 students spent National Youth Service Day 1997 distributing food, cleaning senior citizens' apartments, and tutoring at the local Boys Club. Students at McKinley Middle School in* **Stockton, California,** *cleaned 40 square blocks of a South Stockton neighborhood, removing three truckloads of garbage. In* **East Point, Georgia,** *hundreds of elementary school kids spent the day painting murals, planting gardens, and cleaning up their neighborhoods.*

Go online.

The Web is home to vast amounts of information, links, tips, advice, contacts, stories, and more about service and volunteering. Check out these huge sites:

Action Without Borders
www.idealist.org
A global online resource for nonprofit and community organizations and the people they serve.

Internet Nonprofit Center

www.nonprofits.org

Tons of information on nonprofit organizations and volunteer opportunities.

ServeNet

www.servenet.org

The home of Youth Service America and lots more information about the world of service and volunteering.

VolunteerMatch

www.volunteermatch.org

This nonprofit corporation matches volunteers with opportunities in their area. Don't miss their section on virtual volunteering—serving your community via the Internet (for real!).

DO'S AND DON'TS OF SUCCESSFUL VOLUNTEERING

DO be flexible. It is rare to find the "perfect" fit right away. Keep an open mind—you might discover something new that interests you.

DO be persistent. Volunteer coordinators are often busy, so don't assume they're not interested in you if they don't call you right away.

DO attend orientation meetings. Keep in mind that informed volunteers are the best volunteers. These meetings will help you do the best job possible.

DO take necessary training classes. Ask about them before you decide to get involved and be prepared to learn what will be needed.

DO be responsible. Show up on time and follow through with your commitments. People will be depending on you.

DON'T expect to start at the top. You have to work hard and prove your worth before you are given more responsibility.

DON'T think that volunteering has to be a group effort. You can start on your own volunteer program and do it on your own time.

DO expect to get plenty of personal enjoyment and satisfaction from your volunteer experiences.

From *Catch the Spirit! A Student's Guide to Community Service* published by The Prudential in cooperation with the U.S. Department of Education, © 1996. Used with permission.

In Your Faith Community

● All major faith traditions include a commitment to serve others. Find out what opportunities are available in your faith community, then get involved. If your faith community doesn't already provide ways for youth to serve, start something. You might suggest a goal for your faith community: to engage *every* young person, starting at age 5, in at least *one* service project each year. *Tip:* Service activities are especially powerful when they are followed by *intentional reflection.* In other words, do it—then think about it, talk about it, decide what you've learned from it, and figure out if you'd like to do it differently next time.

● Faith communities often ask their members for financial pledges, and each household (usually the parents) makes one pledge. Suggest that your faith community ask young people to make their own pledges, using their allowance or job earnings.

● Start (or join) a peer ministry/peer helping program—a way to serve others your own age. Kids and teens often go to each other with their problems, which is how peer ministry began.

Assets in Action

High school senior Josh Root gets together weekly with a 12-year-old named Joe for roller-skating, swimming, and trips to the arcade. It's part of a service project organized by his congregation, Mt. Olivet Lutheran in **Minneapolis, Minnesota.** *Josh knows that his volunteer work helps the community, but he also admits to doing it "for very selfish reasons. I help you, you help me—it just gives me a feel-good euphoria."*

With Your Friends

Service is more fun when you do it with a friend—or a group of friends. Get a friend involved with a family service project; join or start a service club with your friends at school or in your faith community. Or connect with a community or national organization. You'll have fun, strengthen your friendship(s), and enjoy the satisfaction that comes from pursuing worthwhile goals together.

For more tips and suggestions on serving others, see assets #26: Caring and #27: Equality and Social Justice.

RESOURCES

For everyone:

Stone Soup for the World: Life-Changing Stories of Ordinary Kindness & Courageous Acts of Service (Berkeley, CA: Conari Press, 1998). Includes more than 100 inspiring stories by or about Nelson Mandela, Mother Teresa, Christopher Reeve, Ram Das, Steven Spielberg, and others, plus an extensive resource guide and directory to service groups and social organizations around the country.

Energize, Inc.
5450 Wissahickon Avenue
Philadelphia, PA 19144
(215) 438-8342
www.energizeinc.com
Founded in 1977, Energize, Inc. assists organizations of all types (health and human service organizations, cultural arts groups, professional associations, schools) with their volunteer efforts. Check out their Web site or call to request a free catalog of books, training materials, and software (which includes resources for youth).

Points of Light Institute
1875 K Street, Fifth Floor
Washington, DC 20006
(202) 729-8000
www.pointsoflight.org
The Points of Light Institute works with a nationwide network of over 500 Volunteer Centers; offers training, products, programs, and services; and calls attention to "Daily Points of Light"—people and organizations making a difference. You can read more than a thousand "Daily Points of Light" profiles on their Web site.

The Prudential Spirit of Community Initiative
www.prudential.com/community
A series of programs that encourage young people to get actively involved in making their communities better places to live. In partnership with the National Association of Secondary School Principals (NASSP), Prudential sponsors the Prudential Spirit of Community Awards to recognize young people ages 11–18 for outstanding self-initiated community service. Go online to meet the winners.

For you:

Catch the Spirit! A Student's Guide to Community Service (The Prudential in cooperation with the U.S. Department of Education, 1996). A free 16-page booklet of tips and ideas. Write to: The Consumer Information Center, Dept. 588C, Pueblo, CO 81009. Or download the booklet from the Prudential Web site.

The Kid's Guide to Service Projects by Barbara A. Lewis (Minneapolis: Free Spirit Publishing, 2009). More than 500 service ideas for youth, from simple projects to large-scale initiatives.

A Student's Guide to Volunteering by Theresa Foy DiGeronimo (Franklin Lakes, NJ: Career Press, 1995). A road map for the who, what, where, when, why, and how of getting involved. Includes the real-life experiences of teens, a directory of national organization resources, and a list of local Volunteer Centers.

For your family:

Volunteer Vacations: Short-Term Adventures That Will Benefit You and Others by Bill McMillon (Chicago: Chicago Review Press, updated often). Lists and describes over 250 organizations offering short-term volunteer opportunities here and abroad; includes vignettes by actual volunteer vacationers.

For your teachers:

National Service-Learning Clearinghouse
www.servicelearning.org
A clearinghouse on service learning, funded by Learn and Serve America.

For your faith community:

Beyond Leaf Raking: Learning to Serve/Serving to Learn by Peter L. Benson and Eugene C. Roehlkepartain (Nashville, TN: Abingdon Press, 1993). Helps faith communities integrate a service-learning philosophy into their youth ministry.

Asset #10

55% of the youth we surveyed have this asset in their lives.

SAFETY

You feel safe at home, at school, and in your neighborhood.

At Home

Make family safety plans.

Have family meetings about ways to stay safe at home. Here are five topics you'll want to cover:

1. What are your family's house rules about answering the telephone, opening the door to strangers, spending time at home alone, using appliances, watching TV, and surfing the Internet? (Work together on rules everyone can understand, learn, and agree to follow.)

2. What would you do in a fire? (Ask your local fire department for advice. Hold family practice drills.)

3. What would you do in other emergencies? (Post emergency numbers by the telephone and keep them current. *Examples:* police, fire, poison control, suicide prevention, the family doctor, the family vet.)

4. What would you do if disaster struck—a flood, tornado, hurricane, earthquake, or. . . ? (Contact your local Red Cross chapter and request copies of disaster education materials including "Your Family Disaster Plan" and "Your Family Disaster Supplies Kit.")

5. If your family owns firearms—handguns, rifles, or shotguns—follow these safety instructions from the National Crime Prevention Council:

- Make sure all firearms are safely stored: unloaded, trigger-locked, and in a locked gun case or pistol box, with ammunition kept separate in its own locked case. Store keys out of reach of children, away from weapons and ammunition, and check frequently to see that storage is secure.

- Make sure all family members are fully trained in firearms safety. Refresh that training at least once a year.

- Teach young children what to do if they find a firearm or something else that might be a weapon: *Stop, Don't Touch, Get Away, and Tell a Trusted Adult.*

FACT:

Having a gun in the home won't make your family safer!

A gun kept in the home is 43 times more likely to kill a family member or friend than to stop a crime. The presence of a gun in the home triples the risk of homicide in the home. It also increases the risk of suicide fivefold.

Each day, 16 children and teenagers in the United States are killed with guns in homicides, suicides, and accidents. At least 50 more are seriously injured.

The safest thing for your family is *not to keep a gun in the home*.

Sources: Center to Prevent Handgun Violence; National Center for Health Statistics.

Make your home a safe house for your neighborhood.

Ask your parents if they'd be willing to participate in the McGruff House Safety Program. This national program establishes neighborhood homes as reliable sources of help for children who are threatened, hurt, or lost. Participating homes display a sign featuring McGruff the Crime Dog. For more information, contact:

McGruff House Safety Programs
National Crime Prevention Council
2001 Jefferson Davis Highway, Suite 901
Arlington, VA 22202
(202) 466-6272
www.ncpc.org

Even if your home isn't an official McGruff House, it can still be a safe house—known as a place that helps and welcomes kids.

Talk with your parents about your fears and concerns.

Is there something that scares you at home, in your neighborhood, at the park, at school, or anyplace else you go? Has anything happened to make you feel worried or afraid? Tell your parents and ask for their help and advice. When you live in fear, you're less likely to take healthy risks, try new things, and make positive contributions.

IMPORTANT: *If you feel unsafe at home with your family, tell a teacher, school counselor, youth group leader, religious leader, or another adult you know and trust. If you can't think of anyone, call a hotline.*

Childhelp National Child Abuse Hotline
1-800-4-A-CHILD (1-800-422-4453)

National Domestic Violence Hotline
1-800-799-SAFE (1-800-799-7233)

National Youth Crisis Hotlines
1-800-442-HOPE (1-800-442-4673)
1-800-999-9999

At School

● With your class or club, take a safety walk around your school. Identify places or things that make you feel unsafe. Come up with ideas for changing them so everyone feels safer, and present them to your principal.

● Survey the students in your school to learn what they think about school safety. Where do they feel safe, and why? Where *don't* they feel safe, and why? What specific things have happened to make them feel unsafe? What ideas do they have for making your school safer? Present the survey results and students' ideas to your principal and/or your school board. Ask how you can help implement some of the ideas.

● Start a Crime Clue Box at your school—a place where students can anonymously report crimes or other suspicious activities they witness personally. Notify your local law enforcement agency or crime prevention council about your Crime Clue Box. They can collect the clues on a regular basis and follow up on the information.

● Work with your class, club, teachers, administration, and community to make your school safer for everyone. *Examples:* Hold a Safety Fair; start an antiviolence poster contest; have an antiviolence rally; ask for a uniformed police officer to be present at your school during school hours and events.

FACT:

If you feel unsafe at school, you're not alone!

In a 1996 survey, 29 percent of high school students knew someone who had brought a weapon to school, 19 percent knew of the presence of gangs at their school, and 12 percent felt unsafe at their own school.

In a 1995 survey, 10 percent of high school students said they had carried a weapon (knife, gun, or club) to school in the past 30 days. Eight percent reported having been threatened or injured with a weapon on school property. Five percent said they had stayed home from school at least one day due to feeling unsafe at school or while traveling to and from school.

Sources: National School Safety Center Statistical Review, School Crime and Violence Summaries from *The 27th Annual Survey of High Achievers; Juvenile Offenders and Victims: 1997 Update on Violence.*

● Encourage your parents and other adults to volunteer in the schools. Especially if you feel unsafe at school, this will give your parents firsthand knowledge of the reasons why. See Asset #6: Parent Involvement in Schooling.

● Establish a peer mediation program so students can help each other resolve conflicts peacefully. See Asset #36: Peaceful Conflict Resolution.

● Encourage your school to set and enforce a zero-tolerance policy regarding weapons, violence, harassment, and racial incidents. Establish an anonymous way for students to report when others violate these boundaries.

Assets in Action

T.C. Williams High School in **Alexandria, Virginia,** *uses parents and grandparents as hall monitors and has a zero-tolerance policy toward guns and drugs. Suspensions are down 40 percent since the policy took effect.*

After two students were shot and killed at Reseda High School in **Los Angeles, California,** *a group of students started a program called W.A.R.N. (Weapons Are Removed Now). Their message is simple:* Students who bring weapons to school aren't your friends. *The students take their message to local middle schools and elementary schools with raps, skits, speeches, and question-and-answer sessions. The W.A.R.N. program is being used in schools across the country. For more information, send a self-addressed, stamped envelope to Dr. Jay J. Shaffer, W.A.R.N., Reseda High School, 18230 Kittredge Street, Reseda, CA 91335.*

At Glen Oaks High School in **Baton Rouge, Louisiana,** *the Security Dads (volunteer fathers) walk the halls, monitor the cafeteria, attend school activities, and listen to students who want to talk. The program is modeled after one that started in Indianapolis five years ago and has since expanded to several high schools. For more information, contact Security Dads, Inc., 11348 Cherry Blossom East Drive, Fishers, IN 46038; (317) 371-4094.*

In Your Community

● Caring neighborhoods are safer neighborhoods. Get to know your neighbors. Do your part to make your neighborhood a place where people notice each other, look out for each other, and are genuinely interested in each other's welfare. See Asset #4: Caring Neighborhood.

● With a group of neighbors, take annual safety walks around your neighborhood. Look for overgrown lots; abandoned buildings, vehicles, and appliances; poorly lit streets, intersections, sidewalks, and alleys; litter; public play areas that are blocked from view; signs of vandalism (broken windows, graffiti); and anything else that concerns you. Clean up what you can. Report problem situations or properties to your neighborhood group, local police, city public works department, or a community information and referral service (*example:* United Way).

Assets in Action

Led by a former elementary school principal, residents of an inner-city neighborhood in **Chicago, Illinois,** *worked together to address safety concerns in their community. They joined forces to evict undesirable neighbors involved in illegal activities, convert abandoned lots into supervised playgrounds, organize a preschool program, and start an after-school recreational program for children and parents.*

When Paul Ohlrogge plans Safe Night in **Wisconsin** *events for his community, he focuses on asset building. Safe Night is a statewide program that began as a citizen action initiative to counter violence in larger cities. Ohlrogge plans several Safe Night events a year to build intergenerational relationships and strengthen a sense of community caring.*

● Choose a safety-related issue that interests you, then get involved in helping your community. *Examples:* You might educate others about fire prevention, seat belt and/or bicycle helmet use, drunk driving, alcohol and drug abuse, home safety, poison safety, Internet safety, or emergency services available in your community. Or you might focus on crime prevention, accident prevention, or disaster prevention and preparation. Or you might teach a class in safety for latchkey kids.

● Work with your community to organize a gun turn-in or buy-back program. People can exchange weapons (including toy guns) for cash, coupons from local merchants, books, or nonviolent toys.

● Get to know the police officers who patrol your neighborhood—on foot or by car—and don't hesitate to call them if you sense or see something wrong.

Learn how to report potentially violent situations or unsafe conditions in your neighborhood. Find out if your local police department offers crime prevention or self-defense classes; if they do, sign up.

● Look around to see what happens to young people after school—especially if schools in your community let students out in the early afternoon or mid-afternoon. What do kids do until their parents get home? Are there supervised programs for younger children? Are there opportunities for teens and preteens to work with children, get or give homework help, tackle neighborhood problems, or learn art, music, sports, or computer skills? *Tip:* In many areas, after-school programs are located in schools themselves and are called Safe Havens or Beacon Schools.

● Speak out when you hear adults blame teenagers for all kinds of crimes. In fact, only about 5 out of 1,000 teens are arrested for violent crime each year. Many more teens are working to *prevent* crime in their communities.

● Join a crimefighting program for youth. Check with your local police to see if a program exists in your area. Or get involved with one of these national programs:

Teens, Crime, and the Community (TCC)
c/o National Crime Prevention Council (see page 93)
www.ncpc.org/programs/tcc

Ignitus Worldwide
9200 South Dadeland Boulevard, Suite 417
Miami, FL 33156
(305) 670-2409
www.ignitusworldwide.org

● Work with your parents and neighbors to start a Neighborhood Watch Program. Contact your local police department or city offices to learn how. Or get your neighborhood involved with the National Night Out program. For more information about National Night Out, contact:

National Association of Town Watch
1-800-648-3688
www.nationaltownwatch.org

DON'T BE A VICTIM:

TIPS FOR AVOIDING CRIME

Teenagers are crime's most frequent targets. They're twice as likely as adults to be the victims of violent crimes. Follow these tips to lower your risk.

1. Whenever possible, go out in a group or with a friend. Try not to go places alone, especially at night. Stay away from poorly lighted, secluded spots. Be aware of your surroundings at all times.

2. Always let a trustworthy person know where you are and when you'll be coming home. Tell a parent, a grandparent, an older sister or brother, a close friend, or a neighbor you can count on.

3. Trust your instincts. If a situation doesn't feel right to you, get away and get help.

4. Always keep change in your pocket for an emergency phone call.

5. Carry your purse or wallet close to your body. Keep valuables out of sight. Lock them in the trunk of your car, keep them in your (locked) locker at school, or leave them at home.

6. Don't hitchhike or go home from parties with strangers or new acquaintances.

7. Don't get involved with drugs or alcohol.

8. Wear clothing and shoes that give you the freedom to run if you have to.

9. Lock your doors and windows, even during the day. Don't open your door to strangers. If you're traveling in a car, lock that door, too.

10. Don't give out personal information (your name, address, etc.) over the phone or the Internet. And never tell anyone that you're home alone.

11. Don't give anyone your house keys or let anyone copy them, not even your friends.

12. Report any crimes or suspected crimes at once. If you're a victim, the best thing you can do is to report it right away. Tell an adult who can help you. Call the police or go to the police.

Adapted from *Kids with Courage* by Barbara A. Lewis. Free Spirit Publishing Inc., 1992, pages 8–9. Used with permission. Teen crime facts from the National Crime Prevention Council.

In Your Faith Community

● Talk with youth and adult leaders about how to make your place of worship a safe place for youth. *Example:* Set clear ground rules for what's okay and not okay between youth and adult leaders. Know what to do if those rules are violated.

● Organize after-school activities for neighborhood children so they have a safe place to go. Organize after-school activities for teenagers, too. Most juvenile violent crimes are committed between 3 P.M. and 6 P.M. Work to keep kids off the streets and out of trouble.

● Teach safety awareness and street smarts to younger kids in your faith community.

With Your Friends

● When you go to unfamiliar places, invite friends to accompany you so you won't be alone.

● If someone you don't know well asks you out, suggest a double date first. Or spend time together in public places until you're sure that he or she is respectful and responsible.

● Practice street smarts together. Watch out for each other. Don't tease or challenge each other to take stupid risks. Make a pact to stay safe together—and to help each other make good choices.

RESOURCES

For everyone:

National Crime Prevention Council (NCPC)
2001 Jefferson Davis Highway, Suite 901
Arlington, VA 22202
(202) 466-6272
www.ncpc.org
The home of McGruff the Crime Dog, NCPC has a wealth of information on staying safe and preventing crime. Go online and take the quiz "What Do You Know About Teens as Crime Victims?"

For your parents:

Safe and Sound: Protecting Your Child in an Unpredictable World by Vanessa L. Ochs (New York: Penguin, 1995). Advice to help parents walk the sometimes thin line between protection and overprotection.

For educators:

Safe and Drug-Free Schools Program
www2.ed.gov/osdfs
The federal government's primary vehicle for reducing drug use, alcohol use, tobacco use, and violence through education and prevention activities in our nation's schools.

BOUNDARIES AND EXPECTATIONS

These assets are about knowing what's in bounds and out of bounds when it comes to your behavior. They're about rules and consequences—and about adults who care enough to follow through. They're also about people who challenge and inspire you to do your best and believe in yourself.

The boundaries and expectations assets are:

11. Family Boundaries
12. School Boundaries
13. Neighborhood Boundaries
14. Adult Role Models
15. Positive Peer Influence
16. High Expectations

43% of the youth we surveyed have this asset in their lives.

FAMILY BOUNDARIES

Your family has both clear rules and consequences for your behavior. They also monitor your whereabouts.

At Home

Look on the bright side.

Boundaries, rules, consequences . . . who needs them? In fact, we all do. Life without them would be chaos. They guide us in making good decisions and provide a structure for our everyday lives. Try thinking of family boundaries as *positives* rather than negatives. And be glad if your parents care enough to bother with them; some parents don't.

Know your family's boundaries.

If you don't know your family's boundaries, ask your parents. How late can you stay up? Where can you go—and not go? Who with? Which behaviors are okay and which aren't? Boundaries should be *clear, concise, consistent,* and *developmentally appropriate.* In other words:

● Boundaries should be brief and to the point. The more complicated they are, the more confusing they get, and the more opportunities there are for loopholes and arguments.

● Parents should agree and stand together on boundaries and consequences. (This makes "Wait-until-your-father-gets-home" or "Wait-until-your-mother-hears-about-this" threats unnecessary. It also means that you can't play one parent against the other.)

● A 17-year-old shouldn't have the same boundaries as a 7-year old (although a 17-year-old still needs boundaries).

● Everyone should know and understand what's expected of them.

Ask what happens if you ignore a boundary or break a rule. Consequences should be *reasonable* and *logical*.

Once you get the answers you need, take some time to think them over. Can you respect and accept your family's boundaries? Why or why not? Tell your parents how you feel and why. Listen to their side. If you can come up with alternatives, maybe your parents will try things your way.

Ask if you can work together as a family to define boundaries, rules, and consequences. When you're part of the process, you can question rules that seem unreasonable and suggest consequences that seem fair.

Tip: This assumes that you and your parents can talk to each other. If you can't, see Asset #2: Positive Family Communication and work on building that asset first.

FACT:

Teens want more family boundaries!

According to a recent nationwide survey of more than 218,000 students in grades 6–12, 53 percent say they either have enough or too much freedom, 35 percent think it's okay for parents to block violent or offensive content on TV, and 30 percent want restrictions on teens' Internet access.

In another survey of 600 youth ages 12–17, 49 percent feel that most kids their age need more guidance and attention from adults.

Sources: "USA Weekend's 10th Annual Teen Report: Teens & Freedom," reported in *USA Weekend*, May 2–4, 1997; *Kids These Days: What Americans Really Think About the Next Generation* (New York: Public Agenda, 1997).

Earn the freedom you crave.

Often there's a painful gap between what teens *want* to do and what their parents will *let* them do. If you and your parents argue a lot, it's probably related to this freedom gap. You want MORE freedom, which makes your parents anxious and fearful. From your perspective, it's a wide, wonderful world out there, full of things you can't wait to have and try. From their perspective, it's a big, bad world out there, full of things that can hurt you or even kill you. You push; they pull. You rebel; they crack down.

If you weren't rebellious to some extent, you wouldn't be a teenager. But there's a better way to gain more freedom: by earning it. In your parents' minds, there's a direct connection between freedom and trust. The more they trust you, the more freedom you'll (probably) have. The less they trust you, the less freedom you'll (definitely) get.

How can you build your parents' trust? Be responsible. Be honest. Think before you act. Keep your promises. Do your homework without being reminded. Do your chores without being told. Let your parents know what's happening in your life—at school, with your friends, in the community. Think of other things you can do that your parents value and appreciate. Prove to them that you can handle the freedom you crave.

THE FINE ART OF NEGOTIATION:

TIPS FOR GETTING **5** MORE FREEDOM

If you're a responsible, trustworthy person, you should be in a position to negotiate for more freedom. Here's how:

1. Set up a meeting with your parents. Pick a time that works for everyone. Plan to show up a few minutes early.

2. Choose a comfortable, quiet place to meet. If home is usually busy and noisy, consider meeting in a park, taking a walk together, or finding a table at a favorite restaurant.

3. Prepare an agenda for your meeting in advance. Write down some of the points you plan to raise. Otherwise you might forget some of the things you want to say, or get distracted by side issues. An agenda will keep you on track.

4. Do your part to keep the meeting positive, upbeat, and civil. This shouldn't be a gripe session. Be clear about what you want; hear what your parents have to say. Try to reach a consensus—an agreement about what you want and what your parents are willing to give.

5. If at first you don't succeed, don't be discouraged. Especially if this is your first attempt at negotiating with your parents, you may get a few wires crossed. If the meeting goes nowhere, suggest that you adjourn and reconvene in a week or so. Then be on your best behavior until you meet again.

CONTINUED ON NEXT PAGE...

It may seem as if you have no freedom, no rights, and no fun; as if your parents don't trust you and want to control every aspect of your life. Maybe you're exaggerating—or maybe they are too strict. Either way, it won't matter for that much longer. Eventually you *will* be leaving home. Part of what your parents are trying to do is teach you the skills to succeed when you're on your own. You might give them a little credit for having good intentions.

Adapted from *The Gifted Kids' Survival Guide: A Teen Handbook* by Judy Galbraith, M.A., and Jim Delisle, Ph.D. Free Spirit Publishing Inc., 1996, page 238. Used with permission.

Keep track of each other's whereabouts.

It's perfectly reasonable for your parents to want to know where you are—and vice versa. If they're going out for the evening, they should let you know where they'll be and how you can reach them in an emergency. This makes good sense and it's respectful.

If your family hasn't yet figured out a way for everyone to communicate their whereabouts, brainstorm some options together. *Examples:*

● Hang a message board or whiteboard on the back of the kitchen door (or whatever door everyone uses most often). Use it to write messages to each other ("Gone to Ben's, back by dinner" or "Play rehearsal—might run late. Yolanda's dad will drive me home").

● Get a calendar with lots of writing space, then put it where everyone will see it. Have everyone in the family start each week by writing down details about where they'll be and when. *Tip:* This also gives your family the chance to identify conflicting schedules and problem solve in advance.

● Get everyone in the family a pager or a cellphone. (If you have a part-time job, offer to pay for all or part of your own cellphone, since you'll probably use it most to talk with your friends.)

Or come up with ideas that fit your family's unique circumstances. Keep trying different ideas until you find one that works for everybody.

Assets in Action

When a father in **Moorhead, Minnesota,** saw an assets bookmark that was being distributed throughout his community, he took special note of the asset that emphasized parental monitoring. His 15-year-old son had been complaining that Dad was being "overprotective" because he always wanted to know where his son was. The father pulled out the bookmark and said "See, son, even the community thinks I need to know where you are. Everybody in the community knows it's important that parents know where their kids are."

Beat your parents to the punch.

If your parents drive you crazy with questions about where you're going, who with, what for, and how long, beat them to it. Give them the information they want *before* they ask. *Tip:* Put it in the form of a question. Instead of "Tam and I are going to the 8:00 movie, then out to eat, and I'll be back by midnight," try "I'd like to go to the 8:00 movie with Tam, then out to eat, and be back by midnight. Okay with you?" Then your parents can graciously give their permission. This way, everyone benefits. They get to feel generous, and you get to go out with your friend.

At School

Ask a teacher if you can have a class discussion about family boundaries. Here are some questions to start with:

● What are some of the boundaries or rules in your family?

● Are these boundaries reasonable? Too strict? Too lenient?

● How would your life be better if your parents didn't set boundaries? How would it be worse?

● What would you tell a friend who had major disagreements with his or her parents about boundaries?

If you learn anything interesting from this discussion, share it with your parents.

In Your Community

● If you see younger kids in your neighborhood doing things that are out of bounds, tell them you're going to speak to their parents. Then do it.

● Ask your community center to sponsor discussion nights for parents and teens on the topic of family boundaries. Invite family counselors or other experts to introduce and lead the discussions.

● Design and create a form that family members can sign, pledging to keep each other informed of their whereabouts. You can use it in your own family— but don't stop there. Introduce the form at a neighborhood or community meeting, and have copies available for everyone who wants one. (*Tip:* This would be perfect for a discussion night about family boundaries.)

𝕱amily 𝖂hereabouts 𝕮ontract

We, the members of the _____ family, promise to keep each other informed of our whereabouts at all times. This means telling someone in the family:

      1) where we'll be
      2) the name(s) of the person(s) we'll be with
      3) a number where we can be reached, and
      4) when we'll be back.

Signed on this date _____

by   _____   _____

      _____   _____

      _____   _____

In Your Faith Community

Make boundaries the topic of your next youth retreat. You might talk about what your faith tradition says about boundaries and discipline in the home; what boundaries and rules are common in your own families; and how you can set boundaries for yourselves.

With Your Friends

● Respect each other's family boundaries.

● Talk with each other about family boundaries, rules, and consequences. Better yet, if everyone is willing, get your family and a friend's family together to talk about boundaries, rules, and consequences. Share experiences and learn from each other.

● With a friend or small group of friends, play "At what age. . . ?" Imagine that you have children. Then imagine at what age you'd allow your children to do each of the following things . . . if ever. (When you put yourself in your parents' shoes, things look a little different.)

At what age would I allow my child to . . .

. . . wear makeup?

. . . work part-time during the school year?

. . . drink alcohol for the first time?

. . . get her or his ear(s) pierced?

. . . get a tattoo?

. . . buy a car?

. . . start dating?

. . . go steady?

. . . stay out past midnight on weekends?

. . . not have a curfew?

. . . rent a hotel room?

. . . go to a boy/girl party?

. . . go to a kegger?

. . . dye his or her hair?

. . . choose his or her own clothes?

. . . stay home alone when parents go out of town?

. . . take a weekend camping trip with his or her friends?

. . . go to an R-rated movie?

. . . take a road trip with a friend?

RESOURCES

For your parents:

Parenting Toward Solutions: How Parents Can Use Skills They Already Have to Raise Responsible, Loving Kids by Linda Metcalf (Upper Saddle River, NJ: Prentice Hall, 1996). Practical ways to create and enforce family boundaries to bring out the best in your children.

Positive Discipline A–Z: 1001 Solutions to Everyday Parenting Problems by Jane Nelson, Lynn Lott, and H. Stephen Glenn (Rocklin, CA: Prima Publishing, 1993). Win-win ways to address and prevent just about every child-raising problem you can think of, in convenient alphabetical order.

Positive Parenting Your Teens: The A to Z Book of Sound Advice and Practical Solutions by Karen Renshaw Joslin and Mary Bunting Decher (New York: Fawcett Columbine, 1997). Quick, clear, workable strategies emphasize cooperation, active listening, and mutual respect. Common problems are arranged alphabetically (from "abstinence" to "zits"), with sample dialogue to guide you in talking with your teen.

Asset #12

46% of the youth we surveyed have this asset in their lives.

SCHOOL BOUNDARIES

Your school has clear rules and consequences for behavior.

At Home

● If your school publishes a student handbook, bring a copy home so your parents can read it. Or read it together.

● Talk with your parents about the school boundaries. Are they clear, concise, consistent, and developmentally appropriate? Are there any you disagree with or don't understand? Are they similar to or different from your family's boundaries?

● If there's a conflict between a school boundary and a family boundary, talk about how to handle it. Maybe it's not a big deal. If it is, meet with the school principal. Calmly state your concern and suggest solutions. If the conflict is related to a religious belief, talk first with your religious leader to learn how this type of conflict has been handled in the past. If the conflict is related to a personal belief, think hard about how important it is to you and whether it's worth fighting about. *Example:* Your school has a rule about students wearing T-shirts printed with certain words. You and your parents believe that this violates your constitutional right to free speech. Are you willing to get suspended or expelled, miss class or go to court over this issue? Or can you find another way to exercise your free speech? *Tip:* Choose your battles carefully and weigh the possible outcomes before you start swinging.

● Encourage your parents to volunteer at your school (see Asset #6: Parent Involvement in Schooling). Or, if they're not able to volunteer, encourage them to visit. Then they can see for themselves what the boundaries are at your school—and whether students respect them.

● Tell your parents when you're feeling pressured to violate a school boundary. Ask for their help and support.

Assets in Action

At Benilde-St. Margaret's High School in **St. Louis Park, Minnesota,** *the Parent Communication Network (PCN) encourages students' parents to communicate with each other about boundaries. Parents who belong to PCN agree to communicate by telephone regarding their students' activities, always chaperon their students' parties, and host and support chemically free activities. Parent members are listed in the student directory.*

At School

Welcome your school's boundaries.

You have the right to attend a school where boundaries are clear, appropriate, and respected by everyone. A school with boundaries is a school where students are free to learn. A school without boundaries—or one where boundaries are ignored or violated—is a school where learning takes second place to survival. If you think that your school's boundaries are stupid, insulting, or too restrictive, consider the alternative.

Assets in Action

Sweetwater High in **National City, California,** *created the Link Crew to promote respect for school boundaries. The Crew—a group of 12th graders—explained the do's and don'ts of behavior to new students and talked with students teachers were struggling with. Grades and attendance improved, and fewer new students spent time in the principal's office.*

Know your school's boundaries.

If your school publishes a student handbook, read it. In addition to the usual stuff about academic and graduation requirements, holidays, and student activities, the handbook should also provide clear and specific information about school standards, student behavior, and sanctions (disciplinary actions). Check to see that your handbook covers these areas (and any others that apply to your school):

- absences (excused/unexcused)
- alcohol/other drugs/paraphernalia
- appearance (dress code/hair code)
- assault
- attendance/skipping classes
- automobiles/parking
- bullying/threats
- cheating/dishonesty
- corporal punishment*
- defiance of authority/disrespect
- destruction of school property/ vandalism
- detention
- discrimination
- disorderly conduct/endangerment
- disruptive devices (boomboxes, firecrackers, etc.)
- distribution of materials (publications, etc.) on school premises
- electronic devices (pagers, cellphones, personal stereos, etc.)
- expulsion
- extracurricular activities/ school-sponsored activities
- fighting
- gang activity/gang association
- homework
- Internet use
- loitering
- plagiarism
- profanity/obscenity
- public displays of affection (PDAs, also known as making out)
- racism/bigotry
- sexual harassment
- smoking/tobacco use
- stealing/theft
- suspension
- tardiness
- verbal abuse
- violent behavior
- weapons (guns, knives, etc.)

If your student handbook doesn't cover these areas—or if it covers them poorly, without specifics and in language that's unreadable or outdated—then it needs a makeover. Ask your principal if one is planned for the near future. If it is, ask if students can sit on the committee responsible for the makeover and offer their input. Or this might be something your student council or school club can handle, with help and advice from the administration. *Tip:* Take a look at other student handbooks. Contact schools in your city or state, or go online. Use a search engine to find "student handbook," then look for URLs (Internet addresses) with ".edu" or "k12."

IMPORTANT: *If you're in a school where boundaries are a joke, get out if at all possible. See if you can transfer to another school in your area—one where conditions are better. If your family can afford private school, find out if this is an option for you. Private schools linked with specific faiths (Catholic schools, Lutheran schools, etc.) are often less expensive than secular (non-religious) private schools; if your family belongs to a church, you might qualify for a scholarship, grant, or reduced tuition. Check into the availability of independent study programs, correspondence courses, charter schools, vouchers (tax credits or other incentives for families whose children attend private schools), and early college entrance. Don't give up!*

---

* Thirty states still permit corporal punishment (swats or paddling) in schools. The other 20 states have banned it.

Respect your school's boundaries.

If some school boundaries seem inappropriate, don't just ignore them. Talk to your teachers, your principal, or the student council about changing them.

If you see someone violating a school boundary, do something about it. Depending on the circumstance, you might intervene personally or report the violation to a teacher or administrator. Or use peer mediation to resolve boundary violations. See Asset #36: Peaceful Conflict Resolution.

Be a role model for other students. Positive peer pressure can be a powerful force. Especially if you're a student leader, it's your responsibility to follow the school rules. And if you're not a student leader, you can still act like one. Use common sense—and good manners. Etiquette can go a long way toward creating a school climate where everyone respects school boundaries.

THE
30
COMMANDMENTS OF CLASSROOM
ETIQUETTE FOR STUDENTS

Thou shalt. . .

. . . listen to thy teacher

. . . think before speaking

. . . clean up after thyself

. . . come to class prepared

. . . raise thy hand to be called upon

. . . be respectful of other people's ideas

. . . compliment each other

. . . remove thy hat in class

. . . address thy classmates and teachers with kindness and respect

. . . keep thy hands and feet to thyself

. . . say "Please," "Thank you," "Excuse me," and "I'm sorry"

. . . find another response for displeasure besides anger

. . . work diligently in class, even if thou must pretend to be interested in a subject or assignment

. . . talk directly to the person with whom thou hast a conflict, rather than to everyone else

. . . remember that teachers have feelings, too.

CONTINUED ON NEXT PAGE...

Thou shalt not. . .

. . . bully others
. . . be physically or verbally aggressive
. . . sexually harass others
. . . ignore a reasonable request
. . . talk when a teacher or classmate is talking
. . . take another's property without permission
. . . backbite or spread rumors
. . . put people down to seem cool
. . . interfere with each other's learning
. . . act bored or fall asleep in class
. . . make hurtful comments about another person's looks, abilities, background, family, ethnic heritage, or sexual orientation
. . . pressure others into doing things that are mean, harmful, or illegal
. . . have an attitude
. . . belch or pass gas on purpose
. . . cause the chalk to squeak.

From *How Rude! The Teenagers' Guide to Good Manners, Proper Behavior, and Not Grossing People Out* by Alex J. Packer, Ph.D. Free Spirit Publishing Inc., 1997, page 193. Used with permission.

Work for stronger boundaries, if that's what your school needs.

Form a committee of other students who feel the way you do. Find an adult sponsor—a teacher, coach, or school counselor—who's willing to work with you. Brainstorm a list of problems at your school. (*Examples:* cheating, stealing, fighting, weapons, drugs, sexual harassment, racial discrimination, skipping class, students loitering in the halls, swearing, bullying.) Then brainstorm boundaries for each area—and consequences for infractions. Refine your lists and summarize your work in a Code of Conduct for your school. Present it to your principal and ask for his or her feedback. Work together on a final version. Make sure it's clear, and keep it as concise as you can—one page if possible. Send copies home to parents and post them throughout your school.

Is your school a *closed campus,* meaning that students must remain on campus during the entire school day? Or is it an *open campus,* meaning that students are allowed to leave the grounds during lunchtime and free periods? If it's open, you might work to close it. (Do this with a group of friends, preferably a *large* group of friends, since you won't be very popular in the process.) Closing a campus helps to strengthen school boundaries. It's also one of the most inexpensive and effective safety measures a school can take.

FACT:

Teens want stronger school boundaries!

According to a recent nationwide survey of over 1,300 high school students, 79 percent say they would learn more if schools enforced being on time and completing homework. Seven in 10 public school teenagers say there are too many disruptive students in their class, and 8 in 10 say that removing unruly teens from regular classes would help them learn more. Half of the teenagers surveyed say that drugs and violence are serious problems in their schools.

In another survey of more than 218,000 students in grades 6–12, 58 percent believe that school officials should have the right to search a student's locker for drugs or weapons without permission, and 75 percent think schools should ban clothing with gang symbols.

Sources: *Getting By: What American Teenagers Really Think About Their Schools* (New York: Public Agenda, 1997); "USA Weekend's 10th Annual Teen Report: Teens & Freedom," reported in *USA Weekend,* May 2–4, 1997.

In Your Community

● Are school boundaries consistent from school to school? It helps when all students hear the same message, no matter what school they attend. Learn about the boundaries at different schools in your area. Encourage the schools to communicate with each other and get together on the issue of boundaries.

● Write an article for your community's newspaper about what schools expect of students. Give examples of how youth are respecting school boundaries.

In Your Faith Community

● Talk with other youth about boundaries in the schools you attend. Which boundaries are the same? Which are different?

● Does your faith community have clear rules and consequences for behavior? If not, why not? Maybe you could work with your youth group to create a "student handbook" for your faith community.

With Your Friends

● Make a pact to support each other in school when there's pressure to violate school boundaries.

● Never pressure each other (or anyone else) to violate school boundaries.

● As a group, model responsible behavior for other students. Show that you respect the school boundaries.

RESOURCES

For everyone:

The Center for Effective Discipline
327 Groveport Pike
Canal Winchester, OH 43110
(614) 834-7946
www.stophitting.com
Corporal punishment of children is unsupported by educational research, sometimes leads to serious injury, and contributes to a pro-violence attitude. CED provides educational information to the public on the effects of corporal punishment and alternatives to its use. CED is headquarters for and coordinates two other organizations: the National Coalition to Abolish Corporal Punishment in Schools (NCACPS) and End Physical Punishment of Children (EPOCH-USA). If your state still permits corporal punishment, CED can help you work to eliminate it.

For your parents:

A Parent's Guide to Innovative Education: Working with Teachers, Schools, and Your Children for Real Learning by Anne Wescott Dodd (Chicago: Noble Press, 1992). Positive strategies for how parents and children can bring out the best in their schools.

For educators:

National School Safety Center
141 Duesenberg Drive, Suite 7B
Westlake Village, CA 91362
(805) 373-9977
www.schoolsafety.us
Created by presidential directive in 1984, NSSC works to promote safe schools—free of crime and violence—and to help ensure quality education for all of America's children.

46% of the youth
we surveyed have this
asset in their lives.

NEIGHBORHOOD BOUNDARIES

Your neighbors take responsibility for monitoring your behavior.

At Home

● Ask your parents what their neighborhoods were like when they were growing up. Did they know their neighbors? Did their neighbors know them? Did adults keep an eye on the kids? Did they step in and say or do something when they noticed inappropriate behavior?

● On your own and as a family, get to know your neighbors. When people know each other, they're more likely to watch out for each other. See Asset #4: Caring Neighborhood.

At School

● Talk with other students about neighborhood boundaries. Do their neighborhoods have boundaries for young people's behavior? How do they know? Which neighbors seem to notice and care about what they do? How do they (the students) feel about that?

● Learn about and respect the boundaries in your school's neighborhood. *Examples:* no littering, no cutting across neighbors' lawns, no loitering on private property, no booming car stereos.

In Your Community

Be glad if your neighborhood has boundaries.

You've probably been warned to stay out of certain neighborhoods in your community. They're the ones with high crime rates, trash in the streets, boarded-up windows, and chain-link fences with Rottweilers behind them. Maybe some neighbors take responsibility for monitoring kids' behavior, but those are the courageous few. The others are afraid of the kids, afraid of the kids' parents—afraid of each other. (If you live in that kind of neighborhood, then you know how bad it is.)

Nobody wants to live in a neighborhood without boundaries. We'd all rather live where people care about each other. So if your next-door neighbor seems nosy, or the neighbor across the street is always nagging you about something, try not to mind too much. Things could be worse. For a lot of teens, things *are* worse.

Assets in Action

Jeff Roy, president of the Lennox Neighborhood Association in **St. Louis Park, Minnesota,** *is a neighbor who believes in boundaries. When three kids roared past him one summer "swearing their heads off," he shouted "Hey!" to get their attention, then said, firmly but calmly, "In this neighborhood, we don't talk that way. You need to go someplace else if you're going to talk that way." With a 10-second intervention, he showed the kids that they were noticed and cared for, and also that the community has expectations for them. Roy advocates continuous relationship building with neighborhood kids to make "street discipline" easier. "Use every opportunity to let children know you like them," he says. "Say 'Hi' and 'How's it going?' It's a risk sometimes, and it takes energy. But there's no shortcut to building a society. If we don't interact with kids today, it'll come back to haunt us in a generation."*

Help to create neighborhood boundaries.

Ideas to try:

● With your family and one or two others, host a front-yard barbecue, block party, or building party for your neighborhood. Talk about neighborhood boundaries and identify three or more that everyone can agree on. *Examples:* Respect people and property; report suspicious activity; supervise children younger than 16; end parties by 11:00 P.M.; talk to neighbors directly about problems or concerns. Publish the boundaries in a one-page newsletter and distribute it door-to-door.

● Produce a neighborhood directory listing the names, addresses, and phone numbers of neighbors who want to be included. Make copies for all neighbors who participate.

● Ask places where neighborhood kids hang out—parks, recreation centers, playgrounds—to set and post boundaries for children and teens. Ask neighborhood businesses to do the same. *Tip:* If kids are involved in setting those boundaries, they're more likely to respect them.

● Work with your youth organization, neighborhood organization, city government, or local service organization to set up a warmline for latchkey kids. A warmline is different from a hotline. Hotlines are for emergency and crisis situations; warmlines are for kids who want or need to talk to someone—about their day at school, about homework, if they're worried or scared, or if they just feel like talking. See if your local government, a TV or radio station, or a business can help by sponsoring and funding your warmline.

Assets in Action

In **Washington, D.C.**, *volunteers staff a PhoneFriend warmline and take calls from kids after school.* In **Pittsburgh, Pennsylvania**, *the University of Pittsburgh sponsors a program called Generations Together. Older residents are matched with latchkey kids, and the adults get in touch with the kids after school in person or by phone.*

Make curfews meaningful.

More and more communities across the nation are setting curfews for kids and teens. There are good arguments against curfews (besides the fact that most teenagers don't like them). *Examples:* Parents, not lawmakers, should decide when their kids are due home; parents, not police, should be responsible for making sure that their kids come home on time. Curfews promote negative stereotypes of youth as troublemakers. They may discriminate against youth of color and poor youth, and they may violate young people's constitutional rights. And it's confusing when adjacent communities have different curfews.

There are also good arguments *for* curfews. *Examples:* Curfews provide clear boundaries and supervision. They give parents an extra tool to keep their children safe (kids who are off the streets at night are less likely to be crime victims). And they give police more resources to fight crime in their communities.

In 1997, the U.S. Conference of Mayors surveyed 347 cities with populations over 30,000. They found that 272 cities (70 percent of those surveyed) had a nighttime curfew. Officials in those cities reported that the curfews are reducing juvenile crime and victimization, curbing gang violence, and helping residents feel safer.

But it's not enough to enforce curfews and punish youth who violate them. And here's where *you* come in. You can start by obeying the curfew in your community (if it has one). Beyond that, you can work with neighborhood and community groups, your school, youth organizations, adult service organizations (Rotary Club, Lions Club, etc.), and your city government to provide alternatives for kids who have nowhere to go and nothing to do but hang out on the streets.

What about opening teen centers in malls? Or keeping community and high school gyms, pools, and recreation centers open at night for supervised activities? (In Phoenix, Arizona, basketball courts and other recreational facilities are open until 2 A.M. Some neighborhoods have experienced a 55 percent drop in juvenile crime.) "Midnight basketball" is a political hot potato in many communities, but it might be something your community needs.

Teens want curfews!

According to a recent nationwide survey of more than 218,000 students in grades 6–12, 50 percent support nighttime community curfews for teens.

Source: "USA Weekend's 10th Annual Teen Report: Teens & Freedom," reported in *USA Weekend,* May 2–4, 1997.

Start watching out for younger kids in your neighborhood.

● Pay attention to what goes on in your neighborhood. Get to know as many kids as you can. Learn their names and something about them. Show that you care about them. See "55 Ways to Show Kids You Care" on page 66.

● Start a club for neighborhood kids. Plan and supervise activities for them. Be a telephone friend to a latchkey kid.

● Keep an eye on neighborhood kids—and intervene when you notice behavior that's out of bounds. This doesn't give you a license to order them around. There are better ways. . . .

12 WAYS TO CORRECT KIDS' BEHAVIOR WITHOUT BEING BOSSY OR RUDE

1. Talk in a natural tone of voice. No one likes to be yelled at. Better yet, talk more softly than usual.

2. Use I-statements, not You-statements. *Example:* Instead of "You shouldn't call each other names," try "I feel sad when you call each other names because you seem like such good friends."

3. Suggest alternatives. *Example:* "If you climb that big tree, you might fall and get hurt. Why don't we go to the park and you can climb on the monkeybars instead?"

4. Keep it short and simple (K.I.S.S.). *Example:* Instead of "Sammy, I saw you drop your soda can on the sidewalk. Now pick it up and put it in the trash can. Don't be a litterbug!" try "Sammy . . . trash can."

5. Find something to praise. *Example:* "Juan, you're a great skateboarder. But when the Kelly kids are playing on the sidewalk, could you pick up your board and carry it past them?"

6. Offer choices. *Example:* "Keisha, instead of teasing Marcy and her friend, you can either go home or help me wash the car. Which would you rather do?"

7. Build cooperation. *Example:* "Luther, if you agree to stop teasing Mr. Mikulski's dog, we can watch a video together."

8. Don't judge. Describe. *Example:* Instead of "Tony, I saw you knock over Ms. Liebow's recycling container. That was a mean thing to do. Now her cans and newspapers are all over the alley," try "Tony, Ms. Liebow's recycling ended up in the alley."

9. Give information and let kids choose to correct their own behavior. *Example:* "When you walk across Mr. Chan's yard instead of using the sidewalk, you trample his flowers."

10. Instead of having a face-to-face conversation about a negative behavior, try a "parallel conversation." Do something fun together (shoot some baskets, bake cookies, play a game) and take advantage of that time to talk.

11. Notice positive behavior. "Zoe, you helped Mrs. Romano pick up her groceries when she dropped them. Good going!"

12. Bite your tongue before using any of these phrases (or others that make kids feel small, stupid, defensive, or patronized):

"You always . . ."	"You should know better than to . . ."
"You never . . ."	"Why did you do that?"
"You shouldn't . . ."	"What were you thinking?"
"You'd better . . ."	"What's wrong with you?"
"I've told you before . . ."	"That was a dumb thing to do."

In Your Faith Community

Work with your youth group and adult members to provide supervised activities for children and youth—with clear boundaries for behavior. Maybe your building can house a drop-in center or host a late-night program for teens.

Assets in Action

Until 1995, the 300-home Raineshaven neighborhood in **Memphis, Tennessee,** *had many latchkey children who were just hanging out after school. So Estelle Paulette and Queen Smith created the Raineshaven Youth Council. Meeting in the neighborhood's Golden United Methodist Church, they hold workshops on such topics as gangs and sexual awareness. They also take students on outings.*

With Your Friends

As a group, set your own boundaries for safety, noise, and other issues. Agree to treat adults with respect. Put your boundaries in writing and present them to your neighborhood council or association. You might print them in a flyer, distribute copies to your neighbors, and post them in public places.

RESOURCES

For your parents and neighbors:

How to Talk So Kids Will Listen and Listen So Kids Will Talk by Adele Faber and Elaine Mazlish (New York: Avon Books, 1991). One of the best books ever written on how to talk with kids of all ages, filled with practical suggestions and examples.

The Youth Charter: How Communities Can Work Together to Raise Standards for All Our Children by William Damon (New York: Free Press, 1997). Presents a detailed, community-based program to raise the intellectual and moral standards of children; explains how to develop and implement a youth charter and how to combat negative media and other external influences that undermine it.

ADULT ROLE MODELS

Your parents and other adults in your life model positive, responsible behavior.

At Home

Take stock.

Who are the adult role models in your life? Think of three people you look up to. Include an adult family member (a parent or stepparent, adult sibling, aunt, uncle, grandparent, or adult cousin), a non-family member (a teacher, coach, neighbor, family friend, or youth group leader), and a national or world figure (a leader, celebrity, author, historical figure, or someone else who's been in the news). Now think of why each person is a role model for you. Why do you admire her or him? What special qualities does each person have? Are these qualities you have or would like to have someday?

If you can't name at least three adult role models . . .

Take action.

Everyone needs role models. They motivate us to dream, plan, set goals, and look forward to the future. By their lives and achievements, they say "I did it, and so can you." If you don't have any role models, find some. They're out there. Here are two ways to start:

1. Talk with your parents about their role models. Who did they look up to when they were teenagers? What about now? Is there anyone they admire that you might want to choose as a role model?

2. Ask your parents to help you identify people who deserve to be respected and imitated. They might clip articles for you from newspapers or magazines, tell you about people they admire, or introduce you to people they know.

FACT:

If you don't have role models, you're not alone!

When 1,000 students from ages 13–17 were asked to name their biggest hero today, 21 percent said "no one." Here's what other teens said:

Who's a hero? According to how many teens?

A parent	16.2%	An actor	4.7%
An athlete	15.0%	An educator	3.2%
A religious leader	6.8%	A business leader	0.7%
A musician	6.4%	A politician	0.3%
A friend	5.5%	A community activist	0.2%

Source: *The Mood of American Youth* (Alexandria, VA: Horatio Alger Association of Distinguished Americans and the National Association of Secondary School Principals, 1996).

Choose your role models carefully.

It's easy to pick celebrities (actors, athletes, rock stars, rappers, talk show hosts, supermodels, etc.) because they seem to be everywhere—in movies and on TV, on the radio, in magazines, in advertisements. Before you choose them, learn more about them.

Don't be fooled by media campaigns that promote celebrities as role models. In a recent article about Tiger Woods, author Jeff Wallach remarked "If this kid becomes a role model for other kids, that's suddenly access to a new realm of golf buyers." When advertisers urge you to "be like Mike" (or emulate some other celebrity), what they really want is for you to buy their shoes, cosmetics, clothes, breakfast cereal, or whatever. Beware!

You might discover that the best role models are people you know. *Tip:* Role models don't have to be perfect. Everyone has flaws; everyone makes mistakes. Role models work to overcome their flaws and learn from their mistakes.

RATE YOUR ROLE MODELS

For each person you consider a role model, answer the following questions. *Note:* A role model might be someone you know or someone you've never met. It might be someone who's living or no longer living, even someone who lived centuries ago. The questions are all in the present tense; you may want to change some to the past tense. *Example:* "Someone who takes positive risks" would become "Someone who took positive risks."

Is the person . . .	YES	NO	DON'T KNOW
1. someone who inspires you?	❏	❏	❏
2. someone who motivates you to do and be your best—to dream big dreams and reach for the stars?	❏	❏	❏
3. someone who helps you believe in yourself?	❏	❏	❏
4. someone who is a positive influence on you and others?	❏	❏	❏
5. someone of principles and good character?	❏	❏	❏
6. someone who exhibits strong personal values and beliefs? (*Examples:* integrity, honesty, loyalty, trustworthiness, courage, compassion, etc.)	❏	❏	❏
7. someone who takes positive risks?	❏	❏	❏
8. someone who behaves wisely and responsibly?	❏	❏	❏
9. someone who uses good judgment?	❏	❏	❏
10. someone who lives a clean and healthy life?	❏	❏	❏
11. someone who respects himself or herself?	❏	❏	❏
12. someone who respects life?	❏	❏	❏
13. someone who values learning?	❏	❏	❏
14. someone who genuinely cares about other people?	❏	❏	❏
15. someone who works for equality and social justice?	❏	❏	❏
16. someone who gives back to the community and serves others?	❏	❏	❏
17. someone who has strong personal goals and a sense of purpose in life?	❏	❏	❏
18. someone who knows how to make plans and decisions?	❏	❏	❏

CONTINUED ON NEXT PAGE...

Is the person . . .	YES	NO	DON'T KNOW
19. someone who has done commendable things?	❏	❏	❏
20. someone who takes responsibility for his or her actions and decisions?	❏	❏	❏
21. someone who has overcome obstacles and adversity?	❏	❏	❏
22. someone who admits and learns from mistakes?	❏	❏	❏
23. someone who gives you hope for the future?	❏	❏	❏
24. someone you want to be like someday?	❏	❏	❏
25. someone who's worth looking up to and admiring?	❏	❏	❏

SCORING: If you answered yes to all or most of the questions, that person is a great role model for you. If you answered no, think again about whether that person is a good role model for you. If you answered don't know, find out more before you make up your mind.

At School

With your class or school, debate this question: *Should celebrities be seen as role models?* Consider the qualities or behaviors that make a person a role model. Here's some food for thought as you prepare your argument:

● In an article on role models for the ezine *Zeen,* 15-year-old Philip Kovnat wrote "Celebrities want their cake and they want to eat it too. They want people to worship them and admire their work, but they don't think people should watch what they do and imitate. You really can't have it both ways."

● Many people today don't trust politicians or care about public figures. (In a 1998 poll of Minnesota adults, only 20 percent could name the state's two senators, and 56 percent couldn't name *either* senator.) Watergate, the O.J. Simpson trial, indictments, scandals, corruption, crime, and screaming headlines have created a role models vacuum.

● Some celebrities don't want to be role models. *Example:* In a Nike ad campaign, NBA star Charles Barkley declared "I am not a role model. I am not paid to be a role model."

● Other celebrities consider it a compliment. *Example:* Olympic gold medalist Jackie Joyner-Kersee has said "I'm glad I can be looked up to. I'm very honored to be a role model."

● Some celebrities use their wealth and influence to benefit others.

Assets in Action

In 1987, Jackie Joyner-Kersee started the **JJK Community Foundation** to support the development of leadership programs in urban areas across the United States. In 1997, she became the official spokesperson for the SuperChallenge, a campaign designed to generate 1 million hours of volunteer time and $1 million for the Boys & Girls Clubs of America.

Through their **David Robinson Foundation,** the San Antonio Spurs All-Star and his wife, Valerie, recently donated $5 million to build an inner-city prep school in San Antonio focusing on character, moral development, and personal responsibility.

In Your Community

● Ask other adults you know and trust to describe their role models—people who have influenced them in positive ways. You might want to learn more about those people or meet them if they live near you.

● Look around you—in your neighborhood, community, and youth organization. Who might make a good role model? Spend time at the library reading about notable people—in biographies, history books, magazines, newspapers, and reference books. *Tip:* Search for people to guide and inspire you, not people to worship.

● Encourage your local media to feature stories about positive role models.

● Get a mentor. See Asset #3: Other Adult Relationships.

● Be a role model for the kids in your neighborhood and community. Model responsible behavior.

Assets in Action

Anne Huey, a 54-year-old database administrator, has arranged her life for the convenience of young people. Her **Seattle, Washington,** condominium is stocked with video games and LEGOs, and her coworkers know she may take days off if a teenager needs her attention. Her generosity takes many forms—from opening her apartment to street teens who need a place to stay, to hosting prom parties.

The Role Models and Leaders Project (RMLP) encourages minority high school students to pursue careers in science, industry, and the professions. Students are introduced to career opportunities, the college admissions process, and financial aid opportunities. Adult mentors advise them during their transition from high school to college. RMLP currently operates in **Washington, D.C., Chicago,** and **Los Angeles.** For more information, contact: The Center for Excellence in Education, 8201 Greensboro Drive, Suite 215, McLean, VA 22102; (703) 448-9062. On the Web, go to: www.cee.org

In Your Faith Community

● Identify role models from your faith tradition. What makes them good role models?

● Look for role models in your faith community. Are there adults you respect and admire? Get to know them better.

● Ask your religious leader to give a sermon or homily about role models. Offer to help by doing a survey of youth in your faith community to find out who their role models are.

● Invite positive role models in the faith community to share their life stories with your youth group.

● Plan intergenerational programs and events so kids can meet adult role models.

With Your Friends

Talk with each other about your role models. For each, give three reasons why he or she is admirable, heroic, commendable, or otherwise worthy of your respect. Do you have any role models in common?

RESOURCES

For everyone:

Giraffe Heroes Project
www.giraffe.org
The Giraffe Heroes Project works to promote civic engagement by inspiring kids and teens to get involved in their communities. Giraffe Heroes are parents, teachers, mentors, leaders, and anyone else who "sticks their neck out for the common good."

Role Model Project for Girls
www.womenswork.org/girls
This site was created to share the notion that girls can grow up to be almost anything. Check out the Role Model Registry (many women describe many careers) and References and Resources (search or link to information about women in the arts, education, mathematics, science and technology, and more); learn about a CD-ROM featuring women professionals talking about their careers.

Asset #15

60% of the youth we surveyed have this asset in their lives.

POSITIVE PEER INFLUENCE

Your best friends model responsible behavior. They are a good influence on you. They do well at school, and they don't do risky things like drink alcohol or use other drugs.

At Home

Revisit old friendships.

You might start by gathering class pictures from your grade school days, old yearbooks, photo albums, scrapbooks, letters—anything that will jog your memory about friendships you've had in the past.

Identify the people who were your friends five years ago, ten years ago, or as far back as you can. Look at their pictures. Think about friends you admired. Why did you admire them? Think about friends who weren't always true friends—people who spread rumors, talked behind your back, or tried to get you to do things you didn't want to do (or weren't supposed to do). What do you remember most about your friends from the past?

The point of this exercise goes beyond nostalgia (although it's fun to think about old friends). Based on what you discover, decide whether you've done a good job of choosing friends up until now. Have your friends modeled responsible behavior? Have they influenced you in positive ways? If your choices haven't been that great, talk with an adult you trust about how to make better choices.

Assess your current friendships.

Think of your three or four best friends—the people you spend the most time with and who influence you the most. Do they build you up or drag you down? Do you support each other in making good choices, even when poor choices are easily available?

Only you know the answers to these questions. Forget about what your parents think or other people say. How do *you* feel about the friends you have now? To find out, you might ask yourself these questions:

• Which of your friends do you most want to be like?

• What do you like most about your friends?

• What bothers you about your friends?

• How do you feel when you're with your friends? Contented . . . or anxious? Cared about . . . or tolerated? Safe . . . or on guard? Supported . . . or put down?

If you're not happy, maybe it's time to make new friends. Here are four groups of likely candidates:

1. people your age who have just moved into your neighborhood

2. people who are new at school

3. people you're acquainted with and could know better if you made the effort

4. people you haven't taken time to get to know, even though they seem interesting (these might be people you've noticed at school, in your neighborhood, in your youth group, at the library, at the park or pool).

There are friends who help you to be your best self, and others you'd be better off without. Be mindful about how you choose your friends, and you'll find yourself with people who influence you positively in many ways. For tips on making friends, see Asset #33: Interpersonal Competence; for tips on resisting negative peer pressure, see Asset #35: Resistance Skills.

Ask your parents what they think of your friends.

You might set some ground rules first—no comments about hairstyles or clothes, for one. And it helps if your parents actually *know* your friends. When your friends come over, do you head straight for your room and close the door? Or do you and your friends share meals with your family, occasionally watch videos together, have conversations, or even take family vacations together? Do your parents make your friends feel welcome in your home?

Parents can be overly critical, but they can also be good sources of advice on friendship (and other topics, too). Ask them what they really think about your friends. Which ones do they like most? Least? Why? Ask them to give specific reasons.

FACT:

Peer pressure can be positive!

When we hear the words "peer pressure," we usually assume the worst. But researchers at the University of Michigan Institute for Social Research are finding that peer pressure among young teens is usually more *positive* than negative. According to Robert W. Roeser, a research associate at the University of Michigan School of Education, "Our study of approximately 1,500 adolescents and their families shows that the vast majority of young teens are not pressured by their friends to drink, smoke, use illegal drugs, or engage in other delinquent behaviors. In fact, friends are much less likely to pressure each other to do wrong than to support each other's efforts to do well."

Source: "Peer Pressure among young teens usually for better, not worse" (Ann Arbor, MI: University of Michigan News and Information Services, June 26, 1996).

At School

By the time you reach your senior year, you'll have spent more than 12,000 hours in school. Most of that will be class time, but a lot of it will be spent in the halls or common spaces between classes, in the cafeteria, in study hall, and other places where you can gather with your friends.

It matters who those friends are. First, because they're likely to be your friends outside of school as well. And second, because they have a huge impact on how you feel about school and whether you're motivated to achieve. If your friends pressure you to cut class, if they give you grief because you study too hard, if they're known as troublemakers or slackers, then you need to find new friends.

It won't be easy. You may worry that you'll be alone. You may fear that you won't fit in anywhere else—and adolescence is a time when everyone wants to fit in. Get advice and support from an adult you trust. If it's too hard to find new friends at school, look elsewhere. Join a youth group in your community or faith community. Find a hobby club or other special interest group. Volunteer in your community. Don't let your social life revolve around school.

If you're wondering whether the friends you have are right for you, see if they pass the Friendship Test.

THE FRIENDSHIP TEST:

15

QUALITIES OF A GOOD FRIEND

For each person you consider a friend, answer the following questions.

Is the person . . .	MOST OF THE TIME	SOME OF THE TIME	HARDLY EVER
1. someone you trust?	❏	❏	❏
2. someone who encourages you to succeed and achieve—and celebrates your successes (instead of being jealous or negative)?	❏	❏	❏
3. someone of good character (meaning: honest, sincere, loyal, respectful, responsible)?	❏	❏	❏
4. someone who resolves conflicts peacefully?	❏	❏	❏
5. someone who has strong, positive relationships with his or her parents and/or other adults?	❏	❏	❏
6. someone who's serious about school?	❏	❏	❏
7. someone who knows how to make plans and set goals?	❏	❏	❏
8. someone who has a positive view of the future?	❏	❏	❏
9. someone who gets along with many different kinds of people—who isn't biased or prejudiced?	❏	❏	❏
10. someone who's kind and compassionate?	❏	❏	❏
11. someone who respects himself or herself?	❏	❏	❏
12. someone who avoids dangerous situations?	❏	❏	❏
13. someone who takes positive risks?	❏	❏	❏
14. someone who gives back to the community and serves others?	❏	❏	❏
15. someone who's a positive influence on you and others?	❏	❏	❏

SCORING: Because nobody's perfect, few people will have all of these qualities all of the time. But the more a friend has, the better that friendship is for you. If a friend hardly ever has many or most of these qualities, you may want to reconsider your friendship. If this is someone you really care about, maybe you can be a positive influence and help him or her develop more of these qualities.

Assets in Action

After a junior at St. Louis Park High School in **St. Louis Park, Minnesota,** *skipped several classes and suffered the consequences, she approached assistant principal John Headlee about starting a peer mentoring program. With Headlee's help, she and other upperclass students identified seven team captains to mentor about 40 underclass students who were at risk for school failure. Each captain worked with five to six students and made sure they went to class. Deon Richardson, one of the team captains, has seen a big difference in the 40 underclass students. "At least 20 to 25 are now doing well," he says. Headlee noticed positive results in the team captains, too: Each developed strong leadership skills.*

In Your Community

● Look around and identify positive influences in your community—people of all ages who seem worth having as friends. Then reach out and get to know them. *Tip:* About the only time in life when friendships are based on age is during your school years—from kindergarten through 12th grade. After that, years matter less and other things matter more—compatibility, common interests, mutual respect, and other factors. But you don't have to wait until you graduate from high school to start making friends who are older (or younger) than you.

● Encourage your local media (TV, radio, newspapers) to profile young people who are setting good examples.

In Your Faith Community

● Learn what your faith community is doing to promote positive relationships among teens. If programs and opportunities already exist, get involved. Or talk with an adult leader about starting one or more of these:

    — regular programs (educational events, choir, plays)
    — social activities and festivals (softball games, picnics, potluck dinners)
    — peer helping programs.

● Make positive peer influence the topic of your next youth retreat. You might talk about teens you know who set good examples for others, and about how you can be a positive influence on each other.

● With your youth group, talk about friendship. Consider how your friendships fit with your values.

Assets in Action

Peer helping is a basic component of the youth program at Annunciation Catholic Church in **Minneapolis, Minnesota.** *Youth who participate in the peer ministry program commit to active involvement. One evening a month, they receive training. Then they serve as small-group leaders and large-group facilitators in the youth program. They also lead a retreat for junior high kids.*

With Your Friends

● Be a positive influence on your friends. When they behave in negative ways or take foolish risks, don't go along. Do your best to talk them out of dangerous behaviors. If you can't, tell an adult you trust. (That's not being a rat. That's being a friend.)

● Sometimes teens who follow the rules get teased or called names (does "brown-nose" or "suck-up" sound familiar?). Decide as a group that you'll encourage positive behaviors and you won't tease each other. If that's not possible, try to ignore the teasing and let it roll off you. If someone in particular gives you a hard time, try talking with the person. For tips on being assertive, see Asset #37: Personal Power.

● Take the Friendship Test (see page 125)—only this time, answer the questions about yourself. Do you have these qualities? Are you a good friend?

RESOURCES

For you:

Teen Central
www.teencentral.net
Get good advice at Teen Central, a Web site with teen stories about peer pressure, friend issues, and health concerns. Then post a story of your own and get a response with options for dealing with the situation you're in.

For your faith community:

Peer Ministry Training: Basic Curriculum by Barbara B. Varenhorst (Minneapolis: Youth and Family Institute of Augsburg College, 1995). A classic curriculum by a peer ministry pioneer, revised and updated.

41% of the youth we surveyed have this asset in their lives.

HIGH EXPECTATIONS

Your parents and teachers encourage you to do well.

At Home

● Tell your parents your hopes and dreams—and what you expect of yourself. Ask for their help and encouragement. See assets #1: Family Support and #2: Positive Family Communication.

● Ask your parents to tell you their hopes and dreams for you. What are their expectations? What would they like you to achieve? Ask them to be specific, then talk about their expectations. Do they seem realistic? Why or why not? *Tip:* There's something about high expectations that bring out the best in all of us. When people we care about want us to do well, we try harder. High expectations boost our self-esteem. We feel more capable and willing to take positive risks.

FACT:

Most parents have high expectations for their children!

In a nationwide survey of 12,700 parents, 98 percent said they expect their children to graduate from high school, 88 percent said they expect them to attend college, and 74 percent said they expect their kids to earn college degrees. About 6,500 youth in grades 6–12 were also surveyed, and their expectations were as high or higher than their parents'.

Source: *National Household Education Survey*, School Safety and Discipline component (Washington, DC: U.S. Department of Education, National Center for Education Statistics, 1993).

● Invite your parents to tell you about the expectations their parents had for them when they were kids. Did they live up to them? Why or why not? (This may help your parents put their expectations for you into perspective.)

● Let your parents know how much you appreciate their support. *Examples:* Thank them for attending school conferences, for showing up at your softball games, for coming to hear your spring band concert. (Parents need strokes, too.)

● Encourage your parents to get involved or stay involved with your school. According to the National Center for Education Statistics, involved parents are more likely to have high educational expectations for their children. See Asset #6: Parent Involvement in Schooling.

● Set high expectations for yourself. Learn skills that will help you meet your goals. See Asset #32: Planning and Decision Making.

● When expectations are high yet realistic, you'll stretch to reach them. When they're too high, you may fear making mistakes. Talk with your parents about why you need room to make mistakes.

REASONS WHY MISTEAKS ARE GRATE

THOUGHTS TO SHARE WITH MOM AND DAD

1. Mistakes are universal. Everybody makes them, from preschoolers to presidents. They give you something in common with the rest of the people on our planet.

2. Mistakes show that you're learning. They inspire you to do better the next time you're in a similar situation.

3. Mistakes show that you're trying something new or different. If you'd spent your whole life so far doing only those things you could master on the first try, you never would have learned to walk, read, or ride a bicycle.

4. Mistakes allow you to see your own improvements. If you videotaped your first attempt at the backstroke, then videotaped yourself again after three months of swimming lessons, you'd notice a significant change for the better.

5. Mistakes allow you to learn from others. When there's something you just can't figure out or do, yet you refuse to get help, you're making a *really* big mistake—the kind that isn't so great.

Adapted from *The Gifted Kids' Survival Guide: A Teen Handbook* by Judy Galbraith, M.A., and Jim Delisle, Ph.D. Free Spirit Publishing Inc., 1996, page 80. Used with permission.

At School

● Tell your teachers what you'd like to accomplish in their classes. Ask for their support. This encourages them to pay closer attention to your progress—and to set high expectations for you.

● Your teachers should clearly explain their expectations for you and the rest of your class at the start of the year (or the semester). If they don't, ask. You can't meet expectations you're not aware of or don't understand.

● Encourage other students to achieve and succeed. Offer to tutor younger students who need help.

● Take advantage of opportunities to lead. Run for student council or campaign to be an officer in your class or club.

● Do your best—without *overdoing* it. Perfectionism is a trap. If you're afraid to take risks or make mistakes; if you're extremely competitive, critical of yourself, critical of others, and never satisfied with anything you do; if you're preoccupied with expectations (yours and other people's); if you set impossible or unrealistic goals for yourself; if you define your self-worth in terms of what you do instead of who you are as a person; if you're stressed out, anxious, and depressed much of the time . . . then you may be a perfectionist.

10 TIPS FOR COMBATING PERFECTIONISM

1. Be average for a day. Allow yourself to be messy, late, incomplete . . . imperfect. Then celebrate your success.

2. Get involved in activities that aren't graded or judged—activities that focus on process, not product.

3. Take a risk. Start a conversation with someone you don't know. Alter your morning routine. Do an assignment without overdoing it. Try something new.

4. Give yourself permission to make at least three mistakes a day. Then go ahead and make them.

5. Stop using the word "should" in your self-talk. Remove "I have to," "I must," and "I'd better" from your conversation.

CONTINUED ON NEXT PAGE...

6. Share a weakness or limitation with a friend you trust. Recognize that he or she doesn't think any less of you as a result.

7. Take an honest look at your expectations of yourself. Acknowledge that they might be too high, even unrealistic.

8. Savor your past accomplishments. Write about how good they made you feel.

9. Ask your friends for help. Maybe they can give you a sign or a word when they notice you being a perfectionist.

10. Join the human race. It's less lonely when we accept imperfections—our own and other people's—and feel part of life.

If you need more help combating your perfectionism, talk with your school counselor or psychologist. Explain your situation and ask for suggestions.

Adapted from *Talk with Teens About Self and Stress* by Jean Sunde Peterson, Ph.D. Free Spirit Publishing Inc., 1993, page 43. Used with permission.

In Your Community

● Parents who are educated about child development are more likely to have realistic expectations for their children. Does your community offer seminars or workshops for parents on this topic? Find out. Check with your community center, mayor's office, or the Community Affairs representative at your local newspaper, radio station, or TV station. Offer to help plan and publicize these events.

● Encourage your local media (TV, radio, newspapers) to spotlight the positive accomplishments of many young people, instead of the negative actions of a few. Learn which reporters typically cover youth issues, then contact them when you hear about someone worth featuring in a story.

● Learn what your community expects of youth. Learn about the laws that affect you—and the consequences of breaking those laws. *Examples:* school attendance, curfews, traffic laws, licenses.

● Find out about neighborhood and community organizations, councils, boards, and committees that welcome teen members, then get involved. See Asset #8: Youth as Resources.

● Hold high expectations for younger kids in your neighborhood. Be clear about the kinds of behavior you want to see—and don't want to see. Tell them you know they can do great things. Encourage them to do well in school.

Assets in Action

The Page Education Foundation encourages minority students in **Minnesota** *to stay in school and continue their education beyond high school. Page Scholars are paired with adult role models (mentors) and serve as role models for younger students, going into grade schools to work with minority children. Founded in 1988 by Alan Page, Minnesota's Associate Supreme Court Justice and an NFL Hall of Fame honoree, the Foundation has granted 1,625 scholarships to more than 820 students. Scholars have studied at 50 different post-secondary schools across Minnesota; 20 have attended or are currently attending graduate schools. For more information, contact the Page Education Foundation, PO Box 581254, Minneapolis, MN 55458-1254; telephone (612) 332-0406. On the Web, go to* www.page-ed.org

In Your Faith Community

● Learn what your faith community expects of you and other teens. Are those expectations clearly communicated? What does your faith tradition say? This might be a good topic for a sermon or homily.

● Tell adults in your faith community what you'd like to accomplish there—and in other areas of your life. Ask for their support.

Assets in Action

Mount Gideon Missionary Baptist Church in **St. Louis, Missouri,** *sponsors a program to recognize outstanding young people. The Youth on a Mission Program is open to youth who:*

· *maintain a grade point average of at least 3.25*
· *submit letters of reference from a teacher and their home church pastor, and*
· *participate in a monthly community service project.*

The membership requirements are an incentive for youth to work hard in their school, faith community, and neighborhood. An especially popular part of the program is the annual ball, where program members are honored with a formal introduction to the assembled gathering.

With Your Friends

● Find and share inspiring stories about people who overcame obstacles in their lives and accomplished amazing things.

● Expect great things of each other. Encourage each other to succeed and achieve. Be your own cheering section.

IMPORTANT: *If the adults in your life don't have high expectations of you— if they don't encourage you to do well, and actually* discourage *you with putdowns, criticism, and other self-esteem smashers—then* find someone who will have high expectations of you. *Don't give up until you do! See Asset #3: Other Adult Relationships.*

RESOURCES

For you:

Perfectionism: What's Bad About Being Too Good? by Miriam Adderholdt, Ph.D., and Jan Goldberg (Minneapolis: Free Spirit Publishing, 1999). Explores the differences between healthy ambition and unhealthy perfectionism and gives strategies for getting out of the perfectionist trap.

For your parents:

Raising a Daughter: Parents and the Awakening of a Healthy Woman by Jeanne Elium and Don Elium (Berkeley, CA: Celestial Arts, 1994) and *Raising a Son: Parents and the Making of a Healthy Man* by Don Elium and Jeanne Elium, rev. ed. (Berkeley, CA: Celestial Arts, 1996). Two indispensable guides for parents chart adolescent development and offer plans for constructive parenting.

The Roller-Coaster Years by Charlene C. Giannetti and Margaret Sagarese (New York: Broadway Books, 1997). Based on the latest findings and surveys of hundreds of teachers, parents, and young adolescents across the country, this user-friendly guide can help you help your child build skills, gain confidence, and prepare for high school. The authors emphasize that kids crave attention from their parents at this age—the last stage of development where parental influence is strong.

CONSTRUCTIVE USE OF TIME

These assets are about having positive, meaningful, interesting, challenging, and fun things to do. They're about getting involved with creative activities (music, theater, other arts), youth programs, a religious community, and other places where you're likely to meet adults who care about kids and teens. They're also about spending quality time at home.

The constructive use of time assets are:

17. Creative Activities
18. Youth Programs
19. Religious Community
20. Time at Home

CREATIVE ACTIVITIES

You spend three or more hours each week in lessons or practice in music, theater, or other arts.

At Home

Get involved.

Participating in the arts—*any* of the arts—is one of the best things you can do for yourself. (For a list of reasons, see pages 140–141.) If you're not already involved, what's holding you back?

Think about what you'd like to do. Have you always wanted to draw? Paint? Sculpt? Dance? Play an instrument? Compose music? Act in a play? Make a movie or video? Write a story or poem? Sing in a choir? Play in a band? Design clothes or buildings? Take photographs? What else? Tell your parents and ask for their help and support.

Say yes to lessons.

Many parents decide that their children should take music lessons. Some kids refuse to take them or resist them so strongly (skipping lessons, refusing to practice) that their parents give up.

If your parents offer to pay for lessons, say yes . . . unless your dreams differ from theirs. *Example:* They want you to play classical piano; you want to play jazz trumpet. You might tell them what you really want to do and see if they're willing to let you do it. Or propose a compromise: If they'll pay for this year's trumpet lessons, you'll study piano next year—or vice versa. (P.S.: Learning piano will make you a better trumpet player. You'll acquire music basics that will carry over to any instrument.)

Add the arts to your family time.

Ideas to try:

● Have a family meeting to talk about ways to experience the arts. Make a date once a month to visit a museum, gallery, or cultural center; attend a play, musical, concert, dance performance, or opera; see a film; or whatever you'd like to do together. Give everyone a chance to choose. *Tip:* As of 1996, the United States had over 8,000 museums, 7,000 community theaters, and 1,800 symphony orchestras.

● Be open to a wide variety of arts-related experiences. Scan the newspapers for notices of free performances. Keep your family informed about school plays, concerts, and exhibits; write them on the family calendar and make plans to go.

● Is your brother in a band? Is your sister in a choir? Are your parents involved with community theater? Show your support by attending each other's performances.

● As a family, take a community education class in one of the arts—drawing, painting, photography, music appreciation, pottery, dance, or whatever else interests you.

● Set up an arts area in your home. Some families have a hobby art room or an art supplies shelf. Others keep a table stocked with construction paper, paint, glue, string, scissors, and other supplies.

● Tour the arts in your home. Talk about paintings, prints, or posters on the walls, the music you listen to, and other signs of art. If you don't have any art on your walls, visit a local museum or gallery; many have inexpensive reproductions available for purchase. *Tip:* Larger museums—like New York's Metropolitan Museum of Art—publish catalogs.

● Tour the arts online. If you have a home computer with an Internet connection, there's a world of music and art at your fingertips. Many music sites have audio files you can download; many museums have Web sites. If you'd like to hear some Mozart (or Madonna)—if you want to visit the Museum of Modern Art in New York, the Louvre in Paris, San Francisco's Asian Art Museum, or the new Guggenheim Museum in Bilbao, Spain—they're all online. *Tip:* A great place to start exploring art on the Web is at the WebMuseum. Go to: *www.ibiblio.org/wm*

Mozart makes you smarter!

Researchers at the University of California at Irvine played a recording of Mozart's Sonata for Two Pianos in D Major for students just before giving them an IQ test. The students' scores were 8–9 points *higher* than when they took the same kind of test after listening to a relaxation tape or sitting in silence.

Source: Frances H. Rauscher, Gordon L. Shaw, and Katherine N. Ky, "Music and Spatial Task Performance" (Irvine, CA: University of California, Center for the Neurobiology of Learning and Memory, 1993).

Go solo if you must.

If your family isn't interested in exploring the arts, and if your parents don't support your interests, don't let that stop you.

- Start by finding out what's available at your school.
- If the offerings there are too meager or not what you're looking for, check out classes offered through community education and arts centers, the YMCA and YWCA, your faith community, and local colleges and universities.
- Learn something on your own by reading books, experimenting, or starting a practice group.
- Find a talented neighbor or relative who's willing to teach you what he or she knows, or get a mentor. See Asset #3: Other Adult Relationships.

At School

Get involved.

If your school offers classes, clubs, and after-school programs in music or the arts, take advantage of these opportunities. If you'd love to play the saxophone but you can't afford to buy one, tell your teacher. Schools with music programs often have instruments available to borrow or rent. If that's not an option, ask for donations from community groups. Contact local newspapers and ask them to write stories about your school's search for musical instruments . . . or art supplies, lighting equipment for the drama club, a portable stereo for the dance club, or whatever else you need.

FACT:

Arts and Music Study = Higher SAT Scores!

Students who study the arts and music score substantially higher on their SATs than those who don't. Here are the statistics for 1997:

Arts and Music: Years of Study	SAT Verbal Score	SAT Math Score
4 or more years	537	533
3 years	515	513
2 years	507	511
1 year	499	509
1/2 year or less	488	499
None	477	491

Source: *1997 Profile of College-Bound Seniors National Report* (Reston, VA: College Board, 1997).

Advocate for arts education.

Your parents (or grandparents) probably remember a time when the arts were part of every child's education. Schools large and small, public and private, urban and rural had bands, orchestras, choirs, drama departments, music departments, and art departments.

Then budgets got tight and cuts were made. The arts were considered less important than the 3Rs (reading, writing, and arithmetic), so those programs were among the first to go. In many of America's 15,000 school districts, arts education went the way of the dinosaurs.

In 1983, the National Commission on Excellence in Education published a scathing report called *A Nation at Risk*. It warned of the "rising tide of mediocrity" in America's schools and sparked the school reform movement. Educators, parents, researchers, and politicians took a hard look at the curriculum and realized that the arts weren't expendable after all.

Here's a brief timeline of what's happened since:

➡ **In 1990,** the Governors and the Congress of the United States adopted eight National Education Goals. One of these goals names the arts—along with English, math, science, foreign languages, civics and government, history, and geography—as something all American students need to learn.

➡ **In 1994,** the *Goals 2000: Educate America Act* formally recognized the arts as a core subject in which all American children are expected to become competent.

➡ **In 1994,** the National Consortium of Arts Organizations published its National Standards for Arts Education, which describe what every U.S. student (grades K–12) should know and be able to do in music, dance, theater, and the visual arts. The Standards are voluntary, not mandatory, but most states have chosen to adopt them in some form.

➡ **In 1996,** the U.S. Department of Education began including evaluations of student knowledge of the arts in its National Assessment of Educational Progress (NAEP).

In other words, the arts are no longer perceived as enrichment subjects, rewards for good behavior, fillers, or frills—at least not officially. Instead, they're viewed as serious academic subjects that belong in the curriculum.

And here's where you come in. You deserve to learn about the arts, and so do students who come after you (maybe including your younger brothers and sisters). You can be a powerful advocate for arts education—in your own school and district, community, and state.

1. Start by learning where your state stands. Call your state's Department of Education and ask what's being done in the area of arts education. Or contact:

National Conference of State Legislatures
7700 East First Place
Denver, CO 80230
(303) 364-7700
www.ncsl.org
The National Conference has a Web site with an online database that summarizes individual states' education policies.

2. Let your legislators know that you support the arts and arts education. (You may not be old enough to vote, but it won't be long before you are.) You might do this as a family project.

REASONS WHY YOU NEED THE ARTS

When you're involved in the arts, you:

1. build skills in creative, complex, and critical thinking, problem solving, risk taking, decision making, flexibility, teamwork, analysis, interpretation, judgment, and communication

2. become more creative, insightful, resilient, innovative, original, perceptive, and imaginative

3. build self-discipline and self-esteem

CONTINUED ON NEXT PAGE...

4. use all of your intelligences and preferred learning styles (if linguistic and logical-mathematical intelligences—the ones schools focus on most—aren't your strengths, the arts give you other ways to succeed and achieve)

5. learn to find structure and meaning where none seems to exist (*examples:* when you make sense out of seemingly random movements in a dance, or shapes in a painting, or notes in a piece of music)

6. learn to cope with uncertainty (*examples:* how will this color look? how will that note sound? what if I read the lines in a play this way instead of that way?)

7. learn to deal with ambiguity (arithmetic, spelling, reading, and punctuation all depend on specific rules to obtain the right answers, but there are no right answers in creating or interpreting art)

8. discover, appreciate, and understand different cultures and cultural values, and feel more connected to your own culture

9. acquire knowledge and meaning you don't get from other subjects (*example:* an artist's interpretation of love, birth, death, or conflict)

10. enhance your performance in other subjects (drawing helps writing; songs and poems make facts memorable; drama makes history vivid and real; creative movement makes processes understandable; sound, movement, space, line, shape, and color are all related to math and science)

11. gain insight into people, ideas, events, and experiences that aren't part of your normal life

12. get more involved in learning, because art makes learning more fun (the arts = *doing,* not just passively absorbing information)

13. learn ways to cope with the ups and downs of adolescence (the arts give you positive, healthy ways to express conflicting emotions and get a grip)

14. gain a different perspective on your life—a chance to imagine a different outcome and develop a critical distance from everyday life (if your life isn't the greatest, the arts are a way to cope).

Plus:

15. Many prominent business leaders have argued that America's economic success depends on the competencies provided by a solid education in the arts. Businesses look for people who can think and create.

Sources: *Reinventing the Wheel* (The Getty Center and The National Conference of State Legislatures, 1992); *Coming Up Taller* (The President's Committee on the Arts and Humanities with Americans for the Arts, 1996); ArtsEdNet Web site.

Assets in Action

*Retired Carleton College music professor Bill Child is a volunteer with the music department at the **Northfield, Minnesota,** public school, coaching kids on wind instruments. His own children are grown, but he understands the value of investing his time in Northfield's young people.*

In Your Community

● Share your artistic abilities with your community. *Examples:* Join a community band or orchestra. Find a building with a big, blank wall that's crying out for a mural, then paint one (with permission, of course). Arrange to display art by children and teens in a public space such as an airport, shopping mall, or community center.

● Work with local arts organizations to create a community arts directory. Get a grant from a local business to produce and print your directory. Make copies available for free, or sell them for a small price—and donate your profits to a struggling arts organization.

● Work to preserve the arts in your community. *Example:* The National Institute for Conservation estimates that almost half of the nation's 27,000 outdoor sculptures are deteriorating.

● Community arts and humanities programs are critical to children's healthy development—especially for children at risk. They create safe places where children and youth can develop positive relationships with their peers and caring adults. See what your community offers. Volunteer to help—or start your own program. If you can't start a program, teach or mentor a younger kid in the arts.

Assets in Action

*When visual artists at City Center Art in **Birmingham, Alabama,** noticed neighborhood children hanging out at their warehouse, they developed an arts program—Space One Eleven—for youth who live in the nearby housing complex.*

*Television director Roberto Arevalo began The Mirror Project at Somerville Community Access Television in 1992 after meeting eight teenagers at a local park in **Somerville, Massachusetts.** He started working with them, helping them explore their neighborhoods with video cameras. Two of the videos won awards, and now, with partial funding from the U.S. Department of Housing and Urban Development, the program operates at housing developments, Boys & Girls Clubs, and community centers in the area.*

In Your Faith Community

● With your youth group and adult leaders, start a community arts program in your building.

● Does your faith community have a youth band, choir, chorus, or other music group? If not, see if you can start one. Or ask if youth can be included in adult groups.

● Identify artistically talented adults and teens who are members of your faith community. Encourage them to offer free lessons to younger kids.

Assets in Action

*The First Presbyterian Church in downtown **Knoxville, Tennessee,** is a community arts school during the daytime hours, providing music lessons for kids who couldn't afford them otherwise. Margaret Bell, who helped start the program, worked with other church leaders to recruit volunteers from within and outside the congregation. They raised funds for teachers and musical instruments from the Junior League, Knoxville Parks and Recreation Department, Knoxville Arts Alliance, Knoxville Housing Authority, and other sources. Now about 40 youth attend the school. In addition to receiving lessons, each youth is paired with an adult artist/mentor from the community. Kids have formed positive relationships, developed stronger self-esteem, and achieved better grades in school—all while experiencing the joys of making music.*

With Your Friends

Make a pact to explore and experience the arts together. Go to museums, exhibits, plays, or concerts as a group (ask about student discounts) and encourage each other's artistic efforts. If you share similar talents and interests, you might paint a mural, start a band, or start a program to teach neighborhood kids how to paint, draw, dance, or put on a play.

IMPORTANT: *Out of all 40 assets, Creative Activities is the one fewest kids have—according to our survey, only 14 percent of boys and 24 percent of girls. Is this because we're limiting arts involvement only to those who have the most obvious talent? Or because arts education in the schools has been underfunded or nonexistent for years? What do you think? Talk about this with your family, teachers, and friends. You may decide to make a special effort to build this asset for yourself and others.*

———————————————— RESOURCES ————————————————

For everyone:

The National Endowment for the Arts
Office of Public Information
1100 Pennsylvania Avenue, NW
Washington, DC 20506
(202) 682-5400
www.arts.endow.gov
An independent agency of the federal government, charged with supporting the arts in America for all Americans (and constantly in danger of having its funding cut). The NEA's reach is vast; its Web site is packed with information.

For educators:

ArtsEdge
www.artsedge.kennedy-center.org
A joint effort of the John F. Kennedy Center for the Performing Arts, the NEA, and the U.S. Department of Education, this site helps educators access and share information, resources, and ideas that support the arts as a core subject area in K–12 curriculum. It also includes pages created by and for students.

The J. Paul Getty Museum
www.getty.edu/education/teachers
This online service supporting arts education includes lesson plans, curriculum ideas, image galleries, and a publications catalog. If you're not online, write or call: The Getty Education Institute for the Arts, 1200 Getty Center Drive, Los Angeles, CA 90049-1679; telephone (310) 440-7300.

59% of the youth we surveyed have this asset in their lives.

YOUTH PROGRAMS

You spend three or more hours each week in sports, clubs, or organizations at school and/or in the community.

At Home

Take stock.

Answer these questions:

● Overall, are you happy with how many different things you do with your time?

● Are the activities you're involved in stimulating and challenging for you?

● Are you making friends with caring, responsible adults in your activities?

● Are you learning new skills and talents and acquiring new knowledge?

● Do your activities teach you more about yourself?

● Are you excited each day to do these activities?

● Do they bring out the best in you?

If you can't answer yes to all or most of these questions, maybe it's because you're not involved in enough (or any) meaningful activities. Or maybe it's because you're not involved in the *right* activities. Either way, you can do something about it.

145

Take action.

Talk with your parents about your interests. What do you like to do? What would you like to try? Ask them to help you research and identify youth programs, teams, clubs, or organizations in your area that match your interests. Or ask any caring adult—a teacher, counselor, youth group leader, faith community leader, or mentor.

There are *many* youth programs out there, just waiting for you to find them. According to the Carnegie Council on Adolescent Development, more than 17,000 national and local youth organizations operate in the United States today. They come in all types. Examples:

- academic clubs
- career education groups
- character-building organizations
- civic education organizations
- conservation groups
- ethnic heritage groups
- hobby and special interest groups
- honor societies
- humane education groups
- patriotic organizations
- peace and global understanding groups
- political organizations
- programs affiliated with museums and libraries
- religious organizations
- self-help groups
- service organizations
- sports organizations
- vocational education groups
- and *many* more.

When you locate programs that look good to you, learn more about them. Write or call for information. Many youth programs have their own Web sites; you can go online to check out descriptions, membership requirements, and chat rooms. When you want to know more about a particular program, follow these suggestions from Judith Erickson, author of the *Directory of American Youth Organizations:* *

1. Get the name of the council, chapter, or club closest to your area, and arrange to go to a group meeting.

2. Prepare questions ahead of time to ask members at the meeting. You might start with these:

- Why did you join this organization? What first got you interested in it?
- How long have you been a member?
- What are some of the things you do as a member?
- What do you like best about this organization?
- Is there anything you don't like about it?

---

* Adapted from *1998–1999 Directory of American Youth Organizations* by Judith B. Erickson. Free Spirit Publishing Inc., 1998, page 2. Used with permission.

- Does this organization hold regular meetings? When and where?
- Has belonging to this organization made a difference in your life? How?
- Have you made new friends by joining this organization?
- What are some other advantages of being a member?
- Why do you think people should join this organization?

3. If you don't feel comfortable asking questions during the meeting, speak with the adult leader afterward. Explain that you're interested in the organization and would like to talk to a member. Ask if the leader can give you a name and phone number, or arrange a time when you can meet with a member.

When you feel that you've done enough research, pick a program to join. Make a six-month commitment to stick with it. Some teens drop out of programs prematurely, or they skip from one to another without giving any a chance. On the other hand, you may need to check out several programs, organizations, or clubs before finding one that feels right to you. Don't get discouraged, and don't give up. With so many choices available to you, you're sure to find a match sooner or later. *Tip:* Sometimes we don't have a clue about whether we'll enjoy something until we try it. This is the kind of risk-taking that leads to new discoveries and adventures.

FACT:

Youth programs build assets!

A youth program is an asset-rich environment. It's one of the best places you can go to build and strengthen a lot of assets at the same time.

You'll form relationships with caring adults (Asset #3). Youth programs are proof that the community values youth (#7). You'll be given useful roles and meaningful things to do (#8), often (depending on the program) including service to others (#9). Youth programs are safe places to go and be (#10). You'll meet and interact with adult role models (#14) and make friends who model responsible behavior (#15). Many youth programs offer creative activities (#17). Most promote positive values (#26–#31), social competencies (#32–#36), and positive identity (#37–#40).

Grand total: 23 assets . . . and maybe more, depending on the program and how involved you decide to be.

At School

- Post information about community youth programs, organizations, and clubs on school bulletin boards, along with information about school activities. (Get permission first.)

● Make sure that your school handbook include descriptions of teams, clubs, organizations, and other after-school activities. If your school has a Web site, they should be listed there, too. Offer to help.

● Find out if your school hosts service clubs for students. *Examples:* Interact Club (sponsored by Rotary International), Key Club (Kiwanis International), Leo Club (Lions Clubs International). If it doesn't, get the ball rolling. Talk to your teachers and principal; meet with members of local Rotary, Lions, and Kiwanis clubs to find out how to start chapters in your school.

● If you're not thrilled by any of the organizations, clubs, or teams at your school, start something. Find five to ten other students who share your interest, then get together and talk about the kind of group you'd like to start. Once you've defined your purpose, decided on your goals, and outlined some possible activities, approach a teacher you like and ask him or her to sponsor you.

Assets in Action

In **Westerfille, Ohio,** *Otterbein College, Big Brothers Big Sisters, and Indianola Middle School joined forces to start the Indianola After-School Project. The project pairs Otterbein students with middle school students in an after-school program on Otterbein's campus. Middle school students travel to the campus once a week for one-on-one sessions that include an hour of tutoring, an hour of family-style dining in the campus cafeteria, and an hour of recreation. The students get a sense of what college life is like and are encouraged to aspire to attend college. The college and Big Brothers Big Sisters support the program by providing transportation, meals, and donations.*

In Your Community

If 59 percent of the youth we surveyed are involved in youth programs, this means that 41 percent aren't. (Remember that 59 percent is an average; in some communities, this number is lower.) Many teens don't participate because they don't know about the programs available to them.

Do what you can to publicize youth programs in your community. You might publish a directory; create flyers, posters, or brochures; or post listings on community bulletin boards and Web sites. Encourage your local media (newspapers, TV and radio stations) to feature stories about youth programs— with contact information.

In cities around the U.S., young people are going block-by-block to canvass their neighborhoods in search of programs, services, places, opportunities, and caring adults available to help them, their families, and their peers. Once these resources are identified, they will be entered into a computer system that makes the data available in a user-friendly way. To find out more about this nation-wide effort—called Community YouthMapping—write or call: Center for Youth Development and Policy Research, Academy for Educational Development, 1825 Connecticut Avenue, NW, Washington, DC 20009; (202) 884-8000. On the Web, go to: *cydpr.aed.org*

Assets in Action

When kids and teens in **Minneapolis, Minnesota,** *want to find something positive to do, they call the What's Up? Youth Info Line. Created in 1996 by the Minneapolis Youth Coordinating Board, it connects young people ages 7–18 to youth programs in the area—from mentorship and job opportunities to athletic and social activities. The staffers are teens from the Minneapolis Public Schools who are trained to use a special database to match activities and resources with callers' needs. In its first year of operation, What's Up? fielded nearly 18,000 calls from young people, parents, and youth program providers.*

In Your Faith Community

● See if your faith community is willing to sponsor an organization or club for young people, or give an existing organization a home. *Tip:* Many scout troops are sponsored by congregations.

● Does the youth program in your faith community deal with issues and topics you and your friends care about? Is it in touch with teens' interests and needs? If not, talk with your friends to find out what changes they would like to see. Prepare a list of suggestions (not demands) and bring them to your youth group leader(s).

Assets in Action

Bethel Temple in **Philadelphia, Pennsylvania,** *sponsors an after-school program for children and youth that includes tutoring and a weightlifting program. The congregation uses the gym in the middle school across the street for a basketball program.*

With Your Friends

Research youth programs in your area and choose one to join as a group. You'll enjoy the benefits together, motivate each other to stay involved, and have more fun.

BUILDING ASSETS WITH YOUR YOUTH PROGRAM:

IDEAS TO TRY

Just as involvement in a youth program builds assets in *you*, it can also empower you to build all 40 assets for other children and teens. Quick tips:

#1: Family Support. Schedule family nights, dinners, retreats, and other special events that bring families together.

#2: Positive Family Communication. Start a newsletter for parents to keep them informed about your youth program.

#3: Other Adult Relationships. Get to know the adult leaders in your youth program. Encourage other kids to do the same.

#4: Caring Neighborhood. Organize informal activities for children and teens in the surrounding neighborhood.

#5: Caring School Climate. Do service projects at neighborhood schools.

#6: Parent Involvement in Schooling. Start a free baby-sitting service for parents attending school conferences and events.

#7: Community Values Youth. Create and perform skits that show how adults in your community treat youth—and how you'd like to be treated.

#8: Youth as Resources. Brainstorm useful roles for younger kids in your youth program. Give them opportunities to lead and make decisions.

#9: Service to Others. Make service projects a regular part of your youth program. Talk about ways to serve others in your everyday lives.

#10: Safety. When planning activities, identify anything that might be unsafe and take appropriate precautions.

CONTINUED ON NEXT PAGE...

#11: Family Boundaries. Talk with each other about family boundaries and how to negotiate appropriate boundaries with parents.

#12: School Boundaries. Get copies of local school policies. Set ground rules for activities in your program that are consistent with school boundaries.

#13: Neighborhood Boundaries. Learn about and respect the boundaries in the surrounding neighborhood.

#14: Adult Role Models. Identify adult leaders in your youth program who are worth looking up to. Encourage each other to view them as role models.

#15: Positive Peer Influence. Make your youth program a positive peer pressure group. Model responsible behavior for each other.

#16: High Expectations. Set high expectations for each other. Challenge each other to do your best in school.

#17: Creative Activities. Form a band, chorus, theater troupe, etc. and share your talents with others.

#18: Youth Programs. Encourage other kids and teens to join youth programs. Welcome newcomers into your program.

#19: Religious Community. Contact members' religious organizations and request copies of their calendars. Schedule your activities so they don't conflict.

#20: Time at Home. Set aside at least one night a week as family night. Don't plan any activities for that night.

#21: Achievement Motivation. Encourage each other to succeed in school. Don't tolerate negative talk or attitudes about school.

#22: School Engagement. Have an annual fund-raiser and purchase school supplies for low-income students.

#23: Homework. Sponsor an after-school study hall. Make tutoring younger children a service activity for your group.

#24: Bonding to School. Attend each other's school events—sports, plays, concerts, debates—as a group.

#25: Reading for Pleasure. Start a book discussion group. Sponsor read-a-thons that encourage youth to read for fun; award prizes.

#26: Caring. Take time during meetings and activities to check in with each other. Find out what's happening in each other's lives.

#27: Equality and Social Justice. Treat each other with dignity, respect, and equality. Do service projects that support human rights and social justice.

#28: Integrity. Do role-plays and simulations that help members stay true to themselves and their values in tough situations.

CONTINUED ON NEXT PAGE...

#29: Honesty. Create an environment where people feel safe and comfortable being honest with each other.

#30: Responsibility. Partner with adults to plan activities and events. Hold each other accountable—and give second chances.

#31: Restraint. Help each other identify and affirm beliefs that keep teens from using alcohol and other drugs or being sexually active.

#32: Planning and Decision Making. Form committees to plan activities and events. Give everyone a chance to make decisions.

#33: Interpersonal Competence. Make training in peer helping part of your program's focus.

#34: Cultural Competence. Include games, arts, music, stories, food, etc. from different cultures in your program's activities.

#35: Resistance Skills. Help each other practice ways to say no. Role-play various tough situations. Support each other.

#36: Peaceful Conflict Resolution. Train everyone—kids, teens, and adults—in peaceful conflict resolution.

#37: Personal Power. When your group faces big problems or issues, break them down into manageable pieces. Address them one at a time.

#38: Self-Esteem. Take time to affirm each other and celebrate accomplishments.

#39: Sense of Purpose. Identify people in your community who have accomplished great things. Invite them to speak to your group about their motivation and sense of purpose.

#40: Positive View of Personal Future. Talk with each other about your dreams for the future—and ways to make your dreams come true.

RESOURCES

For community leaders:

A Matter of Time: Risk and Opportunity in the Nonschool Hours (New York: Carnegie Council on Adolescent Development, 1994). Describes the special problems today's teens face, the potential of community organizations to support youth development, and ways to strengthen community programs for youth. You may purchase a copy of the full report or obtain an abridged version free of charge. Write or call: Carnegie Corporation of New York, 437 Madison Avenue, New York, NY 10022; (212) 371-3200. On the Web, go to: *www.carnegie.org*

64% of the youth
we surveyed have this
asset in their lives.

RELIGIOUS COMMUNITY

**You spend one or more hours each week
in religious services or spiritual activities.**

At Home

● If you're active in a faith community, think about your experiences. What was your most positive experience? Most negative? How do you feel about your current involvement? What, if anything, would you like to change? Talk with your parents about these issues.

● Have a family meeting to discuss your family's spiritual involvement. What do people like about it? What don't they like? Is participation something your parents require, or do family members (including children and teens) have a choice? If you don't have a choice about whether to participate, are there other choices you do have? *Examples:* Can you attend a later service than the ones your parents go to? Can you sit with your friends instead of your family? Can you wear what you want (within reason)? *Tip:* Having choices makes people feel powerful. The more choices you have about your spiritual involvement, the more likely it is that you'll stay involved. (You may want to share this tip with your parents.)

● If your parents aren't involved in a faith community, this doesn't mean you can't be. Perhaps you can join a friend's faith community. Or visit the places of worship in your neighborhood or nearby and talk with the people who lead the youth program.

● What if your parents are involved in a faith community, but their choice doesn't seem right for you? Try telling them how you feel. Maybe they'll agree to help you find a community that meets your spiritual needs.

9 REASONS TO STAY INVOLVED OR GET INVOLVED WITH A FAITH COMMUNITY

1. Faith communities reduce risky behaviors. Youth who are involved in a church, synagogue, parish, mosque, or other spiritual community are half as likely as those who aren't to use alcohol or other drugs, have sex too soon, or attempt suicide.

2. Faith communities teach values. This leads to responsible decision making and positive choices. Teens who say no to risky behaviors often do so because of their values. *Tip:* Many schools and other organizations shy away from teaching values. Your faith community may be the only place you spend time (outside your family) where people talk openly about values. You need adults in your life who aren't afraid to say "This is right" or "That's wrong"—even if you don't always agree with them.

3. Faith communities are intergenerational. You'll meet, worship with, and get to know people of all ages—adult leaders, younger teens, children, grandparents. *Tip:* Society is increasingly age-segmented. Your faith community may be one of the few places you go where you have regular contact with principled, caring adults.

4. Faith communities provide caring and support. You'll form relationships with religious education teachers, youth group leaders, peers, friends, relatives, and mentors who care about you and are there for you in good times and bad.

5. Faith communities have high expectations for their young people. They motivate teens to grow and mature, succeed and achieve.

6. Faith communities provide opportunities to be contributing members of a group. You'll participate in meaningful activities and perform useful roles. Along the way, you'll learn and practice problem solving, decision making, and goal setting.

7. Faith communities encourage service to others. All major faith traditions include an emphasis on service, and many places of worship make service an integral part of their youth program.

CONTINUED ON NEXT PAGE...

8. Faith communities nurture social competencies and leadership. Most give youth opportunities to lead, plan programs, become peer ministers, and care for younger children.

9. Faith communities offer security and stability. Over the course of your lifetime, many things will change. You'll graduate from schools, leave home to live on your own, move into and out of neighborhoods, and probably switch careers more than once. But no matter where you go, you can always find a community of people who share your faith and values. Most large religious organizations have places of worship around the world. Your faith community can be a source of support, encouragement, and affirmation throughout your life.

Source: Search Institute.

At School

● Unless you attend a private religious school, your faith community may be separate from your school life. But that doesn't mean you can't live by your values and beliefs at school (or anywhere else). Let them guide you to do and be your best.

● Give your teachers and principal copies of your faith community's calendar, listing religious holidays and other special events. Request that they not schedule school activities that conflict with religious holidays.

● Ask your teachers to include information about various religious holidays and traditions in class discussions. (This isn't permitted in some schools, but it won't hurt to ask.)

Assets in Action

In **Town and Country, Missouri,** *Trinity Lutheran Church and the Parkway School District are working together to build assets in their community. "My job and the school's have very similar goals," says Rob Rose, a youth minister at the church. "We want the betterment of kids. Part of our church's philosophy is that Trinity needs to be a community center. We need to be more than just a building."*

In Your Community

Work to build religious understanding and tolerance.

The more people know about each other's spiritual beliefs, the more accepting and tolerant they become. Bias and prejudice are built on ignorance and fear. Especially if your community has problems with discrimination, violence, or hate crimes based on religious differences, do your part to change things for the better. Be respectful of people whose beliefs are different from yours; don't tolerate religious slurs or offensive jokes; get to know people of all ages and many spiritual beliefs.

On a larger scale, you might see if your community is willing to sponsor a series of presentations on different faiths within your community. Talk with community leaders and offer to help.

What other ideas do you have for building religious understanding and tolerance in your community? Talk with your parents, your spiritual leaders, your friends, and other community members. *Tips:* Your youth group might attend services at other places of worship; you might get together with other youth groups for social functions and service projects.

Join a national religious organization for youth.

You'll connect with other teens who share your faith, and you'll have plenty of opportunities for leadership, sports, activities, achievement, service, spiritual growth, camping, and fun. Here are just a few examples of national religious organizations; to learn about more that fit your beliefs, contact local places of worship or ask your youth leader or other spiritual leader.

B'nai B'rith Youth Organization
2020 K Street, NW, 7th Floor
Washington, DC 20006
(202) 857-6600
www.bnaibrith.org
An international Jewish youth-led organization for teens.

Student Venture
100 Lake Hart Drive
Orlando, FL 32832
1-800-699-4678
www.studentventure.com
The high school ministry of Campus Crusade for Christ.

Young Life
PO Box 520
Colorado Springs, CO 80901
1-877-438-9572
www.younglife.org
A nondenominational, community-based program for Christian junior high and high school students.

In Your Faith Community

Use your faith community as a home base for asset building.

Like a youth program (see Asset #18), a faith community is an asset-rich environment. Involvement builds assets you need and strengthens those you already have. It's also a great place to build all 40 assets for other children and teens. For tips, see the In Your Faith Community sections throughout this book; every asset chapter has one.

Assets in Action

For four days each week, 50 African American boys ages 6–18 come together for a meal, activities, ceremonies, tutoring, computer classes, and more at Liberty Hills Baptist Church in **Little Rock, Arkansas.** *They're part of the Brother to Brother Program, which weaves together social rituals, cultural information, and educational enrichment within the context of values. For many of the boys in the program, the real world is one of crime, gangs, violence, racial isolation, and stereotyping. Brother to Brother doesn't try to shield them from the world. Instead, it gives them the skills, support, and sense of identity they need to deal with it.*

Don't just drop out.

Many young people drop out of their faith communities during their teens. Organized religion no longer seems relevant to their lives. Their parents may want them to stay involved, but eventually they decide that it's not worth arguing about. Don't drop out until you try one or more of these alternatives:

● If you haven't already joined the youth program, make the effort. Stick with it for a few months and see what happens.

● If you feel that your faith community is out of touch with young people, speak up. Talk with the people who lead the youth program. Come with ideas and offer to help. *Examples:* Have a roundtable discussion so teens can express their opinions, thoughts, and needs. Start a suggestion box so kids can contribute their ideas for activities, programs, and special events.

● Instead of expecting your faith community to serve you, figure out ways you can serve. *Example:* If you'd like your faith community to offer services especially for kids and teens, get a team together and make a plan.

● Lobby for classes and discussion groups that address real-life issues important to teens—alcohol and other drug use, peaceful conflict resolution, sexuality, independence, relationships, depression—within a context of faith and values.

● If you experience a serious crisis of faith, talk with your youth leader, pastor, minister, rabbi, priest, or other spiritual leader. Believe it or not, they've heard it all before. You're not the first teenager to decide that religion is meaningless or lame. Explain how you feel; listen to what the other person has to say.

● Remember that the more involved you are, the less likely you'll be to walk away.

FACT:

Teens give faith communities high marks!

When Search Institute surveyed 1,100 young people in Minneapolis (Minnesota), Durham (North Carolina), and St. Louis (Missouri) about faith communities in their city, here's what we learned:

• 82% said that faith communities are safe places to be.
• 77% said that faith communities welcome young people.
• 65% said that faith communities don't discourage young people from asking questions about their beliefs.
• 63% said that faith communities offer a variety of meaningful activities.
• 63% said that faith communities offer a variety of fun activities.
• 51% said that faith communities are good places to go for help about serious issues like alcohol, other drugs, or sex.

Young people we surveyed also said that faith communities help them feel good about themselves and gain a sense of purpose in life.

Source: Search Institute.

With Your Friends

● Don't give each other grief about being spiritual or being active in a faith community. Support each other's commitment to a good thing. Go as a group to events and activities in each other's faith communities.

● If you and your friends feel comfortable talking about religion, you might consider these questions:

— How many of your role models are involved in religion? (You may need to do some research to find out.) For those who are involved, how does that seem to affect them?
— How does religious involvement affect other teenagers you know?
— Is it important to know a person's spiritual beliefs when deciding whether to be friends? Why or why not? What about when deciding whether to date someone?

RESOURCES

For everyone:

How to Be a Perfect Stranger: A Guide to Etiquette in Other People's Religious Ceremonies, volumes 1 and 2 (Woodstock, VT: Jewish Lights Publishing, 1995 and 1996). When you visit other faith communities, these books will tell you what to expect and how to act. Vol. 1 covers larger faiths, from the Assemblies of God to the United Church of Christ. Vol. 2 covers U.S. religions with smaller memberships.

For your faith community:

Building Assets in Congregations: A Practical Guide for Helping Youth Grow Up Healthy by Eugene C. Roehlkepartain (Minneapolis, MN: Search Institute, 1998). Everything you need to create an asset-building faith community. Includes a discussion of Developmental Assets, a planning guide, worksheets, strategies and ideas for infusing assets into youth programs, tips for creating intergenerational programs and parent workshops, and reproducible bulletin inserts.

Asset #20

50% of the youth we surveyed have this asset in their lives.

TIME AT HOME

You go out with friends with nothing special to do two or fewer nights each week.

At Home

Don't go ballistic.

You may disagree with this asset. You may view it as a prison sentence. Spend *more* time at home than you already do? FIVE NIGHTS A WEEK? Don't scream or skip this asset until you understand it fully.

● **First,** it doesn't mean that you have to spend five nights at home each and every week. It means that you shouldn't spend more than two nights out with friends with *nothing special to do.* Unstructured time is vastly different from having *something special* to do. If you're attending a community meeting, doing a service project, doing an activity with your youth program, practicing for the school play, or playing basketball with your friends, you're not just hanging out. You're doing something positive.

● **Second,** this is a general guideline, not a hard-and-fast rule. Depending on your activities, interests, and commitments, there may be weeks when you're hardly ever home. What's important is to find a balance between time at home and time away.

● **Third,** time at home is a matter of *quality*, not just quantity. Five nights (or any number) won't matter if you spend them alone in your room or in front of the TV. What you need is family time—being together, interacting, getting serious, having fun.

Social scientist Reed Larson has found that in early adolescence, youth spend 35 percent of their waking time with family; in late teens, that falls to 14 percent. Try to spare a few hours for your family now and then. It's worth it.

Tip: Maybe your parents already limit the amount of time you can spend away from home. If they don't, try setting your own limits. Focus more on your schoolwork and your family and see what happens.

FACT:

Everyone wants more family time!

According to a University of Maryland study, parents today spend only 17 hours per week with their children—40 percent fewer than in 1965.

- When the Family and Work Institute surveyed 3,381 adults nationwide, they found that 66 percent wanted more time with their children.
- A 1995 Gallup poll found that nearly half of all parents feel that they spend too little time with their children.
- In a Search Institute study, almost 20 percent of 6th–12th graders said they hadn't had a good conversation—lasting for at least ten minutes—with either one of their parents in more than a month.
- Three-quarters of the children who watch more than two hours of TV each day say that if they could choose between spending time with their families and watching TV, they would choose family time.

Source: Family Research Council.

Make the most of your family time.

Like a youth program (see Asset #18) or a religious community (Asset #19), a home where people care about each other is an asset-rich environment. You can build and strengthen many assets with your family. For ideas, see Asset #1: Family Support and Asset #2: Positive Family Communication. Also see the At Home sections throughout this book; every asset chapter has one.

Start by discussing these questions as a family:

- How can we balance our commitments and our family time?
- How do we feel about the time we spend together?
- How can we make our time at home more appealing?

Then set some goals and ground rules. *Examples:*

1. We'll spend at least one evening together each week. Do something you all enjoy or want to try. Give everyone a chance to make suggestions and choices.

2. We'll eat at least one meal together every day. This is a tried-and-true technique for getting and staying close as a family. *Tip:* Talk about the good things that happened that day. Save the complaints for one-on-one conversations or family meetings called for the purpose of problem solving.

3. We won't answer the phone during family time. *Tip:* Turn on the answering machine or let calls roll over to voicemail. If this makes everyone anxious, or if there are some calls you can't miss, consider getting caller ID.

4. We'll be kind, caring, and respectful toward each other. Why not make your time together pleasant for everyone? Good manners make a big difference.

THE
30
COMMANDMENTS OF FAMILY ETIQUETTE

Thou shalt. . .

. . . say "Please" and "Thank you"
. . . use proper table manners
. . . disagree without being
disagreeable
. . . ask without yelling
. . . listen attentively
. . . be willing to compromise
. . . treat others as thou would like
to be treated
. . . share willingly
. . . treat each other's property with
care and respect
. . . apologize sincerely when apologies are called for
. . . rejoice in each other's successes
. . . empathize with each other's pain
. . . be thoughtful of each other—
especially if thou knowest a
family member is having a
difficult day
. . . take responsibility for thine own
actions and words
. . . smile.

Thou shalt not. . .

. . . lie
. . . hit
. . . snoop
. . . whine
. . . interrupt
. . . use crude language
. . . take each other's belongings
without first asking
. . . tell each other's secrets
. . . ignore each other's requests
. . . be afraid to speak up when thou
feelest something is wrong
. . . spend all day or night on the
telephone
. . . embarrass thy parents or siblings
or children in front of their
friends
. . . schedule commitments for each
other without clearing them in
advance
. . . forget to do thy chores
. . . treat each other discourteously.

Adapted from *How Rude! The Teenagers' Guide to Good Manners, Proper Behavior, and Not Grossing People Out* by Alex J. Packer, Ph.D. Free Spirit Publishing Inc., 1997, page 120. Used with permission.

Turn off the TV.

The average high school graduate will have spent 15,000 to 18,000 hours in front of a television but only 12,000 hours in school—and a lot fewer with their families.

Cut down on the number of hours you spend watching TV. How many hours is that? Keep a log for one week; record what you watch and when; add up the hours at the end of the week. That's how many.

Consider making one day each week TV-free. If you have a TV in your room, force yourself to watch less. If this isn't possible, move the TV out of your room.

Blah, blah, blah . . . you've heard it all before. The Evils of Television, The Decline in Quality Programming, the Idiot Box! That's old news. But here's more recent news that might interest you.

FACT:

TV Makes You Fat!

When researchers at Johns Hopkins University School of Medicine, the Centers for Disease Control and Prevention, and the National Institutes of Health studied 4,063 children and youth ages 8–16, they found that:

- 20% reported two or fewer bouts of vigorous physical activity per week (the kind that makes you breathe hard and sweat)

- 26% watched 4 or more hours of TV per day

- 67% watched at least 2 hours of TV per day

- Those who watched 4 or more hours per day had greater body fat and body mass than those who watched less than 2 hours per day.

Source: *Journal of the American Medical Association* 279 (1998), pages 938–942.

Assets in Action

When their children were eight, six, and three years old, a family in **Minneapolis, Minnesota,** *tried an experiment with the television. On school days, they kept the set off to encourage the kids to read and focus on homework. On weekends, the kids could watch as much TV as they wanted. For the first month, the children flocked to the set after school on Friday and could hardly tear themselves away until Sunday afternoon. But gradually, over the next few months, they began to lose interest in it. The freed-up time on weeknights had encouraged them to play games together and explore other activities. Today all three kids perform well in school, pursue a wide range of activities (from karate to viola to creative writing), and spend hours together playing Monopoly, chess, or card games.*

If you have a part-time job . . .

According to the University of Michigan's Institute for Social Research, about a quarter of high school seniors work between 11 and 20 hours per week. Recent studies show that working long hours can:

- lower your grades
- boost your levels of stress, irritability, and fatigue
- make you feel frustrated and cynical about future careers (especially if your job is boring)
- increase the chances that you'll use cigarettes, alcohol, and marijuana.

Plus work cuts into your homework time, family time, extracurricular activities, creative activities, and other good things you need in your life.

When researchers at a university in Pennsylvania studied 1,800 high school students, they learned that those who work more than 15 hours a week have more problems than those who work fewer hours. You may not have a choice; you may have to work more than 15 hours a week to help support your family. In this case, you're doing the best you can under the circumstances. But if you do have a choice, keep your hours to a minimum.

Tip: If you can get along without a part-time job during the school year, this may be the way to go. A majority of teachers (51 percent) who participated in a recent Phi Delta Kappa poll say that part-time work hurts students' academic performance. Only 8 percent say it has a positive effect.

IMPORTANT: *For some teens, home is not a good place to be. Their families are messed up, their homes are dangerous, or nobody else is ever around and they're left there all alone. If you feel that your home is unhealthy and you've done your best to make things better, spend more time in positive environments—your youth group, club, faith community, or friends' homes where people support and encourage each other (and the parents are present). Don't give up until you find a place where you feel welcome and safe.*

At School

Request that your school spread special events over the whole school year instead of grouping them around holidays or other occasions when family time is especially important.

In Your Community

Working with other schools and youth groups, create a community calendar that includes all kinds of activities—in schools, places of worship, community organizations, etc. Distribute it widely (through a community newspaper, cable access, or a community Web site) so families can plan and set priorities together.

In Your Faith Community

With your youth group, brainstorm suggestions for activities and projects families can do together. Publish them in worship bulletins.

With Your Friends

● Encourage each other to spend more time at home.

● If you know someone who's in a negative environment, explain the situation to your parents. See if they'll agree to make that person welcome in your home.

● Invite friends over on some of your nights at home. Spent part of the time with your family and the rest doing things with your friends.

RESOURCES

For your family:

Don't Sweat the Small Stuff with Your Family: Simple Ways to Keep Loved Ones and Household Chaos from Taking Over Your Life by Richard Carlson (New York: Hyperion, 1998). Strategies for easing stress at home.

303 Great Ideas for Families by Phyllis Pellman Good and Merle Good (Intercourse, PA: Good Books, 1997). Hundreds of free or inexpensive ideas for enjoying your time together as a family.

365 TV-Free Activities You Can Do with Your Child by Steven J. Bennett and Ruth Bennett (Holbrook, MA: Adams Publishing, 1996). The revised and updated version of the popular bestseller offers hundreds of fast, easy family-centered play activities.

BUILDING INTERNAL ASSETS

20 good things you need in yourself and how to achieve them

COMMITMENT TO LEARNING

These assets are about taking school seriously and making the most of every opportunity to learn. Getting an education is important to your life; being curious and open to learning new things—and developing the skills you need to learn them—are vital to your success now and in the future. These assets will help you feel motivated to do well in school and continue your education.

The commitment to learning assets are:

21. Achievement Motivation
22. School Engagement
23. Homework
24. Bonding to School
25. Reading for Pleasure

63% of the youth we surveyed have this asset in their lives.

ACHIEVEMENT MOTIVATION

You want to do well in school.

At Home

● Keep your parents informed about what you're doing in school. Don't wait for report cards to deliver the news (whether good or not so good). *Tip:* Keeping parents informed is especially important when you need their help with a school project. If you wait until the last minute, they might not be available—and they definitely won't be happy.

● Encourage your parents to get involved or stay involved with your school. The National Center for Education Statistics has found that involved parents are more likely to have high educational expectations for their children. When expectations are high (yet realistic), you'll reach to achieve them. See Asset #6: Parent Involvement in Schooling. (If you feel that your parents are pushing too hard, see Asset #16: High Expectations.)

● If you're having problems at school, talk to your parents and explore the reasons why. Is school too easy for you, or too hard? Are you getting the help and support you need? Do you feel safe at school? Arrange a meeting between you, your parents, and your teachers; brainstorm ways to change things for the better. *Tip:* If you're having problems *now*, don't procrastinate. Talk to your parents today.

● Ask your parents to support your efforts to do well in school. Tell them about your successes—and your failures. (They can celebrate the former and empathize with the latter. Chances are their school experience wasn't smooth sailing all the way.)

● Don't limit your learning to school. Read books that interest you, take community education classes, hang out at the library, explore the Internet. Learning is a continuum and a process; it isn't divided into neat little compartments. What you learn at the science museum may help you in your science class at school—and other classes, too.

● Do your homework. See Asset #23.

● If you have a part-time job during the school year, limit your work schedule to 15 or fewer hours per week. See Asset #20: Time at Home for reasons why.

● Be a role model for your younger brothers and sisters. Show them that you think school and learning are important.

At School

Be motivated from the inside.

To succeed in school (and in life), you need to be motivated from the *inside*, not the outside. Rewards (parents who pay you for A's; teachers who give special privileges) and punishments (parents who ground you for D's; teachers who withhold privileges) are external motivations. If you're motivated from the outside, you're likely to choose the fastest, easiest ways to learn—and you won't learn much.

Take this quiz to learn where your motivation lies:

	OFTEN	SOMETIMES	NEVER
1. Do you lose track of time while learning?	❏	❏	❏
2. Do you discover new things about yourself while learning?	❏	❏	❏
3. Do you enjoy learning for its own sake?	❏	❏	❏
4. Do you love the challenge of figuring out a difficult subject, problem, or concept?	❏	❏	❏
5. Are you curious about many different things?	❏	❏	❏

CONTINUED ON NEXT PAGE...

	OFTEN	SOMETIMES	NEVER
6. When you have a choice between a learning experience and entertainment, do you choose the learning experience?	❏	❏	❏
7. When you're interested in a topic, do you pursue it beyond what you get from your teachers and textbooks?	❏	❏	❏
8. Do you seek out extra credit projects and opportunities for independent study?	❏	❏	❏
9. When you have a question about something, do you hunt for the answer, even if it has nothing to do with your schoolwork?	❏	❏	❏
10. Do you delight in learning new things?	❏	❏	❏

SCORING: If you answered often or sometimes to most questions, you're inner-motivated. If you answered never to most questions, take a look at what motivates you.

FACT:

Most teens want to succeed in school . . .

According to a recent survey of over 1,300 high school students, most teenagers believe that getting an education is important to their lives. They would like to do well in school, and they admire classmates who make good grades.

. . . but a lot admit to just getting by!

Of the teenagers surveyed, 96 percent say they enjoy doing well in school, but 65 percent admit that they could do much better if they tried—and 83 percent usually can't wait for the school day to end.

Source: *Getting By: What American Teenagers Really Think About Their Schools* (New York: Public Agenda, 1997).

Take charge of your education.

If you sometimes (or often) feel like school is a waste of your time, do something about it. Set goals for yourself, ask questions in class, and find an ally—a teacher or school counselor who can help you get more out of school.

Are you having a problem with a class or an assignment? Can you see room for improvement in how a subject is taught? Do you have a better idea for a special project or term paper? Don't just tell your friends. Talk to the teacher. *Note:* Most teachers will be happy to talk with you. They *want* students in their classes who are involved, interested, successful—and awake.

TIPS FOR TALKING TO TEACHERS

1. Make an appointment to meet and talk. This shows the teacher that you're serious and you know he or she has a busy schedule. Tell the teacher how much time you'll need, be flexible, and don't be late.

2. If you know other students who feel the way you do, consider approaching the teacher together. There's strength in numbers.

3. Think through what you want to say before you go into your meeting with the teacher. Make a list of the items you want to cover. You may want to copy your list for the teacher so both of you can consult it during your meeting—or give it to the teacher ahead of time.

4. Choose your words carefully. *Example:* Instead of saying "I hate doing reports; they're boring and a waste of time," try "Is there some other way I could satisfy this requirement?"

5. Don't expect the teacher to do all the work or come up with all the answers. Be prepared to make suggestions, offer solutions, even recommend resources.

6. Be diplomatic, tactful, and respectful. Teachers have feelings, too. And they're more likely to be responsive if the purpose of your meeting is conversation, not confrontation.

7. Focus on what you need, not on what you think the teacher is doing wrong. The more the teacher learns about you, the more he or she will be able to help. The more defensive the teacher feels, the less he or she will want to help.

8. Don't forget to listen. Many students need practice in this essential skill. The purpose of your meeting isn't just to hear yourself talk.

9. Bring your sense of humor. Not the joke-telling sense of humor, but the one that lets you laugh at yourself and your own misunderstandings and mistakes.

10. If your meeting isn't successful, ask another adult for help. "Successful" doesn't necessarily mean getting what you want. Even if the teacher nixes your request, your meeting can still be judged successful. If you had a real conversation—if you communicated openly, listened carefully, and respected each other's point of view—congratulate yourself on a great meeting. If the air crackled with tension, the meeting fell apart, and you felt disrespected (or acted disrespectful), it's time to bring in another adult—perhaps the school counselor or another teacher you know and trust. Once you've found help, approach your teacher and try again.

Adapted from *The Gifted Kids' Survival Guide: A Teen Handbook* by Judy Galbraith, M.A., and Jim Delisle, Ph.D. Free Spirit Publishing Inc., 1996, page 155–156. Used with permission.

Make the most of what school offers.

You won't be in middle school or high school forever, although it may seem that way today. Before too long, you'll be long gone. School success is your ticket to a good job, college or trade school admission, scholarships, financial aid, and other important steps toward becoming independent and achieving your goals. That's why you need to take it seriously.

Here are a few more tips to try:

● Get to know your teachers. Personal attention and interest from a teacher can help your motivation soar.

● Don't skip the small stuff. Often, grades are a combination of factors: assignments done, papers turned in on time, test scores, class participation. Don't make the mistake of skipping assignments or turning papers in a day late. What seems like an insignificant little worksheet can affect your final grade.

● Develop a love of learning. See Asset #22: School Engagement.

● Work to make your school a better place for everyone—including you. Do your part to create a school that's caring (see Asset #5) and safe (#10), with clear rules and consequences for behavior (#12). Advocate for arts education (#17); schools with strong arts programs have students who are more motivated to learn.

Assets in Action

In **Gloucester, Virginia,** *the PAWS for Success Program helps kids at risk succeed in school. (PAWS stands for Positive Achievement with Students.) Children at T.C. Walker Elementary School who have been identified as at-risk or are performing below grade level are matched with tutors from Gloucester High School, who come to the elementary school from one to three times a week. The tutors follow lesson plans provided by the teachers and report back to the teachers on how the sessions went. Tutors also act as positive role models, learning about the younger kids' interests and dreams.*

In Your Community

● Find adults in your community who model achievement motivation and lifelong learning. Get to know them. See Asset #14: Adult Role Models.

● Volunteer to be a tutor or a mentor for younger kids. Show that you value learning by donating your time and expertise.

● With your class, club, or youth program, start a Speakers' Bureau of high achievers in your community—including both adults and students. Publicize their availability to speak at area schools.

Assets in Action

Since 1987, Wegmans grocery chain in **Rochester, New York,** *has helped hundreds of young people graduate from high school, learn responsibility, and go to college. Through the Work-Scholarship Connection, teens get academic support, job readiness training, and part-time jobs in Wegmans stores or company-sponsored community relations projects. Workplace mentors make sure the students succeed; full-time youth advocates, housed in the schools, coordinate work and scholarship efforts and nurture partnerships with parents. Graduates with a C average or better get a bonus: full-time jobs at Wegmans or tuition assistance at the college of their choice.*

In Your Faith Community

Make school a regular topic of conversation in your youth group. Encourage each other to achieve; celebrate each other's successes. *Tip:* For some students, success means going from a D to a C.

Assets in Action

First Church of the Brethren in **Brooklyn, New York,** *actively encourages young people in the primarily Hispanic community to continue their education through college. Tutoring begins in elementary school and continues through high school. The Sunday school teachers and pastors make periodic visits to the schools and check with principals, teachers, and counselors about their students' progress. Church members also help the young people apply for college admission and scholarships.*

With Your Friends

Consider your friends' attitudes toward school. If you're spending most of your time with kids who hate school and do the minimum work needed to pass, maybe you need new friends. See assets #15: Positive Peer Influence and #33: Interpersonal Competence.

— **RESOURCES** —

For you:

Making the Grade: The Teen's Guide to Homework Success by Janice Gabe (Indianapolis: Professional Resource Publications, 2000). Tips for school success in an easy-to-use format.

School Power: Study Skill Strategies for Succeeding in School by Jeanne Shay Schumm, Ph.D. (Minneapolis: Free Spirit Publishing, 2001). How to get organized, take notes, study smarter, write better, handle homework, and more.

For your parents and teachers:

Bold Parents, Positive Teens: Loving and Guiding Your Child Through the Challenges of Adolescence by Karen Dockrey (Colorado Springs, CO: Waterbrook Press, 2002). Ideas for parents looking to instill in teens the traits they need to succeed.

How to Talk So Kids Can Learn at Home and in School by Adele Faber and Elaine Mazlish (New York: Simon & Schuster, 1997). The authors of the bestselling *How to Talk So Kids Will Listen & Listen So Kids Will Talk* show parents and teachers how to motivate kids to learn and succeed in school. The stories and examples are about younger kids, but the wisdom is applicable to all kids.

Asset #22

64% of the youth we surveyed have this asset in their lives.

SCHOOL ENGAGEMENT

You like to learn new things.

At Home

● Talk with your parents about school and learning. Tell them every day what you did in school, what you learned, what you liked about school, what you didn't like about it. Invite them to tell you what *they* learned that day.

● Ask your parents to help you explore all the learning options available at your school. You may have choices you're not aware of—special classes, enrichment programs, opportunities for independent study, mini-courses.

● Start each day rested and ready to learn. Get enough sleep and don't skip breakfast, even if it means grabbing a banana on your way out the door. If you have a part-time job during the school year, don't work late on school nights and do try to limit your hours. See Asset #20: Time at Home for more on the topic of part-time jobs.

● Take learning risks. Rent a foreign film on video (subtitled, not dubbed). Explore a Web site on a topic that's new to you (economics? architecture? politics? Buddhism?). Listen to music that's completely different from anything you've ever heard before (Japanese shakuhachi flute? Brazilian samba? New Orleans jazz?). Read a book on a subject you know nothing (or pitifully little) about. *Tip:* A great place to start is with any book that has *For Dummies* or *The*

Complete Idiot's Guide in the title. Written by experts, each assumes that you're starting at ground zero, then gives you tons of information in plain English. *Examples:*

. . . For Dummies (all published by IDG Books Worldwide)	*The Complete Idiot's Guide to . . .* (all published by MacMillan General Reference)
Accounting . . .	. . . Astronomy
Art . . .	. . . British Royalty
Auto Repair . . .	. . . Classical Mythology
Chess . . .	. . . Elvis
Classical Music . . .	. . . Genealogy
Gourmet Cooking . . .	. . . Golf
Hockey . . .	. . . Philosophy
Investing . . .	. . . Skiing
Law . . .	. . . Tae Kwon Do
Opera . . .	. . . Tennis
Politics . . .	. . . Turtles and Tortoises
Weight Training . . .	. . . Yoga

● Model the love of learning for your younger brothers and sisters. Involve them in your hobbies and interests; show enthusiasm for theirs. Learn a new skill together.

● Make it a goal to get excited about *something* new ASAP—today, this week, this month. Then learn as much as you can (or want to) about it.

FACT:

Curiosity is good for you!

Roper Starch Worldwide, a leading marketing, public opinion, advertising, and media research firm, has identified 10 percent of Americans as the opinion leaders of today. These "Influential Americans" have several characteristics in common: More than 75 percent have been to college; about 25 percent have done post-graduate study; nearly 48 percent are extremely satisfied with their careers, as compared to 27 percent of the total public.

The Influentials also share a strong *intellectual curiosity*. The subjects they're most interested in are current events, investing, medicine and health, computers, economics, other countries and culture, and history. Nearly half say they would like to know more about these topics, as compared to 31 percent of Americans as a whole.

According to the Roper Starch publication *The Public Pulse*, "Curiosity may have killed the cat in the children's nursery rhyme. But in the current economy, it seems to be one of the keys to getting ahead. Having it can make it easier to adopt technologies, troubleshoot workplace problems, and adapt to changing conditions in one's field."

Source: *The Public Pulse*, Roper Starch Worldwide (1997).

At School

Get a new attitude.

You'll spend 13 years of your life in school—longer if you continue your education in college, trade school, and graduate school. You can view school as a drag or an adventure; it's up to you. Your teachers can try to inspire you; your parents can try to encourage you; but what you get out of school depends on *your* attitude and *your* willingness to learn.

If you're already excited about school, that's great. If you're not, how can you get excited? What can you do to make learning more appealing and enjoyable? Some tips to try:

● Even in the dullest class, you can probably find *one* thing that sparks your interest. Pursue it.

● Relate what you're learning to real life.

● Tell your teachers (and your parents) that you want to get more excited about learning. Ask for their support and suggestions.

● Make the effort to stay awake in class and keep up with the assignments.

● Participate in class discussions. Ask questions if there's something you don't understand.

● Deepen your understanding of a subject by doing a special project or interviewing an expert.

● Investigate something you're curious about.

Assets in Action

In **Nampa, Ohio,** where the Healthy Youth initiative slogan is "It's better to build a young person than to rehabilitate an adult," teachers are praising a highly personalized tutoring program for fourth-, fifth-, and sixth-grade students who need extra academic help. The after-school program also helps bilingual students polish their language skills. Teachers say the program raises grades and boosts students' self-esteem.

If you have a choice, sit up front.

It's tempting to beeline for the back of the classroom and hope you'll go unnoticed. But if you can sit wherever you want, hotfoot it for the front. Teacher Randall McCutcheon shares these reasons why:*

---

* Adapted from *Get Off My Brain: A Survival Guide for Lazy Students* by Randall McCutcheon. Free Spirit Publishing Inc., 1998, pages 13–15. Used with permission.

● Bright, ambitious students tend to sit in the front row.

● Front-row students are more likely to take good notes you can borrow if you miss class.

● If you don't understand some of the material and the teacher is usually busy after class, these students are the next best thing.

● You're less likely to fall asleep when sitting in the front row. Snoring is visible, noisy, and embarrassing. So is drooling on your desk.

● By sitting up front, you give the teacher a chance to know you. You're not just another face in the crowd.

● When you sit in the front row, your confidence level increases. You speak out more, ask more questions, and feel more positive when studying for exams.

Stand up for your right to learn.

If school is deadly for you, don't just whine about it. And don't just give up. Do something! See Asset #21: Achievement Motivation for tips on being motivated from the inside, how to talk to teachers, and more.

Dr. Roger C. Schank, a leader in the field of artificial intelligence and multimedia-based interactive training, believes that students should have some say in their education. "Students can determine what interests them," he says, "and they should have the right to complain when outmoded teaching methods are in use." He's written a Student Bill of Rights that might inspire you to lobby for an education that's more exciting, meaningful, and fun. *Warning:* Some teachers will perceive this as a radical manifesto. If you decide to pursue the rights it describes, proceed with caution. Choose one at a time to work on, and enlist support from other students and teachers.

THE STUDENT BILL OF RIGHTS

by Dr. Roger C. Schank
Director, Institute for the Learning Sciences,
Northwestern University

1. Testing: No student should have to take a multiple-choice or fill-in-the-blank test.

2. Real-Life Skills: No student should have to learn something that fails to relate to a skill that is likely to be required in life after school.

CONTINUED ON NEXT PAGE...

---

3. Memorization: No student should be required to memorize any information that is likely to be forgotten in six months.

4. Clarity of Goals: No student should be required to take a course, the results of which are not directly related to a goal held by the student, nor to engage in an activity without knowing what he or she can expect to gain from that activity.

5. Passivity: No student should be required to spend time passively watching or listening to anything unless there is a longer period of time devoted to allowing the student to participate in a corresponding active activity.

6. Arbitrary Standards: No student should be required to prepare his or her work in ways that are arbitrary or to jump through arbitrary hoops defined only by a particular teacher and not by the society at large.

7. Mastery: No student should be required to continue to study something he or she has already mastered.

8. Discovery: No student should be asked to learn anything unless there is the possibility of his or her being able to experiment in school with what he or she has learned.

9. Defined Curriculum: No student should be barred from engaging in activities that interest him or her within the framework of school because of breadth requirements imposed by the curriculum.

10. Freedom of Thought: No student should be placed in a position of having to air his or her views on a subject if the opposing point of view is not presented and equally represented.

Reprinted from *Engines for Education,* © 1994, The Institute for the Learning Sciences. Used with permission.

In Your Community

Take advantage of learning opportunities within your community. Check out libraries, museums, community centers, and local colleges. That's right, *colleges.* In Minnesota, students enrolled in the Postsecondary Enrollment Options Program take college-level courses at state expense. Between 1985 and 1995, tens of thousands of students signed up for courses at state universities, private colleges, vocational schools, and industrialization centers while still in high school. This option is available in other states, too.

Assets in Action

*Since 1987, the Love of Learning Program at Davidson College in **Davidson, North Carolina,** has helped African American youth succeed in school. Starting in the 9th grade, qualified students are involved in residential summer programs, internships, and college preparatory seminars; during the academic year, they meet at least twice a month for workshops, cultural and social events, and other activities. The program focuses on enriching the students' academic, physical, spiritual, social, and cultural development, and parents are expected to participate fully. Love of Learning graduates have experienced dramatic changes in their attitudes toward school and their achievement levels, and the program has served as a model for similar programs at other colleges and universities.*

In Your Faith Community

Work to make your faith community a learning faith community. Talk with your youth group leader; come up with ideas and offer to help. *Examples:* You might discuss sacred writings as a faith community, form intergenerational groups to discuss specific topics, or visit local art museums to view religious paintings and sculpture.

With Your Friends

Talk about your school experiences. You might start with these questions:

- What makes a teacher a *good* teacher?
- How does a good teacher make learning exciting and fun?
- What's the *best* class you've ever taken, and why?
- What's the *worst* class you've ever taken, and why?
- What about learning is most exciting to you?
- How can you get excited about learning when the subject or teaching method seems boring?

If you feel daring, you might invite a teacher or two to listen in on your discussion.

RESOURCES

For everyone:

Engines for Education by Roger C. Schank and Chip Cleary (Mahwah, NJ: Lawrence Erlbaum Associates, 1995). Describes what's wrong with our current educational system, how to reform it, and the role of educational technology in that reform.

For you:

Neuroscience for Kids

faculty.washington.edu/chudler/neurok.html

Want to know more about how you learn? Check out this fun and fascinating site. It includes experiments, activities, brain games, facts about the brain and nervous system, resources, links, and *much* more for elementary and secondary students and their teachers. You can also sign up for the Neuroscience for Kids Newsletter.

For your parents:

The Complete Idiot's Guide to Parenting a Teenager by Kate Kelly (New York: MacMillan General Reference,1996). While you're expanding your mind with *The Complete Idiot's Guide to Astronomy* (or *Elvis*, or whatever), your parents can learn a few things from this stress-reducing approach to raising teens. It offers comforting, down-to-earth advice and tips for coping with everyday issues concerning *you* . . . with humorous sidebars that put things into perspective.

Your Child's Growing Mind: A Guide to Learning and Brain Development from Birth to Adolescence by Jane M. Healy, Ph.D. (New York: Main Street Books, 1994). Tips for guiding your child's learning from birth through the teen years.

HOMEWORK

You do at least one hour of homework every school day.

At Home

Accept it.

Homework is a fact of life. You can run, but you can't hide. Besides, it's good for you! Here's the scoop from *School Power* author Jeanne Shay Schumm:

- Homework encourages you to practice skills you haven't fully learned.
- It gives you opportunities to review skills you might forget.
- It enriches your store of general knowledge.
- It teaches you responsibility.
- It allows for tasks that are too time-consuming to finish during regular school hours.

So stop making excuses and . . .

Just do it.

Make homework your first priority—before TV, time with your friends, extracurricular activities, even a job.

What if you don't have at least five hours of homework in a typical week? Spend the time reading more about a particular subject, practicing your skills, or reviewing your books and notes. If you haven't yet formed the homework habit, do it *now*. You'll need it if you go to college, where you'll have more homework than you ever dreamed possible.

P.S. "At least one hour of homework every school day" is a *general* guideline for grades 6–12. Experts recommend (and teachers expect) that the older you are, the more homework you'll do. Diane Heacox, author of *Up from Underachievement*, suggests these specific guidelines:

- Grades 6–8: Up to 1 hour a day, 6 days a week.
- Grades 9–12: Up to 3 hours a day, 6 days a week.

FACT:

Teens don't do enough homework!

When 1,000 students from ages 13–17 were asked about their homework habits, 69 percent said they spend seven hours or less per week on homework, while 29 percent said they spend *two* hours or less.

Students who give their schools high ratings do more homework than those who don't. Girls spend nearly 1 1/2 hours more per week on homework than boys do, and private school students study more than public school students.

Sources: *The Mood of American Youth* (Alexandria, VA: Horatio Alger Association of Distinguished Americans and the National Association of Secondary School Principals, 1996); *The State of Our Nation's Youth 1997–1998* (Horatio Alger Association, 1997).

Build the skills to do it right.

According to Judy Dodge, author of *The Study Skills Handbook*, there are three types of skills you need to do homework well:

1. Organizational skills. Find a quiet, comfortable, well-lit place to do your homework without distractions. Have everything you need close at hand: pencils, pens, paper, textbooks, notebooks, reference materials, assignment sheets, etc. Keep your study environment neat so you won't waste time shuffling papers and books.

2. Time management skills. Schedule a specific time each day to do your homework, then stick with it. Learn to project how long assignments will take. For tips on tackling long-range assignments, see Asset #32: Planning and Decision Making.

3. Study strategy skills. If you don't know how to study, get help. Ask your teacher for suggestions; ask your librarian to recommend books. Two are listed in the Resources on page 190.

Make it easier on yourself.

● Prioritize your homework and do the hardest assignments first.

● Have the resources you need when you need them. Start a personal reference library and keep it current. Begin with the basics: dictionary, thesaurus, almanac, desk encyclopedia, atlas. Add reference books on specific topics related to your classes or interests. If you have a computer, consider buying an encyclopedia on CD-ROM.

● If you have a part-time job during the school year, limit your work schedule to 15 or fewer hours per week. See Asset #20: Time at Home for reasons why.

● If it's impossible to do your homework at home, go somewhere else—the library, a community study center, the youth room at your religious organization, or a friend's house.

Homework matters more in the upper grades!

Psychologist Harris Cooper of the University of Missouri gathered data on 709 students in grades 2–4 and 6–12. For students in the lower grades, he found "a significant *negative* relationship between the amount of homework assigned and student attitudes." But in grades 6 and up, the more homework students did, the higher their achievement. Many studies have found that homework doesn't start paying off until middle school.

Source: *Newsweek,* March 30, 1998, pages 50–51.

Go online.

An Internet connection gives you access to vast amounts of homework help and information. Check out these Web sites:

B.J. Pinchbeck's Homework Helper
www.bjpinchbeck.com
This site offers hundreds of links divided into categories including science, English, and math.

Fact Monster
www.factmonster.com
Atlases, almanacs, dictionaries, and encyclopedias make this a one-stop Web resource.

HomeworkSpot
www.homeworkspot.com
Links to subject areas, must-see reference resources, science fair project ideas, and much more.

Homework help is also available in newsgroups and their FAQ (Frequently Asked Questions) files, and through commercial services (CompuServe, America Online). In fact, there's so much on the Net that finding what you need without getting frustrated or sidetracked can be overwhelming. That's when a book (remember books?) comes in handy. Look for the latest editions of these titles:

● *Internet Homework Helper* (Upper Saddle River, NJ: Prentice-Hall Computer Books, 1996). Designed for students in grades 7–12, this book comes with a CD-ROM of links to educational resources.

● *Net Study: Your Complete Guide to Academic Success Using the Internet and Online Services* by Michael Wolff (New York: Dell, 1997). An affordable mass-market paperback with reviews and URLs for sites in all major academic areas.

If you need frequent access to an encyclopedia, the *Britannica* is now online. Go to *www.eb.com* for a free trial and subscription information. Depending on how often you use this resource, your family may want to spring for a monthly or annual subscription.

At School

Since your teachers expect you to do homework, it's only fair for *you* to have a few expectations, too.

● Homework shouldn't consume your life. If it does, either your teachers are assigning too much or there's some other problem that needs addressing.

● Homework shouldn't cover brand-new territory. It should build on what you're learning in school.

● Homework assignments should be clear. If there's something you don't understand, ask.

● Homework should be meaningful. It should help you grasp a concept or process, prepare for a test, strengthen a skill, or build your knowledge in a specific subject area.

● Homework should be interesting, engaging, creative, and even (at times) *fun*. It should foster a love of learning, not fill you with dread or bore you to death.

● Homework shouldn't fall into a black hole. You deserve feedback, whether it comes in the form of grades or comments. Otherwise it's just busywork.

If your homework doesn't meet your expectations, talk to your teacher. See Asset #21: Achievement Motivation for tips on how to do this.

HOW TO HANDLE HOMEWORK PROBLEMS

PROBLEM	SOLUTION
"I have a lot of other things to do, so I don't have time for homework."	Homework is not an option. Eliminate some of your other activities.
"I let my homework go until the last minute."	Use an assignment sheet or calendar. Write down *all* of your assignments. Check your sheet or calendar daily so homework doesn't sneak up on you.
"I don't pay attention to how important homework is for my grade. Then it's too late."	Listen to your teachers when they tell you what counts in their classes. Most teachers will base at least part of your grade on your homework.
"I forget to take my books home, or I forget to bring my homework to class."	Keep your materials (books, papers, assignment sheet, calendar) organized. Check your sheet or calendar before you leave school each day. Use it like a shopping list to decide what you need to take home from your locker. Check it in the morning to find out what you need to bring to school.
"I forget the instructions. Sometimes I don't understand them in the first place."	Write down all assignments and directions. If there's something you don't understand, ask the teacher or a friend for help.
"I spend a lot of time on homework, but I still can't get it all done."	Are distractions keeping you from working (TV, phone calls, the Internet, noise, interruptions)? If distractions aren't the problem, talk to your teachers. See if they have any suggestions. (Maybe they're assigning too much homework and you're not the only one who can't get it all done.)
"All of my teachers assign homework on the same day. Then they give tests on the same day. I can't keep up!"	Use assignment sheets or a calendar to organize the assignments you know about in advance. (Write down what's due when.) Ask your teachers if they can give you longer lead times on some assignments. If your work still piles up, talk to your teachers. See if they're willing to compare their schedules and give assignments and tests on different days. If this doesn't work, take your problem to the school counselor or student council.

Adapted from *School Power: Strategies for Succeeding in School* by Jeanne Shay Schumm, Ph.D., and Marguerite Radencich, Ph.D. Free Spirit Publishing Inc., 1992, page 110. Used with permission.

In Your Community

● Be a homework helper for younger kids in your neighborhood. Schedule a time each week after school to sit with them, answer their questions, and monitor their progress.

● Work with teachers, administrators, and community leaders to set up a homework hotline staffed by volunteers (teachers, other adults, high school and college students). *Tip:* This would be a great service project for your school or youth program.

● Work with your neighbors and community leaders to create a neighborhood study center. Find a large room that's not in use after school or on weeknights (check with public libraries, religious organizations, youth organizations, and community centers). Stock it with resources and reference materials; staff it with teachers, parents, and older students.

Assets in Action

In **Moorhead, Minnesota,** *the Moorhead Public Library converted a van into a "Library to Go" that visits neighborhoods after school with resources and homework help.*

Carrie and Tom Barndt, owners of four McDonald's restaurants in suburban **Madison, Wisconsin,** *give their student employees generous leaves of absence when they need time for sports activities or rehearsals. Plus a "McStudy" option lets them add one hour of paid study time before or after their work shifts, up to three hours a week. Students are expected to sit alone during that time and do schoolwork; in exchange, they're paid regular wages for the study hours. The Barndts have benefited, too—in lower staff turnover and more committed workers.*

In Your Faith Community

● See if your place of worship is willing to open the youth room after school as a study and homework center. Staff it with adult and teen volunteers.

● When planning activities for your youth program, scale back during the school year. Schedule week night activities for later in the evening, after homework is finished.

● Set up a homework hotline staffed by adults and high school students from the faith community.

With Your Friends

Start a study group; it's less lonely and more fun than studying alone. To improve your chances of success, keep it small (3–4 members), meet frequently for shorter sessions instead of rarely for marathons, follow an agenda, and hold everyone responsible for being prepared and making a contribution.

Words to the wise from teacher and author Randall McCutcheon: "Do not form a 'study group' unless you plan to study. Otherwise, you end up with a social group that gets together to avoid the loneliness of *not* learning."

RESOURCES

For you:

Becoming a Master Student by David B. Ellis (Boston, MA: College Survival, 1997). Written for college freshmen, this book is also valuable for junior high and high school students who need help learning how to learn.

Last Minute Study Tips by Ron Fry (Franklin Lakes, NJ: Career Press, 1996). Cramming isn't ideal, but for times when you don't have a choice (because of other commitments or procrastination), these accelerated study techniques can help.

Asset #24

51% of the youth
we surveyed have this
asset in their lives.

BONDING
TO SCHOOL

You care about your school.

At Home

● Talk with your parents about school. Tell them what you like about it—and what you don't like about it. What can you do to change the things you don't like?

● Usually it's the people—teachers, administrators, friends—who make a school worth caring about. Is there someone at your school who looks forward to seeing you every day? Who misses you when you're absent? Are there people you enjoy seeing? Try to identify at least *one* adult and *one* peer. Ask your parents to tell you about people who made school special for them.

● Invite a teacher to dinner at your home. You'll get to know each other better outside of class, and you might form a closer relationship. See Asset #3: Other Adult Relationships.

● Set up a school bulletin board in your home. Post the school calendar and school notices. Have a family meeting once a month to choose which school activities you'll attend as a family.

At School

Know the benefits of bonding to school.

Good things happen—and bad things don't—when students bond to their schools. Research shows that students who care about school are . . .

. . . *more* likely to achieve in school
. . . *more* likely to care about their communities
. . . *less* likely to get involved with alcohol and other drugs
. . . *less* likely to get involved in gangs
. . . *less* likely to develop violent behavior
. . . *less* likely to drop out.

Know why some students don't bond to their schools.

A study of 20,000 students in California and Wisconsin found that about 40 percent of high school students, although physically present in school, are psychologically disconnected from it.* Causes include:

• parents who aren't involved with school
• the influence of peers who devalue school achievement
• too many hours (more than 20 per week) spent working or in extracurricular activities
• too little time spent on homework.

If you're feeling disconnected from your school for one of these reasons, you can do something about it.

• If your parents aren't involved with your school, see Asset #6: Parent Involvement in Schooling.
• If your peers devalue school achievement, see Asset #15: Positive Peer Influence.
• If you spend too many hours working or in extracurricular activities, see Asset #20: Time at Home.
• If you spend too little time on homework, see Asset #23: Homework.

Find something to like about your school.

You spend every weekday there during the school year, and if you can't find *something* to like, either you're not trying or you're in a terrible school. If you're not trying, you're cheating yourself and wasting your time. If you're in a terrible

---

* Reported in Larry Steinberg, Bradford Brown, and Sanford M. Dornbush, *Beyond the Classroom: Why School Reform Has Failed and What Parents Need to Do* (New York: Simon & Schuster, 1996).

school, do what you can to get out of there. See Asset #12: School Boundaries, page 105.

Teens find lots to like at school!

When 1,000 students from ages 13–17 were asked to name their reasons for liking school, here's what they said:

What's to like?	According to how many teens?
Friends	87.2%
Sports	51.9%
Social activities	47.2%
Classes	43.1%
Cocurricular activities	41.4%
Teachers	40.2%
Learning	37.0%
Preparing for college	35.5%
Preparing for a job	26.5%

Source: *The Mood of American Youth* (Alexandria, VA: Horatio Alger Association of Distinguished Americans and the National Association of Secondary School Principals, 1996).

Sign up or start something.

If you can't think of things you like about your school, identify *one* thing you enjoy doing, then find out if your school offers anything—a class, a club, a team—that matches your interest. If it doesn't, start one. Find an adult sponsor (usually a teacher) who's willing to support you. Write a proposal and present it to the principal, faculty, or activities coordinator at your school. Then advertise your class, club, or team to attract new members.

Here are more ways to care about your school:

● Don't badmouth your school to your friends, neighbors, or anyone else. When you wear a school shirt, jacket, or cap in public, remember that you're representing your school.

● Discourage cliques. Work to make everyone feel welcome and valued.

● Volunteer to tutor younger kids. Encourage them to care about school.

● Contact alumni and invite them to write guest articles for your school newspaper, yearbook, or Web site about what the school has done for them.

● Advocate for arts education in your school (see Asset #17: Creative Activities). Schools with strong arts programs have higher attendance among students and teachers, and their students are more engaged with school.

Assets in Action

Rickey Wheeling, a student at Gaylesville High School in **Gaylesville, Alabama,** *thought his small, rural school should offer students the latest in computer technology. But the school had barely enough money for necessities, much less "luxuries" like computers. So Rickey won the support of his school newspaper, student government, and principal, initiated several fund-raisers, secured matching grants, and arranged for a donation from Hewlett-Packard. Then he spent his summer break building and networking the computers and installing the software. Now he's training younger students in computer assembly so the project can continue after he graduates.*

John Bollhardt, a student at Mount Anthony Middle School in **Bennington, Vermont,** *coordinated a clothing drive to help purchase textbooks for his school. He enlisted support from his principal and classmates, arranged for a recycling company to purchase the used clothing, advertised the clothing drive, and mobilized volunteers to collect the donations. The result: nearly $400 for textbooks.*

Daniel Aguirre, a student at Northview Middle School in **Ankeny, Iowa,** *volunteers 10 hours each week to help his school janitorial staff clean the school.*

Note: *These students have something in common besides caring about their schools. All were State Honorees in the 1998 Prudential Spirit of Community Awards program. To learn more about this program, contact The Prudential Spirit of Community Initiative; see page 84.*

Build school spirit.

You may think that school spirit is corny, but it helps students care about their school. Plus it links students who might otherwise have little or nothing in common.

WAYS TO BUILD SCHOOL SPIRIT

1. Does your school have a symbol, logo, slogan, song, fight song, and/or cheer? If not, have a contest to generate ideas. Then have a vote so everyone (students, teachers, and administrators) can choose their favorites. *Tip:* If your school already has a symbol, logo, slogan, etc. but it's outdated, unpopular, or offensive, form a group of students who feel the same and lobby for change.

2. Show your school pride. Buy and wear T-shirts, sweatshirts, jackets, caps, or other clothing printed with your school's name or logo. Ask your parents to display a school bumper sticker or window sticker on the family car.

CONTINUED ON NEXT PAGE...

3. Start a Spirit Club at your school. Plan events and activities to boost school spirit; create inspiring banners or posters to display in the halls.

4. Hold an annual Spirit Week at your school. Schedule it for just after homecoming or during the February slump. Offer a variety of after-school activities and events. *Examples:* a mural contest, a student bake-off, a pie-eating contest, relay races.

5. Put your school in the news. Find out which reporters cover schools in your area and learn how to contact them. Keep them informed of important events and achievements at your school.

6. Come up with fun and unique ways to attract community and media attention to your school. Work with your class or club to plan projects and events. *Examples:* An all-school banquet featuring the world's largest submarine sandwich; a school play where admission is free to anyone who donates canned goods or other nonperishables for your local food shelf.

7. Support your school's athletes. Go to their games and matches and cheer them on. Have tailgate parties before football games. Post game schedules on school bulletin boards; if your school has a Web site, post them there, too. Use the morning announcements to recap recent games and encourage everyone to attend upcoming games. Support other school events, too—plays, concerts, musicals—by showing up and applauding.

8. Honor all types of achievers at your school, not just the athletes. What about awarding letters for academic achievement? For service? For the arts? Give monthly School Spirit Awards to the most caring, enthusiastic, and involved students, teachers, administrators, support staff members, and volunteers.

9. Start a friendly rivalry with another school in your community. Figure out ways to compete with each other that boost school spirit. *Examples:* Pit your school's best debaters against theirs; have an academic tournament (like College Bowl); see which school can generate the most volunteers for a local Habitat for Humanity project.

10. Make a special effort to welcome incoming classes and new students. Produce "survival kits" for newcomers. Each kit might include a school map, directory, calendar, and handbook, a list of activities and clubs at your school, descriptions of upcoming events (including dates and times), PTA/PTO information for parents, and . . . what else? What would be helpful? What would be fun?

Don't even think about dropping out.

Nearly half a million young adults drop out of school each year. Teens who leave school before graduating face a number of potential problems:

- More dropouts than high school graduates are unemployed.
- Dropouts who are employed earn less money than graduates.
- Dropouts are more likely to receive public assistance.
- Young women dropouts are more likely to have children at younger ages and are more likely to be single parents.

For some teens, dropping out isn't something they mean to do. Instead, it sneaks up on them. They don't feel like going to school for a day (or a few days, or a week), and by the time they think about returning, they're so far behind that they're afraid they'll never catch up. Or they find part-time jobs that seem more relevant than school. Or illness keeps them out of school for several days or weeks, and the prospect of going back is too scary. Regardless of your reason(s) for wanting to leave school, *don't drop out*. Talk to your school counselor; there may be a program for students in your situation.

Need a bottom-line reason to stay in school? According to the U.S. Census Bureau, the difference in lifetime earnings between a student who doesn't graduate from high school and one who does is more than $200,000. For a student who receives a bachelor's degree or higher, the difference is almost $1 million. These are 1994 figures; those for your lifetime will likely be higher.

In Your Community

● Ask your parents and neighbors to support school fund-raising events. *Examples:* bond issues, read-a-thons, book sales.

● If all the kids in your neighborhood don't attend the same school(s), find out which ones they do attend. Go to plays and concerts at each other's schools.

● Encourage the local media to feature positive stories about schools.

● If your school has serious school spirit problems, find one or more schools in your community where spirit is strong. Learn what they're doing differently. Talk with students, teachers, and administrators; read the school paper; attend a play, concert, or athletic event; go to an open house and look around. Bring some of their ideas back to your school.

In Your Faith Community

● Talk in your youth group about where people go to school and what they like about their schools. Go as a group to events at each other's schools.

● Publicize school events in your faith community's weekly bulletin or newsletter.

With Your Friends

● As a group, make a pact to stay in school and graduate. Offer support and encouragement to anyone who struggles with school.

● Go as a group to events at each other's schools.

● Give each other school spirit gifts (T-shirts, caps, banners) on birthdays and other special occasions.

RESOURCES

For you:

Surviving High School by Mike Riera (Berkeley, CA: Celestial Arts, 1997). Author Mike Riera has been a high school counselor for ten years. In this book, written in a lively dialogue format, he covers the hot topics and strikes a balance between guidance and choice.

For educators and community leaders:

Boxed In and Bored: How Middle Schools Continue to Fail Young Adolescents and What Good Middle Schools Do Right by Peter C. Scales (Minneapolis: Search Institute, 1996). Summarizes the latest research on young adolescent development and offers remedies to help middle schools and communities become healthier, more nurturing environments for youth.

READING FOR PLEASURE

You spend three or more hours each week reading for pleasure.

QUICK QUIZ

1. You're reading this because:
a) you have to.
b) you want to.

2. Reading is:
a) a waste of time.
b) a basic life skill.

If you answered a) to both questions, you probably need to build this asset. Please keep reading. If you answered b) to both questions, you probably have this asset already. Please keep reading anyway. You'll discover ways to make reading even more enjoyable—and ways to get others excited about reading.

At Home

Get help if you need it.

If you hate to read, or if reading is hard for you, *get help.* Talk to your parents; they may not be aware of the problem. If they don't give you the support you need, talk to your teachers. See also the list of resources on pages 202–203.

Reading is vital to your current and future success. The more you read, the stronger your reading skills become. Skilled readers do better on tests, read more quickly and easily, and retain more of what they read. They're more likely to ask questions when they don't understand something; to look up words they don't know; and to take notes on what they read.

Reading for pleasure—reading because you want to—makes you a better reader. If you haven't yet formed the habit, it's not too late to start. Think of something (anything!) you'd like to know more about, then visit your school or public library. Ask the librarian to help you find a book or magazine on that topic. Once you've read that, read another. Three hours of reading per week may seem like a lot, but it's less than 26 minutes a day.

Bonus: The more you read, the easier it becomes, and the more you enjoy reading. Many people *love* to read. In 1995, Americans spent an estimated $20 *billion* on books. They know something you can, too: Reading is one of the great joys in life. Books take you places you've never been and show you things you've never seen; they broaden your mind and touch your emotions. It's hard to believe that print on paper can do all that (and more), but it can. See for yourself. Be a reader.

Make reading a family affair.

● Spend time reading as a family every day (or whenever schedules allow). Gather in the living room, family room, or den for an hour or half-hour before or after dinner, or any time that works for everyone.

● Start a family book club. Ask everyone what books they'd like to read, then decide on one to start with. Talk about it afterward. Be willing to read all kinds of books—bestsellers, classics, children's books, YA (Young Adult) novels.

● Make frequent visits to the library. Everyone in your family should have his or her own library card.

● Keep books, magazines, and newspapers around the house. Read them aloud to each other.

● Give each other books and magazine subscriptions as gifts.

● Read aloud to your younger brothers and sisters. You might do this at bedtime or any time. Reading aloud is a perfect activity for cold winter evenings and lazy summer afternoons. Or take the kids to the library, let them pick out books, and read to them there.

● If you see a movie or watch a video based on a book, read the book, too. Talk about the similarities and differences between the film and the book.

● Play word games (Scrabble, Boggle) together. Put magnetic words and letters on the refrigerator; write messages and poems to each other.

● Volunteer as a family to tutor others in reading. For tips on volunteering as a family, see Asset #9: Service to Others.

FACT:

Teens are reading!

When 1,000 students from ages 13–17 were asked to name the types of books they read for pleasure, here's what they said:

What do you read?	According to how many teens?
Mystery/murder	45.1%
Horror/thriller	41.2%
Fantasy	26.7%
Science fiction	26.7%
Sports	24.2%
Romantic fiction	20.5%
Classic literature	15.1%
History	14.0%
Biography	12.8%
Religious/inspirational	12.6%
Do-it-yourself	5.5%
Self-help	4.6%

BUT . . . only 43 percent of the teens named reading as a hobby or special interest. AND . . . younger teens read more than older teens.

Source: *The Mood of American Youth* (Alexandria, VA: Horatio Alger Association of Distinguished Americans and the National Association of Secondary School Principals, 1996).

Go online.

If you have access to a computer with an Internet connection, you can read for pleasure online. The Internet has movie files, sound files, and other eye and ear candy, but it's still primarily text-based—people go there to *read*. Late-breaking news, major newspapers, popular magazines, favorite authors' Web sites, even whole books are online.

It matters where you go and what you read; not all sites are created equal in terms of content or value. But if you're a savvy navigator, you can truthfully tell your parents, "What do you mean, turn off the computer? I'm READING!"

Tip: You can also go online for advice on great books to read. Check out these sites:

The Children's Literature Web Guide
www.ucalgary.ca/~dkbrown

Favorite Teenage Angst Books
www.grouchy.com/angst

Young Adult Library Services Association (YALSA) Booklists
www.ala.org/yalsa/booklists

At School

- If you have free time at school—before or after classes, during study hall or lunch—spend it reading. Carry a book in your backpack at all times.

- Form a student committee to read and recommend books to feature in the school library or media center.

- Write book reviews for your school newspaper or Web site.

- Start a reading club at your school.

- Work with your student council to plan activities and events that get everyone excited about reading. *Examples:* book fairs, read-a-thons, essay contests about "a book that changed my life," awards for reading achievement.

- Help younger students write their own stories and produce them in book or dramatic form. (It's more interesting to read other people's stories once you've written your own.) Organize an event for the children to read or perform their written work.

- Ask parents, businesses, and community groups to donate books and other reading materials your school needs. Make sure that these include books in Braille, large-print texts, and books on tape.

- Volunteer as a reading tutor for younger kids or peers.

Assets in Action

At Garfield Junior High in **Hamilton, Ohio,** the Teens for Literacy group helps students with developmental disabilities become better readers. These eighth and ninth graders also help run their school's book fair.

In **St. Louis Park, Minnesota,** girls on the high school basketball team read books on Saturday mornings to younger children at the public library.

Each Thursday during the school year, eighth grade students from West Tallahatchie High School in **Webb, Mississippi,** read to their Book Buddies at two local elementary schools. By reading to younger students, the eighth graders improve their own reading and self-esteem levels.

Founded by a Harvard student in 1996, the Harvard Emerging Literacy Project (HELP) in **Cambridge, Massachusetts,** began with just a few undergraduate students volunteering to read with a group of preschoolers once a month. Today HELP places volunteers in every Head Start classroom in Cambridge.

In Your Community

Promote literacy.

Forty percent of America's fourth graders can't read at the basic level on national reading assessments. Ninety million adults—about 47 percent of the U.S. population—performed at the two lowest levels of literacy in a 1992 national survey. Businesses estimate that they lose between $25 billion and $30 billion a year nationwide in lost productivity, errors, and accidents due to poor literacy.

Contact one or more of the following organizations to learn how you can help—or get help. You can also contact your local Boys & Girls Club of America, YMCA/YWCA, Girl Scouts or Boy Scouts, Lions Club, etc. Many local and national youth organizations have literacy initiatives.

America Reads Challenge
U.S. Department of Education, 7th Floor
400 Maryland Avenue, SW
Washington, DC 20202
1-800-USA-LEARN (1-800-872-5327)
www.ed.gov/inits/americareads
The America Reads Challenge calls on all Americans to help ensure that every child can read well and independently by the end of third grade.

The Center for the Book
Library of Congress
101 Independence Avenue, SE
Washington, DC 20540-4920
(202) 707-5221
www.loc.gov/loc/cfbook
The Center for the Book in the Library of Congress stimulates public interest in books, reading, libraries, and literacy through projects, partnerships, events, and publications.

Literacy Information and Communication System (LINCS)
www.lincs.ed.gov
The Literacy Information and Communication System, commonly referred to as *LINCS*, is a national dissemination, resource gathering, and professional development system providing information on a wide variety of literacy topics, issues, and resources. Find literacy research on kids through adults, publications, webcasts, and more at their website. Use their literacy directory to help you find programs and assistance in your area.

National Center for Family Literacy
325 West Main Street, Suite 300
Louisville, KY 40202
(502) 584-1133
www.famlit.org
This organization, emphasizing the importance of literacy development within families, offers volunteer opportunities.

ProLiteracy Worldwide
1320 Jamesville Avenue
Syracuse, NY 13210
(315) 422-9121
www.proliteracy.org
This national organization delivers free tutoring services through a network of trained volunteers. Its mission is to reach adults whose literacy skills are limited or nonexistent.

THINGS YOU CAN DO TO HELP CHILDREN READ WELL AND INDEPENDENTLY

TIPS FROM AMERICA READS CHALLENGE

1. Become a learning partner/reading tutor to a child in your neighborhood or from your local elementary school. Volunteer to read to or with the child for 30 minutes a week for at least eight weeks. Take the child to the library to get a library card.

2. Help start a community reading program. You might work with adults to set up an America Reads Challenge: READ*WRITE*NOW! program or volunteer as a reading tutor. Call 1-800-USA-LEARN for more information.

3. Ask your public librarian how you can help at your local library. Offer to volunteer after school in the children's section, reading stories or helping children pick out books. Offer to develop a program or support an existing summer reading program at the library.

4. Encourage community businesses and nonprofit organizations to support community reading programs. Visit local businesses and organizations; encourage them to donate supplies and to allow their employees time off to volunteer in local schools.

CONTINUED ON NEXT PAGE...

5. Collect and donate children's books to an early childhood center or parent/child play group. Organize a program in which members volunteer to read to children in these programs each week.

6. Encourage other volunteers to read with children. Ask teachers and parents to identify children who need extra help in reading; contact volunteer groups at nearby colleges, high schools, community organizations, religious groups, businesses, or senior centers and enlist their help.

7. Take neighborhood kids on a field trip to the local library. Contact the head librarian to arrange for a guided tour and explanation of how students can use the library. Any child who doesn't already have a library card can sign up for one during this visit.

8. Help motivate children to read for enjoyment. Talk with them and ask what they're interested in. Direct them to books, magazines, books on cassette, videos, computer software, and other library resources. Ask a librarian for suggestions.

Adapted from *Simple Things You Can Do to Help All Children Read Well and Independently by the End of Third Grade.* Washington, DC: America Reads Challenge: Read*Write*Now!, U.S. Department of Education, 1997.

Fight censorship.

Question: What do these books have in common?

The Adventures of Huckleberry Finn by Mark Twain
Bridge to Terabithia by Katherine Paterson
Catcher in the Rye by J.D. Salinger
The Chocolate War by Robert Cormier
Forever by Judy Blume
The Goosebumps Series by R.L. Stine
I Know Why the Caged Bird Sings by Maya Angelou
It's Perfectly Normal by Robie Harris
My Brother Sam Is Dead by James Lincoln Collier and Christopher Collier

Answer: They were the most frequently challenged books of 1996, according to the American Library Association. When a book is *challenged,* a person or group asks that it be removed from the curriculum or library. Most challenges are unsuccessful. A successful challenge results in a *ban*—a book is actually removed. Which means that people (including you) can't read it.

Books are usually challenged with the best intentions. People (usually adults) want to protect others (usually children and teens) from difficult ideas and information. But what *you* read should be up to you and your parents. And that's why you and your parents should join the fight against censorship. Here's how:

1. When you learn that a book or author is being challenged, speak up. (Challenges often make the local news.)

2. Support Banned Books Week. Sponsored by the American Library Association, the American Booksellers Association, and others, this annual promotion (held in September) celebrates the freedom to read. Ask about it at your local public library or contact: Banned Books Week, American Library Association, 50 East Huron, Chicago, IL 60611; 1-800-545-2433. On the Web, go to: *www.ala.org/bbooks*

3. Get informed and stay informed about electronic "book bans" in public schools and libraries. Special filtering software is being used to block potentially offensive Internet sites. As of this writing, this controversy is just heating up, and court fights are underway. For the latest news, contact your local ACLU (American Civil Liberties Union) office. On the Web, go to: *www.aclu.org*

In Your Faith Community

● Work with adult leaders to create a library and reading room for children and youth in your faith community.

● Volunteer to tutor younger kids in your faith community who need help building reading skills. This would be a great service project for your youth group.

Assets in Action

When the U.S. Department of Education launched the America Reads Challenge in 1997, many religious denominations quickly got involved. Examples:

• **The Presbyterian Church (U.S.A.)** *declared 1998 the "Year of Education" to focus congregations' attention on reading and tutoring.*

• **The Progressive National Baptist Convention** *addressed the challenge at its annual convention of 15,000 delegates.*

• **The Union of American Hebrew Congregations** *made plans to mobilize 100,000 volunteers.*

• **The United Methodist Church** *began publishing resources for churches to use in supporting education in their communities.*

With Your Friends

● Talk about your favorite books. Recommend books to each other; share books you enjoy. Give each other books for birthdays and holidays.

● Start a book group. Decide each month on a book you'd all like to read. Set a deadline for reading it, then get together and talk about it. *Tip:* Visit a local library or bookstore for suggestions. Ask for information about starting a book club.

RESOURCES

Publications and other materials about reading and literacy are also available through the organizations listed on pages 202–203.

For everyone:

"Read With Me: A Guide for Student Volunteers Starting Early Childhood Literacy Programs" by Chandler Arnold (Washington, DC: National Institute on Early Childhood Development and Education, 1997). Chandler Arnold started the Harvard Emerging Literacy Project (HELP) when he was an undergraduate student. View the document online at: *www.ed.gov/pubs/ReadWithMe*

The Reading Group Handbook: Everything You Need to Know to Start Your Own Book Club by Rachel W. Jacobsohn (New York: Hyperion, 1998). Just what the title says.

The Reading Tutor's Handbook by Jeanne Shay Schumm, Ph.D., and Gerald E. Schumm Jr., D. Min. (Minneapolis: Free Spirit Publishing, 1998). Written for anyone who wants to share the joy and power of reading, this comprehensive guide covers everything tutors need to know.

For you:

Ask for these books at your library's reference desk:

The Bookfinder or *The Best of Bookfinder: A Guide to Children's Literature About Interests and Concerns of Youth Ages 2–18.* If you're facing a specific challenge in your life, *Bookfinder* can direct you toward books that will help. It groups and describes books by topics including peer pressure, communication with parents, loneliness, and depression.

Magazines for Kids and Teens, edited by Donald R. Stoll (Newark, DE: International Reading Association, 1997). Lists and describes hundreds of periodicals for children and youth.

Something About the Author (Detroit, MI: Gale Research, several volumes). Learn about your favorite authors—and books by them you might have missed.

For educators:

The Reading Connection: Bringing Parents, Teachers, and Librarians Together by Elizabeth Knowles and Martha Smith (Englewood, CO: Teacher Ideas Press, 1997). Shows how to encourage literacy and reading by establishing a book club for parents, teachers, librarians, and students in grades K–8 (and struggling readers in grades 9–12).

POSITIVE VALUES

According to the *Who's Who Among American High School Students 26th Annual Survey of High Achievers*, America's top teens identify the "decline of social and moral values" as today's greatest national crisis, as well as the biggest problem facing their own generation.

These assets are about building a strong inner core of positive values. They're about forming beliefs and convictions that guide your choices and decisions, shape your priorities, and influence what you do and say. They're about caring for others—and honoring yourself. Your values reflect who you are.

The positive values assets are:

26. Caring
27. Equality and Social Justice
28. Integrity
29. Honesty
30. Responsibility
31. Restraint

43% of the youth we surveyed have this asset in their lives.

CARING

You believe that it's really important to help other people.

At Home

● Make your home a place where people care about and help each other. See assets #1: Family Support, #2: Positive Family Communication, and #20: Time at Home.

● Talk as a family about ways to develop empathy for others—to feel their feelings (or at least try). *Examples:* When you hear that people are having a hard time or struggling to overcome problems, don't just blame them. Put yourself in their shoes. If possible, get to know them. *Tip:* It's always easier to care about someone you know.

● Talk about things that can make you less caring and desensitize you to the feelings, needs, and values of others. *Examples:* Putdowns, racial jokes, and stereotypes undermine your care for people who are different from you. Excessive violence and disrespect on TV and in the movies can make you less sensitive to others and less able to be empathetic and caring.

● Have family meetings to brainstorm ways to help people outside your family. There are two kinds of caring: direct and indirect. *Direct caring* involves spending time with people who need care, interacting with them, and getting feedback from them. *Indirect caring* involves collecting money, food, or other items to give to organizers or volunteers who distribute them to people in need. Your family should participate in both kinds. For tips on serving as a family, see Asset #9: Service to Others.

● Instead of spending money on holiday gifts for each other, identify a family in need. (Ask at your school, community center, and/or religious community.) Then work together to make a list of gifts and necessities and shop for them. Have everything delivered anonymously.

Assets in Action

A family in **New Canaan, Connecticut,** *decided to show an elderly widow they cared about her by cleaning up her yard and planting flowers. The five children were so excited about the idea that they told their friends. On the day of the project, 15 kids showed up, and the parents had to ask neighbors to help drive everyone to the woman's home. After completing the project, the young people decided to start what they called the Kids Care Club and began planning their next event. This time, 25 kids showed up. They packed bag lunches (and decorated them) for a soup kitchen.*

Since then, the Kids Care Club has been a model for other families, neighborhoods, communities, congregations, and schools. You can start your own Kids Care Club in your family with one small project. Then register your club with the National Kids Care Clubs. Write a letter explaining why you want to help others and send it to: Kids Care Clubs, 975 Boston Post Road, Darien, CT 06820; telephone (203) 656-8052. On the Web, go to: www.kidscare.org

WAYS TO SHOW YOU CARE

IDEAS FROM THE KIDS CARE CLUB™

1. **Friendship Boxes.** Fill a shoebox with small toys and games for a needy child.

2. **Bedtime Snacks.** Make healthy bedtime snacks for homeless kids.

3. **Bear Hugs.** Collect new teddy bears for police officers to give children injured in accidents.

4. **Bag Lunches.** Make sandwiches and cookies for soup kitchens that serve the hungry.

5. **Project Linus.** Make a quilt for a child who is suffering through cancer therapy or AIDS.

6. **Love Letters.** Write letters or make hand-designed cards for children who are very sick.

7. **Care Posters.** Make colorful posters to decorate the walls of homeless shelters.

8. **Spring Bags.** Fill bags or baskets with Easter treats and/or toiletries for needy kids.

CONTINUED ON NEXT PAGE...

9. Promise Placemats. Laminate decorated paper to make fun placemats for kids or elderly persons.

10. Table Tops. Create table arrangements for soup kitchens or nursing homes.

11. Elderly Assistance. Help an elderly neighbor with yard or housework, or just visit.

12. Reading Robinhood. Collect used children's books for inner city schools or shelters.

13. Books on Tape. Read children's books on cassette tapes for blind children to hear.

14. Bags of Love. Collect baby items for new moms without money to buy diapers and bottles.

15. Play Kits. Make game or craft kits for hospitals to offer children who are in bed.

16. Home Warming Baskets. Fill a laundry basket with household items for relocated homeless families.

17. Cool Hats. Collect crazy and fun hats for kids going through chemotherapy who have lost their hair.

18. Wish List Party. Have a party and invite guests to bring canned food or toiletries for a shelter.

19. Lend a Hand. Write or read letters for elderly patients in nursing homes.

20. Back to School Bags. Collect school supplies for kids who are not able to afford them.

21. Handicapped Friendly. Be a friend to a handicapped or lonely child in your school.

At School

● Work to make your school a caring, encouraging, supportive place for everyone. See Asset #5: Caring School Climate.

● Promote and support service learning at your school. See Asset #9: Service to Others.

● Start a Kids Care Club at your school. See Assets in Action on page 209 for contact information. (Schools pay an annual registration fee to use the Kids Care Club name and logo, and also receive a Kids Care Start Up Kit with materials and information.) *Tip:* If you think a Kids Care Club is too young for your school, start one at a local elementary school.

● Work with your student council to start a Most Caring Person awards program. Each month, honor a student, teacher, administrator, staff person, or volunteer who goes the extra mile to help others. Contact local media and ask them to feature stories about the winners.

● Show that you care in simple, everyday ways. Do small acts of kindness for your friends, classmates, and teachers. Say something nice to or about another person. Leave a gift or a thoughtful note in a friend's locker or on a teacher's desk. Or just smile at someone. When you decide to be a caring person, the possibilities are endless.

FACT:

Girls care more than boys!

According to Search Institute researchers, girls are much more likely than boys to value caring. Of the girls surveyed, 82 percent said helping other people was important to them, and 73 percent said it was important to help make the world a better place. For boys, the numbers were 60 percent and 57 percent, respectively.

Source: Search Institute.

In Your Community

Get to know people who are different from you.

One of the best ways to become a caring person is to get to know other people and learn more about their lives. Make an effort to spend time with people who are different from you—because they're older or younger than you; of different races, cultural backgrounds, ethnic groups, or religions; differently abled; from a different type of family than yours . . . or whatever. Make a *special* effort to get to know people who are stereotyped by the media or the community. Reach out to people in your neighborhood; make new friends by tutoring or mentoring someone through a program, organization, or agency.

Find role models.

There are many opportunities within your community to help others. Countless young people have made (and are making) a difference in people's lives. Look around you for examples. You might have to look carefully, because children and teens who help others usually don't make a big deal about it and might not get much recognition. Ask adults you know to point you toward youth who serve. Talk with those kids and teens and ask them why they do it. You'll probably hear that the more they give, the more they get—respect, self-esteem, and the satisfaction that comes from having an open hand and an open heart.

Volunteer with a national helping organization.

Two large organizations that do a world of good are the American Red Cross and Habitat for Humanity International. The Red Cross is there when disaster strikes and provides a variety of health and safety services in non-emergency situations, including CPR and first aid training. Habitat for Humanity brings families and communities in need together with volunteers and resources to build decent, affordable housing. To date, Habitat has built more than 60,000 houses around the world. Both organizations welcome youth volunteers. Contact your local chapters or:

American Red Cross
2025 E Street, NW
Washington, DC 20006
1-800-733-2767
www.redcross.org

Habitat for Humanity International
Campus Chapters and Youth Programs Department
121 Habitat Street
Americus, GA 31709-3498
1-800-422-4828
www.habitat.org (home page)
www.habitat.org/ccyp (youth pages)

See Asset #9: Service to Others for a list of national programs that promote youth service.

Assets in Action

*When **Shepherdsville, Kentucky,** was hit hard by flooding in 1997, hundreds of people turned to a Red Cross shelter for help. The manager of the shelter was an 18-year-old high school senior named Jeremy. A veteran Red Cross volunteer—he served his first cup of coffee to a disaster victim when he was 7 years old—Jeremy organized meals, acquired cots and other bedding materials, and made sure that enough volunteers were available to staff the shelter. "If there were any time in my life I couldn't volunteer," he says, "I'd go crazy. It means a lot, before I go to bed, that I've done something without pay."*

Give yourself a break.

Consider your options for your next school break. You could be a couch potato, party every day—or do something meaningful. Students across the nation are spending their breaks helping others. It's a cheap way to travel and it feels good.

● Habitat for Humanity offers **Collegiate Challenge,** a weeklong service program for high school and college students ages 16 and older. During spring break of 1997, more than 5,400 students volunteered at 128 Habitat sites throughout the country. For more information, contact Habitat (see page 212).

● **Break Away: The Alternative Break Connection** works with 350 schools to connect students with groups in need. Write or call: Break Away, 2451 Cumberland Parkway, Suite 3124, Atlanta, GA 30339, 1-800-903-0646. On the Web, go to: *www.alternativebreaks.org*

You can also spend your breaks volunteering in your own community. Check with local service organizations to learn what's available.

In Your Faith Community

● With your youth group, plan and do a service project.

● Start (or join) a peer helping program—a way to serve others your own age.

● Learn what other faith communities in your area are doing to help others. You may want to join forces with their youth group(s) and work together.

Assets in Action

Mt. Olivet Lutheran Church in **Minneapolis, Minnesota,** *includes four hours of service as a requirement of the confirmation program. In addition to whole-group service activities, youth also help in the church nursery, work on food drives, and serve in other ways.*

At Ginghamsburg United Methodist Church in **Tipp City, Ohio,** *youth coordinate and lead after-school and summer activities that serve 50 children each week in inner-city Dayton.*

With Your Friends

● Many schools and faith communities offer training in peer helping, which teaches you ways to show care and concern to your friends. Take advantage of these opportunities so you can really be supportive when your friends need your care.

● Are you chronically short of cash for family birthdays and holidays? Give Helping Coupons as gifts. This would be a fun group project. Make your coupons by hand or design them on a computer, then think of ways to help your parents, siblings, and other relatives. For each coupon, fill in the person's name and what you're offering to do. Then sign it to show you're serious.

COUPON

For: _____

I Can Help By: _____

_____

Signed: _____

RESOURCES

For everyone:

Random Acts of Kindness, More Random Acts of Kindness, and *Kids' Random Acts of Kindness* by the editors of Conari Press (Emeryville, CA: Conari Press, 1993 and 1994). Inspiring true stories of people who have been the givers or recipients of caring and compassion.

For your parents:

Teaching Your Kids to Care by Deborah Spaide (Secaucus, NJ: Citadel Press, 1995). The founder of the Kids Care Clubs, Deborah Spaide believes that children have a natural instinct to help others. In this practical, inspiring book, she describes 105 projects that develop the charity instinct in children and youth from preschool through high school.

For educators, youth leaders, and community leaders:

The Giraffe Heroes Program. Now used in 47 states, this powerful curriculum helps teachers and youth leaders build courage, caring, and responsibility in kids from 6–18 years old, then guides kids in designing and implementing their own service projects. Businesses, service clubs, and other organizations can become Giraffe Partners. For more information, write or call: The Giraffe Project, PO Box 759, Langley, WA 98260; (360) 221-7989. On the Web, go to: *www.giraffe.org*

Asset #27

45% of the youth
we surveyed have this
asset in their lives.

EQUALITY AND SOCIAL JUSTICE

**You want to help promote equality and
reduce world poverty and hunger.**

At Home

Get smart.

We are all citizens of the world. Communication technology has made it possible to stay on top of news from almost anywhere. As a family, watch CNN, listen to public radio, read newspapers and magazines, and/or search the Internet to educate yourselves about the world's people and their cultures, contributions, and challenges. Talk about what you learn, what you think, how you feel, and what you can do.

Talk about equality and social justice.

As a family, discuss and give your opinions about the following issues. For each, decide if 1) you're very concerned about it, 2) you're somewhat concerned about it, or 3) you don't think it's a problem.

- racial discrimination
- gender discrimination
- poverty
- sexual orientation discrimination
- hunger
- ethnic/cultural discrimination
- religious discrimination
- age discrimination
- disability discrimination
- class discrimination

Opinions will probably differ; talk about that, too. Has anyone in your family had personal experience with discrimination, poverty, or hunger? How have people in your family (including your ancestors) taken a stand on equality and social justice issues?

FACT:

Girls are more concerned than boys!

According to Search Institute researchers, girls are much more willing than boys to promote equality and social justice. Here are the percentages who say it's important to:

	Girls	Boys
Help reduce hunger and poverty in the world	82%	60%
Help make sure all people are treated fairly	53%	33%
Speak up for equality	73%	57%

Source: Search Institute.

Read and discuss the Universal Declaration of Human Rights.

On December 10, 1948, the General Assembly of the United Nations adopted and proclaimed the Universal Declaration of Human Rights. Following this historic act, the Assembly called upon all member countries to publicize the Declaration and "cause it to be disseminated, displayed, read and expounded principally in schools and other educational institutions." You can read it at home, too. Copies are available at your local library and at many sites on the World Wide Web (*example:* Project Diana; see Resources, page 223).

The UDHR lists and describes 30 basic human rights that belong to everyone. *Examples:*

• the right to equality
• freedom from discrimination
• the right to life, liberty, and personal security
• freedom from interference with privacy, family, home, and correspondence
• freedom of belief and religion
• freedom of opinion and information
• the right to participate in government and in free elections
• the right to education.

Many Americans view human rights violations as other countries' problems. In fact, human rights are violated in the United States every day. Crime, racism, homelessness, poverty, inadequate health care, inadequate education, and the destruction of the environment are all violations of basic human rights.

Which of these rights and freedoms are most important to you and your family? Why? How have people in your family (or other people you know) stood up for these rights? What responsibilities do you have to protect and advocate for these rights?

Take action.

You and your family can't stop a war or save a nation, but you can make a difference. Help support a relief, economic development, or human rights organization. Join a letter-writing campaign (see page 218); get involved with your local Habitat for Humanity chapter (see page 212). Volunteer at a local service organization or through your faith community. Advocate for people with disabilities. Every effort, however small it may seem, has the potential to profoundly change someone else's life—and yours. Here are more ideas to try:

● Write letters to the editor on social issues that concern you. Highlight the positive benefits and potential for addressing these issues.

● Register voters in your neighborhood and community. Contact your local League of Women Voters for information on how to do this.

● Support candidates who take a stand on equality and social justice.

● Volunteer at a soup kitchen, homeless shelter, or food pantry. For tips on volunteering as a family, see Asset #9: Service to Others.

● Join marches and demonstrations for equality and social justice.

● Help others improve their literacy skills. See Asset #25: Reading for Pleasure.

● Take part in community cleanups.

● Don't wait for disasters or major problems to happen before you get involved. Join organizations that keep you informed about issues you care about. As a family or on your own, regularly contribute money to organizations that promote equality and social justice.

● Work to make December 10, International Human Rights Day, important in your community.

Assets in Action

Trevor Ferrell was just 11 years old when he saw a news story about homeless people. That evening, he begged his parents to drive him to downtown **Philadelphia, Pennsylvania,** *to hand out blankets and pillows to people with no homes to go to. The next night, he and his family delivered hot food to people in the same neighborhood. By the time Trevor was 16, he and his family had opened a 33-room shelter called Trevor's Place where homeless people can stay for a short time before eventually finding jobs and moving on to permanent housing. The Philadelphia City Council passed a resolution praising Trevor as "an example of the good that lies in the human heart."*

*In **St. Paul, Minnesota,** Chaica Mendoza Ramirez works with Hispanic and Hmong immigrants, helping them prepare for American citizenship. Mai Houa Thao acts as an interpreter at resident meetings for Hmong families in her neighborhood. In 1998, Chaica and Mai—who are both involved in many types of volunteer and service activities—were honored as Youth Heroes by United Way of St. Paul.*

Join a letter-writing campaign.

When thousands of letters start pouring in from all over the world, leaders (and human rights violators) take notice. Various organizations sponsor and encourage letter-writing campaigns. Two of the biggest and most respected are Amnesty International and Human Rights Watch; each also has extensive information available on human rights issues. Write, call, or visit their Web sites to learn how you can make a difference.

Amnesty International USA
5 Penn Plaza
New York, NY 10001
(212) 807-8400
www.amnesty-usa.org

Human Rights Watch
350 Fifth Avenue, 34th Floor
New York, NY 10118
(212) 290-4700
www.hrw.org

If you'd like to help end hunger, you might get involved with Bread for the World, which also encourages letter-writing campaigns. This respected organization (with strong Christian roots) provides credible, balanced reporting on hunger-related issues. If you'd like to address the justice needs of America's children, particularly those who live in poverty, join a letter-writing campaign for Children's Defense Fund or take part in CDF's Stand for Children day, held on June 1 of every year. For more information, write, call, or visit the Web sites.

Bread for the World
425 Third Street, SW, Suite 1200
Washington, DC 20024
1-800-82-BREAD (1-800-822-7323)
www.bread.org

Children's Defense Fund
25 E Street, NW
Washington, DC 20001
1-800-233-1200
www.childrensdefense.org

At School

Learn about and work for equality and social justice.

● Work to eliminate discrimination at your school based on race, gender, and other differences. Look for inequities and find ways to address them. *Examples:* Do boys have more opportunities in sports than girls? Are some students excluded from activities because they can't afford to pay for them?

- Promote tolerance and acceptance. See Asset #34: Cultural Competence.

- Invite representatives from international service, relief, and human rights organizations to speak to classes, groups, and assemblies.

- Promote and support service learning. See Asset #9: Service to Others.

- When you're assigned special projects, try to pick ones that allow you to study social justice issues.

- Start a club that focuses on equality and social justice issues—international development, equal rights for women, equal rights for people of color, child labor, elderly people, or anything else that concerns you. If you're especially interested in human rights, consider starting an Amnesty International chapter at your school. Ask a teacher or your principal to contact the Human Rights Educators' Network for information; see the Resources at the end of this chapter.

Assets in Action

Amnesty International USA students at a high school in the **Midwest** *arranged a weekend "lock-in" one Saturday night each year with plenty of pizza, pop, and letter-writing. Hundreds of students attended and dozens joined the campus AI chapter.*

In **Colorado,** *a dozen AI high school chapters put on a spring "Jamnesty" with half a dozen bands, each of which gave a pro-human-rights rap before performing. Almost a thousand students attended and signed petitions on behalf of prisoners of conscience—people who are detained for their beliefs or because of their ethnic origin, gender, color, or language and who have not used or advocated violence.*

Advocate for human rights education.

As part of the United Nations Decade for Rights Education (1995–2004), many countries, states, and school districts have launched human rights education projects. Ask your teachers what's happening in your school and how you can help.

Assets in Action

From 1992–1997, Partners in Human Rights Education—a coalition of more than 850 teachers, lawyers, and community advocates—donated thousands of hours to educate students in **Minnesota** *about their human rights and responsibilities. More than 15,000 students learned about the Universal Declaration of Human Rights and its relevance in their daily lives.*

In Your Community

Find ways to serve.

● Work with your school district, scouts, or other organization on a food drive, clothing drive, or other project.

● Contact your city or state's Human Rights Commission. Are youth involved in meaningful ways? If not, why not? See Asset #8: Youth as Resources.

● Work with community leaders to plan and promote discussions and workshops about equality and social justice. Invite representatives from service, relief, and economic development organizations to speak.

● When you see or hear news stories about equality and social justice issues in your community, find out how you can lend your support and get involved. When you learn about someone who's working to address these issues, send a note or find another way to thank and encourage him or her.

● Join a national organization that promotes youth service. See Asset #9: Service to Others.

● Post fact sheets about hunger, poverty, inequality, and injustice on community bulletin boards. Distribute brochures from service and relief organizations.

STEPS TO SOCIAL ACTION

1. Choose a problem. Look around your neighborhood, school, or community for ideas. Or you might choose a problem that affects your nation or the world.

2. Do your research. Survey your school or neighborhood to find out how other people feel about the problem you want to tackle. Telephone officials for information; write letters; read magazines and newspapers; watch news channels on TV; search the Internet.

3. Brainstorm possible solutions and choose one. Think of what you might do to solve your problem. After you've made a long list of potential solutions, look at each one carefully, then choose the solution that seems the most doable and will have the greatest impact.

4. Build coalitions of support. Find people who agree with your solution and invite them to work with you. The more people you have on your team, the more power you'll have to make a difference.

CONTINUED ON NEXT PAGE...

5. Work with your opposition. For every good solution, there are people, businesses, and organizations that might oppose it. Identify possible barriers before you run into them, then make plans to overcome other people's objections. *Tip:* It's tempting to think of people who oppose your solution as "bad guys." But it can be more useful to see them as people with different needs and opinions. Get to know them; you might have more in common than you think. And you might find ways to compromise.

6. Advertise. TV, radio, and newspaper reporters love stories of children and youth taking social action. Write letters, make phone calls, distribute flyers, and/or send out news releases.

7. Raise money. After letting people know about your project, you might try to raise funds to support it. This isn't essential, and many wonderful projects can be tackled without this step. But sometimes you have more power if you put money where your mouth is.

8. Carry out your solution. Make a list of all the steps you need to take. Then do it!

9. Evaluate and reflect. Have you tried everything? Should you change your solution or your approach? Do you need to talk with more people? What have you learned? What have you actually accomplished?

10. Don't give up. Unless *you* think it's time to quit, don't pay too much attention to people who don't agree with your solution. If *you* believe your cause is important, keep working at it.

Adapted from *The Kid's Guide to Social Action* by Barbara A. Lewis, rev. ed. Free Spirit Publishing Inc., 1998, pages 12–13. Used with permission.

Start a teen court.

Teen courts (also called student courts or youth courts) try first-time offenders ages 16 and under for minor crimes (*examples:* underage drinking, drug use, theft, vandalism, or disorderly conduct). The judge is usually (but not always) an adult; the jurors, attorneys, bailiffs, and clerks are all teens. The teen jurors decide on the sentence, which usually involves community service, classes, and jury duty for a future teen court. Defendants who complete their sentence have the charges dropped from their record.

Find out if there's a teen court in your community. If there isn't, contact your principal, mayor, state representative, or governor and ask that one be started. Meanwhile, you can learn more about teen courts on your own. Call the Juvenile Justice Clearinghouse at 1-800-851-3420 and request a free copy of *Peer Justice and Youth Empowerment: An Implementation Guide for Teen Court Programs.*

In Your Faith Community

Most faith communities promote equality and social justice. Many contribute to international service, relief, and human rights organizations that work to alleviate poverty, hunger, and homelessness around the world. Some send their members—adults and youth—on helping trips and missions. Find out what your faith community is doing and get involved. If you don't feel that your faith community is doing enough, talk to your youth leader and other leaders in your faith community.

Assets in Action

Bethel Temple in **Philadelphia, Pennsylvania,** *is committed to providing support and care for young people in the community. Several times, a congregation member or staff person has become a temporary foster parent for a young person whose parents are incarcerated or in treatment for alcohol or other drug addictions. The congregation also becomes an advocate and support network to help family members put their lives back together again.*

With Your Friends

Talk with each other about equality and social justice. Which problems in the world bother you the most? Why? What can you do as a group to make a difference? You can start by trying any of the suggestions in this chapter. See also assets #9: Service to Others and #26: Caring.

RESOURCES

For everyone:

Anti-Defamation League (ADL)
605 Third Avenue
New York, NY 10158
(212) 490-2525
www.adl.org
ADL fights anti-Semitism, terrorism, and hate crimes and works for equality and social justice around the world.

Human Rights Resource Center

229 19th Avenue South, Suite N-120

Minneapolis, MN 55455

(612) 626-0041

www.hrusa.org

Human Rights Resource Center educates people in the United States about their human rights and encourages community-based action.

National Association for the Advancement of Colored People (NAACP)

4805 Mt. Hope Drive

Baltimore, MD 21215

1-877-622-2798

www.naacp.org

The oldest, largest, and strongest civil rights organization in the United States, the NAACP works to ensure the political, educational, social, and economic equality of minority group citizens.

National Organization for Women (NOW)

1100 H Street, NW, Third Floor

Washington, DC 20005

(202) 628-8669

www.now.org

NOW works on behalf of women's rights—in politics, the workplace, the community, and the home.

Project Diana

avalon.law.yale.edu/subject_menus/diana.asp

An extensive online human rights archive at Yale Law School, with links to many other sites. Updated frequently, searchable, and easy to navigate.

For you:

The Kid's Guide to Social Action by Barbara A. Lewis, rev. ed. (Minneapolis: Free Spirit Publishing, 1998). This award-winning guide includes everything you need to make a difference in the world, from inspiring true stories to fill-out forms and up-to-date resources.

For educators:

Human Rights Educators' Network

Amnesty International USA

5 Penn Plaza

New York, NY 10001

(212) 807-8400

www.amnesty-usa.org/education

Membership includes a subscription to *Human Rights Education: The Fourth R*, educational materials, and more. Request information about organizing a student chapter of Amnesty International at your school. Visit the Web site for sample lessons, *First Steps: A Manual for Starting Human Rights Education*, and more.

GANDHI

MOTHER TERESA

JIM SMITH

INTEGRITY

You act on your convictions and stand up for your beliefs.

At Home

Talk about your family values.

Values shape our relationships, our behaviors, our choices, and who we are. The more positive our values, the more positive our actions.

What are your family values? Here's a list of possibilities to start thinking and talking about:

caring	integrity	respect
compassion	kindness	responsibility
courage	love	self-control
dependability	loyalty	self-discipline
equality	mercy	self-reliance
fidelity	moderation	sensitivity
friendliness	peacemaking	social justice
honesty	promise keeping	

If anyone mentions other values, write them down. Then try to agree on the 10 values that are most important to your family. List them on a clean sheet of paper, write Our Family Values at the top, and post it where everyone will see it. Or, if you're feeling creative, make a poster, painting, collage, or mobile of your family values.

Talk about how to live these values with integrity. How will you affirm each other for living the values? How will you hold each other accountable? How will you support and encourage each other when it's hard to live with integrity because of pressures you face?

Talk about integrity.

Talk as a family about integrity—what it means to you and why it's important.

Come up with a family definition of integrity. You might want to start by reading and discussing other people's definitions. Author Barbara Lewis, who writes about character, service, and social action, has this to say:

> When you have integrity, you're honest with yourself and others. But integrity involves more than telling the truth. You talk the talk and walk the walk. You match what you do to what you believe. . . . You do the right thing, even if it isn't the easiest or most popular thing.

Tell each other about times when you stood up for something, even though it was hard to do. Explain how you felt. Then tell about times when you didn't stand up for something because you were afraid. Why is it easier to act on your convictions in some situations than others?

Identify people who have integrity. These might be people you know (family members, friends, neighbors, teachers, religious leaders, etc.) and people you don't know personally but by reputation (politicians, community leaders, celebrities, etc.). What makes you think each person has integrity?

RATE YOUR INTEGRITY

Read each of the following statements and decide if it's true for you.

	SOMETIMES	MOST OF THE TIME	IT DEPENDS
1. I'm honest with myself.	❏	❏	❏
2. I'm honest with other people.	❏	❏	❏
3. I ask for what I want and need from others.	❏	❏	❏
4. I know what I believe.	❏	❏	❏
5. I stand up for my beliefs, even when it's not popular.	❏	❏	❏
6. I make choices based on what I believe, not what others believe.	❏	❏	❏

CONTINUED ON NEXT PAGE...

	SOMETIMES	MOST OF THE TIME	IT DEPENDS
7. When someone says something I disagree with, I tell that person how I feel.	❏	❏	❏
8. When a clerk gives me too much change, I tell the clerk.	❏	❏	❏
9. When someone blames me for something I didn't do, I speak up.	❏	❏	❏
10. When someone praises me for something I didn't do, I speak up.	❏	❏	❏
11. My family and friends know what I believe.	❏	❏	❏
12. With me, what you see is what you get.	❏	❏	❏

SCORING: If a statement is true for you most of the time, that's a sign of integrity. If it's true for you some-times, that means you're trying. If it depends, you may need to look at what you believe. Maybe you worry too much about what other people might think. Or maybe you change your beliefs and behaviors depending on the circumstances.

At School

Promote integrity.

Ask your teachers if you can discuss integrity in the classroom. You might start with one of these thought-provoking quotations:

● "This above all: to thine own self be true."—William Shakespeare

● "Keep true, never be ashamed of doing right; decide on what you think is right and stick to it."—George Eliot

● "What lies behind us and what lies before us are small matters compared with what lies within us."—Ralph Waldo Emerson

● "Integrity without knowledge is weak and useless, and knowledge without integrity is dangerous and dreadful."—Samuel Johnson

● "A person of integrity lurks somewhere inside each of us: a person we feel we can trust to do right, to play by the rules, to keep commitments."—Stephen L. Carter

You might create an Integrity Bulletin Board and feature people who acted with integrity (*examples:* Gandhi, Martin Luther King Jr., Mother Teresa). Or nominate people you know—including each other.

Get the scoop on character education.

For years, teachers avoided teaching values at school. Values education was linked to prayer in schools, sex education, and other hot potato topics. Many people insisted that values should be taught in homes and places of worship, not in schools . . . especially not in *public* schools.

Things are changing because of a widespread belief that many positive values have declined in recent decades. And it's not just adults who are concerned. When 1,000 students from ages 13–17 were asked to name the most important problems facing America today, the decline of moral and social values was #2— right after crime and violence. Those same teens listed poor morals as among the worst influences facing today's youth.*

Now thousands of schools across the country are teaching character education. The U.S. Department of Education has given millions of dollars in grants to states to promote character education. There's conflict raging around this issue—whose values are the *right* values?—but it seems to be a trend.

● Find out how your school and district are approaching character education. What's being done? Who's in charge? Decide if you agree with how character education is being taught in your school. If you do, ask how you can help. If you don't, talk with your parents and teachers.

● What if your school doesn't teach character education and you think it should? Form a group of students who feel the way you do, and talk with your teachers and principal. Get a dialogue going about which values can and should be taught in your school. *Tip:* Character education programs in schools are more likely to be accepted if they focus on broad values (honesty, respect, giving, responsibility) and involve *everyone*—teachers, students, administrators, and parents.

Teens want values education at school!

Most middle and high school students believe that values and principles of right and wrong should be taught in school. In a nationwide survey, public school students in grades 7–12 were asked if lessons on values belong in the classroom. Sixty-three percent said yes.

Source: *The Metropolitan Life Survey of the American Teacher 1996: Students Voice Their Opinions on Learning About Values and Principles in School,* conducted by Louis Harris and Associates, Inc.

---

* Reported in *The Mood of American Youth* (Alexandria, VA: Horatio Alger Association of Distinguished Americans and the National Association of Secondary School Principals, 1996).

Assets in Action

At Jefferson Junior High in **Washington, D.C.,** *character education is part of the curriculum. Weekly hour-long lessons are reinforced with assemblies that emphasize positive character traits; mentors, tutors, and community youth organizations lend support. The school has seen improvements in student behavior, school safety, and academic success.*

A high school in **Carver County, Minnesota,** *had eight flags sewn, each displaying one of the eight shared values identified by the community. The flags are displayed in the school's entrance hallway. The school has also named its hallways, gym, lunchroom, offices, and other areas after the eight values, and a local business funded the painting of the values in the lunchroom.*

In Your Community

● Ask people you trust and respect—your teachers, youth leaders, spiritual leaders, other adults—for their definitions of integrity. You might want to write them in your journal, if you keep a journal.

● Model integrity wherever you go. Be someone who talks the talk and walks the walk. Support your peers and younger kids when they act with integrity.

● Work with your community to launch a campaign on the value of integrity. Use billboards, posters, grocery bags, flyers, local media, and the Internet to spread the word. Hold community events—speeches, workshops, roundtable discussions—that are open to people of all ages.

● Read character-building stories to younger children at a local elementary school, community center, or public library. Ask a librarian for suggestions. Or find a copy of *Books That Build Character* (see Resources on page 229).

Assets in Action

Ellen Bigger of **Key Largo, Florida,** *had every reason to have strong beliefs and not act on them. When she was five years old, she and a group of her kindergarten classmates got caught in the crossfire between a sniper high on drugs and a police SWAT team. When she was 10, someone high on drugs killed her Girl Scout leader. Ellen could have lived in fear and cynicism, but she believed she could make a difference. So she started a program called Drug-Free Homes. She spent $500 of her own money creating and printing a brochure explaining the program and the dangers of drugs. On the back was a pledge for people to sign. Those who signed the pledge received a decal saying "This Is a Drug-Free Home. Every Member Within Has Signed a Pledge to Live a Drug-Free Life." By showing what can happen when youth act on what they believe, Ellen is an example of integrity—and a positive influence on others.*

In Your Faith Community

While schools and youth organizations often shy away from discussing values, most faith communities don't. Take advantage of this opportunity to explore values with your peers, youth leaders, and other adults. Find examples of people in your faith community who model integrity and get to know them. Talk about integrity (and other values) within your youth group. Help teach younger kids the values that are important to your faith.

With Your Friends

● Try to surround yourself with people of integrity—friends who act on their convictions and stand up for their beliefs. Then you can support each other during tough or challenging times. See Asset #15: Positive Peer Influence.

● Talk to each other about your values. Help each other clarify what you stand for—and what you won't stand for.

● Congratulate each other for acting on your values—especially when you're pressured to do otherwise.

● Read books about integrity and other values; talk about them as a group. See Asset #25: Reading for Pleasure.

RESOURCES

For everyone:

Books That Build Character: A Guide to Teaching Your Child Moral Values Through Stories by William Kilpatrick, Gregory Wolfe, and Suzanne M. Wolfe (New York: Simon & Schuster, 1994). Lists and describes hundreds of novels, myths and legends, biographies, and more that celebrate virtues and values. Chapters are divided into age levels: 4–8, 8–12, and 12 & up. You might use it to find stories to read aloud to younger kids.

Integrity by Stephen L. Carter (New York: HarperCollins, 1997). An in-depth look at what integrity is and why it's important.

For you:

What Do You Stand For? For Teens: A Guide to Building Character by Barbara A. Lewis (Minneapolis: Free Spirit Publishing, 1998). Explore and practice honesty, kindness, empathy, integrity, tolerance, patience, respect, and more with the stories, dilemmas, activities, and resources in this big book.

For your parents:

The Moral Intelligence of Children: How to Raise a Moral Child by Robert Coles (New York: Plume, 1998).
The respected child psychiatrist and Harvard professor gives sound advice about developing character
in children, discusses children's moral development and dilemmas characteristic of different stages, and
suggests appropriate responses to children from the early years through adolescence.

For educators and youth leaders:

Character Counts!
9841 Airport Boulevard, Suite 300
Los Angeles, CA 90045
(310) 846-4800
www.charactercounts.org
A nationwide initiative to support nonpartisan character education. Ask about lesson plans and products based on the "Six Pillars of Character": trustworthiness, respect, responsibility, fairness, caring, and
citizenship.

HONESTY

Asset #29

You tell the truth—even when it's not easy.

At Home

● Talk as a family about honesty. You might decide to make honesty one of your family's 10 most important values. (See Asset #28: Integrity.) Discuss what each of you would do if someone asked you to be dishonest, if you found it hard to tell the truth, and if you told a lie. Describe times when you noticed other people acting honestly and dishonestly.

● Work together to come up with family rules about honesty and consequences for dishonesty. See Asset #11: Family Boundaries.

● When you watch TV shows and videos together, notice when characters are honest or dishonest. Are there positive consequences for honesty? Negative consequences (or any consequences) for dishonesty? Are the consequences realistic? Talk about times when they *aren't* realistic. What message(s) does this send?

● Set a good example by being honest with your parents, your siblings, other family members, friends, teachers, neighbors—and yourself. When you fudge the truth, admit it and apologize.

● Make a personal commitment to tell the truth. Tell someone you trust about your commitment—a parent, teacher, close friend, youth group leader—and ask for support. Go to her or him when being honest is especially hard for you.

GREAT REASONS 8 TO TELL THE TRUTH

1. Telling the truth lets everyone know what really happened. There's less chance of misunderstanding, confusion, or conflict.

2. Telling the truth protects innocent people from being blamed or punished.

3. Telling the truth allows everyone to learn from what happened.

4. You usually get into less trouble for telling the truth than for lying (and getting caught).

5 Other people trust you more when you tell the truth.

6. You don't have to tell (and remember) more lies to keep your story straight.

7. You gain a reputation for being truthful—a trait most people value.

8. Telling the truth helps you feel secure and peaceful inside.

From *What Do You Stand For?* by Barbara A. Lewis, Free Spirit Publishing Inc., 1998, page 116. Used with permission.

At School

● Most schools have clear boundaries and consequences for lying, cheating, stealing, and plagiarism. Learn your school's rules. Are they published in the student handbook? Are they written clearly so everyone can understand them? See Asset #12: School Boundaries.

FACT:

Teens are cheating!

When 3,200 high-achieving high school students from ages 16–18 were asked about cheating:

- 88% said that cheating was widespread in their school; 65% said that it would be easy to obtain test questions or answers at their school.
- 76% admitted they had cheated on their schoolwork; 38% said they had cheated on a test or quiz.
- 60% of those who cheated said "it didn't seem like a big deal."

Source: *Who's Who Among American High School Students 28th Annual Survey* (Lake Forest, IL: Educational Communications, Inc., 1997).

- Ask your teachers if you can study honesty in the classroom. Ideas to try:

  — Role-play what to do and say when it's hard to tell the truth; when telling the truth might hurt someone's feelings; when you're caught telling a lie.

  — Create a classroom display about honesty. Feature people in history who told the truth, inspiring quotations about honesty, books about honesty, and stories about honesty from newspapers and magazines.

  — Have students give examples from their own lives about people who acted honestly and dishonestly.

  — Write a Code of Honesty for your classroom or school.

Assets in Action

When Jana Benally was in fifth grade, she got caught cheating on a social studies assignment, and she promised herself that she would never cheat again. Years later, when Jana was a sophomore at San Juan High School in **Blanding, Utah,** *her promise to herself was severely tested. She was a star on her school's volleyball team, and they were battling another team for the state championship. During a heated game, Jana blocked a winning point by the other team. She felt her arm brush the net (which is illegal in volleyball). No one saw it; no one knew but Jana. She hesitated for only a moment before she told the referee. The other team got the point—and the game—but Jana knew she had done the right thing.*

In Your Community

Take a stand for honesty.

Did a clerk at the store give you too much change? Give it back. Did you accidentally send a baseball through a neighbor's window? Tell your neighbor and offer to repair or replace it. Form the habit of honesty and people will respect you for it.

Ask your local media to feature stories about honesty. Did someone discover a wallet full of money and return it—with nothing missing? Did a politician admit to making a mistake instead of trying to cover it up? (Now *that's* news.)

Make it easy for others to be honest.

Sometimes we make it easier for others to be *dishonest* by making fun of honesty or pressuring them to be dishonest (so we can win, gain personal advantage, or avoid embarrassment). Find ways to make it easy for others to be honest.

Examples: If you're playing a game, don't put too much pressure on a team-mate—pressure that might make it tempting to cheat. Don't get mad at friends or younger kids when they're honest with you, even if you don't like what they have to say. And when you notice people being honest, don't tease them. Praise them for doing the right thing.

Don't be duped.

Wearing clothes with designer labels won't make you popular. Potato chips don't make a party. And smoking won't make you cool . . . no matter what commercials and billboards say.

Each day, you're bombarded by advertisements. They may look and sound different, but they share the same goal: to get your money. Don't believe the hype. Decide what's important to *you,* then pursue it.

If you want to know more about advertising, check out *Adbusters,* a quarterly magazine for people who are tired of TV and magazine ads full of stereotypes, sexism, and propaganda. See if your library subscribes. Visit the Web site for articles from past issues, previews of upcoming issues, TV "uncommercials," information about Buy Nothing Day (the first Friday after Thanksgiving), and more.

Adbusters
The Media Foundation
1243 West 7th Avenue
Vancouver, BC V6H 1B7
Canada
1-800-663-1243
www.adbusters.org

In Your Faith Community

● With your youth group, commit to being honest. You might write and sign an Honesty Pledge to formalize your commitment.

● Talk to each other when you feel pressured to cheat or be dishonest in other ways.

● Help teach younger kids in your faith community about honesty. Read stories, create and perform skits, and do role-plays.

Assets in Action

In **Northfield, Minnesota,** the school district and the ministerial association worked together on a Year of Values for their town. Here are some of the things that happened:

· Every family in the community received a wallet-size card listing seven values for the healthy family: equality, self-control, promise keeping, responsibility, respect, honesty, and social justice.

· The parent-teacher organization offered workshops to help parents learn how to talk with their children about values.

· Elementary school children designed posters about values.

· A grocery store printed information about the Year of Values on 50,000 grocery bags.

· Faith communities featured sermons on each of the key values, culminating a month later in an ecumenical Thanksgiving service.

· A national speaker came to town to talk about the media and values.

With Your Friends

Know the difference between honesty and tact.

What do you say when . . .

. . . a friend who's been gaining weight asks "Do you think I'm getting fat?"
. . . a sibling with a hideous haircut asks "How do you like my new do?"
. . . a grandparent who gave you an ugly sweater asks "Have you worn it yet?"

Honesty gets tricky when we know we can hurt someone's feelings by telling the truth. Often it's easier—and more tactful—to tell small lies.

In your own life, you'll need to judge this on a case-by-case basis. When telling the truth would be hurtful, ask yourself "What good will it do to hurt this person?" If it won't do any good, choose the kinder route. *Examples:*

• To the friend who's been gaining weight: "You're not getting fat. I worry about getting fat, too. That's why I go to the Y every day and swim a few laps. Want to come with me next time?"

• To the sibling with the hideous haircut: "It's totally unique. Just like you."

• To the grandparent who gave you an ugly sweater: "I'm saving it for a special occasion. How about if I have Mom take a picture of me wearing it? I'll send you a copy."

Surround yourself with friends who value honesty.

These are people who don't lie about losing their homework when they just didn't do it; who don't tell their parents they're going one place when they're really going somewhere else; who don't spread gossip and rumors. Reinforce each other's efforts to be honest.

WAYS TO ATTRACT THE TRUTH

You can't force other people to tell you the truth, but you can make it more likely that they will. You can become the kind of person it's easier to be truthful with.

1. Become known as a truthful person. Wouldn't you rather be truthful with people who are honest with you?

2. Keep secrets. If someone shares a confidence with you, keep it confidential. Make this one of your personal trademarks, and people will trust you with their truths. (*Exceptions:* when a friend is in danger; when the potential consequences of keeping a secret are worse than telling a trusted adult.)

3. Be careful how you use other people's truths. *Example:* A friend confides that he is afraid of spiders. Later, you make fun of his fear in front of a crowd of your peers. Or you use it to get back at him the next time he makes you angry. Your friend will wish he had never been truthful with you in the first place—and he won't repeat his mistake.

4. Don't be critical. If sharing the truth with you is an unpleasant experience—if you always respond with criticism—people will stop doing it.

5. Resist the urge to give advice unless it is asked for. Are you likely to share the truth with someone who immediately replies "Here's what you should do" or "Here's what you should have done"?

6. Don't be overly sensitive. It's hard to be truthful with someone whose feelings are always getting hurt, or who interprets every little remark as a personal insult.

7. Keep an open mind, and be willing to change your mind. If you're set in your ways, no one will tell you truths that don't fit with your beliefs. Instead, be receptive to new facts and information. Seek out both sides of any issue that's important to you. You're most likely to be misled when all you know is one side.

8. Don't jump to conclusions. Suspend your judgment until most of the facts are in. Ask questions to gather more facts. Wait to make a decision until you feel ready.

9. Be a good listener. People are more likely to tell you the truth when you give them your full attention without interrupting.

From *The First Honest Book About Lies* by Jonni Kincher. Free Spirit Publishing Inc., 1992, pages 148–149. Used with permission.

RESOURCES

For you:

The First Honest Book About Lies by Jonni Kincher (Minneapolis: Free Spirit Publishing, 1992). Examples, games, and thought-provoking questions encourage you to develop honesty as a personal value.

For your parents:

Teaching Your Children Values by Linda Eyre and Richard Eyre (New York: Fireside, 1993). Age-appropriate ideas for helping children (from age two to the teenage years) develop honesty, respect, and other important values.

60% of the youth we surveyed have this asset in their lives.

RESPONSIBILITY

You accept and take personal responsibility for your actions and decisions.

At Home

Get serious about responsibility.

You can accept and take more responsibility in all areas of your life. Start by thinking about ways to take more responsibility at home. Are there chores you could be doing? Other ways you could be helping? Could you take more responsibility for meeting your own needs? Imagine what your life would be like if you were living on your own. Who would do your laundry? Prepare your meals? Clean your room? Manage your money? Make sure you get to school (or work) on time? How many of these tasks are your parents doing for you? How many could you do for yourself? *Tip:* The more responsibility you take, the stronger and more capable you'll feel.

Know the benefits of being responsible.

Most parents notice and appreciate responsible behavior in their kids, and they tend to reward it with more privileges and freedom. (See Asset #11: Family Boundaries.) But this isn't the only benefit that awaits you.

When you're responsible . . .

. . . you're less susceptible to negative peer pressure. Instead of worrying about fitting in or being rejected, you make decisions based on what you think is best for you.

. . . you're more likely to ask questions and weigh the options available to you, less likely to just follow orders.

. . . you still might make bad choices—but they'll be *your* choices. You won't blame others for your actions or try to weasel out of the consequences. Instead, you'll learn from experience and make better choices next time.

. . . you're more confident about your ability to do the right thing. You're less concerned about what others might think or say.

. . . you believe that you have the power to shape your own life, because you do.

Be responsible on a daily basis.

● When you make a commitment, follow through. If possible, deliver even *more* than you promise.

● When you can't or don't do something you should, don't make excuses. Talk with your parents about ways to avoid similar situations in the future.

● Watch your language. Don't say "He made me do it" or "She wouldn't let me" or "It was their fault" or "I couldn't help it." Own up to your actions.

● If you think your parents expect too much of you, talk to them. Your responsibilities should be realistic and appropriate for your age and abilities.

● Take on more responsibilities as you get older. This will equip you for life on your own, which isn't that far in the future.

● Be a role model for your younger siblings and their friends. When they make poor choices, don't cover for them. Hold them accountable.

● Don't take on more responsibility than you're ready for. Know and respect your limits. At the same time, take opportunities to stretch and grow.

TIPS FOR BEING A RESPONSIBLE TEEN

1. Get things clear. Be sure that you and your parents recognize existing limits, rules, and expectations to mean the same thing.

2. Make lists of agreed-upon responsibilities. Post them if you'd like. There'll be no question whether Tuesday is your night for dishes or rubbish, whether tying up the newspapers is something you do for extra money or as part of your chores.

CONTINUED ON NEXT PAGE...

3. Make contracts. Write out the precise understandings, obligations, and conditions underlying agreements and commitments between you and your folks.

4. Come up with a schedule. This is an especially good idea for those space cadets among you who forget they have music lessons on Wednesdays and orthodontist appointments on Thursdays after school.

5. When in doubt, check it out. Why risk trouble just because of confusion or misunderstanding? Ask and ye shall find out.

6. Observe your behavior. Often there are patterns to a person's irresponsible behavior. Analyze yourself. Do you tend to goof up only in certain areas? If so, why? If you can discover patterns, you can find solutions.

7. Write yourself a note. Leave it in a place so obvious that it screams to be noticed.

8. Do it NOW. A lot of irresponsibility is good, old-fashioned forgetfulness. The longer you put something off, the greater the chances you'll forget or something else will come along to entice you away. Get it over with, whether it's a chore, a phone call, a practice session, or an appointment.

9. Take the bull by the horns. Be active. Don't let problems occur through passivity or inattention. Responsibility exists; look for it, talk about it, and ask your parents to be specific when they accuse you of irresponsibility.

10. Give advance notice. Anticipate problems so you can work them out ahead of time. *Example:* If you agree to baby-sit your little brother next Friday night and you've just been invited to a party at the same time, don't wait until Friday afternoon to say you can't baby-sit. Bring it up as early as you can. You'll avoid looking irresponsible and inconsiderate, and you'll increase the chances that plans can be changed.

11. Get in trouble for a good reason. If you're going to be labeled irresponsible, try to be irresponsible on a high plane of behavior—one where you can take an action based on careful consideration, high principle, and integrity. Be sure your parents realize that the course you charted was a conscious choice and not mindless stupidity.

12. Make that call. When you don't turn up on schedule, it's parent nature to assume the worst. This can be avoided with one phone call. You're not a baby checking in; you're smart enough to know what's in your best interests, which in this case happens to coincide with your parents' best interests. *Tip:* If the emergency change you keep for this purpose has a way of getting spent, you can call home collect, even if it's a local call.

Adapted from *Bringing Up Parents: The Teenager's Handbook* by Alex J. Packer. Free Spirit Publishing Inc., 1992, pages 80–83. Used with permission.

At School

● Make a commitment to learning. Build assets #21–25 and you'll also build responsibility—for getting an education, succeeding in school, doing your homework, and making the most of opportunities to learn.

● Expect your friends to be responsible—and hold them accountable. When they don't follow through, don't try to protect them by covering up or excusing their irresponsibility. When they do follow through, thank them.

● Respect your school's rules and expectations. See Asset #12: School Boundaries.

● Take responsibilities that are available to you—or create your own. Join or start a service club; run for student council; offer to serve on a committee. Ask for real responsibilities within the classroom as opposed to busywork.

Assets in Action

Arturo Alvarez was once a failing student who spent his free time with gang members in his **Los Angeles, California,** *neighborhood. Today he travels over an hour on three buses just to get to school, where he's an honors student. Arturo also volunteers at his church, and he never misses a class or club meeting. He was recently presented with an American Youth Character Award from Character Counts. In the words of Mikel Jollett, a student advisor at Arturo's local YMCA, "Considering the neighborhood he lives in, Arturo risks his life every day just to fulfill his responsibilities. He is my hero."*

In Your Community

● Find a mentor who models responsible behavior. Learn from him or her. See assets #3: Other Adult Relationships and #14: Adult Role Models.

● Be a responsible citizen. Find ways to give back to your community and serve others. Once you start looking for opportunities, you'll find that many exist, and your biggest problem will be choosing just one. See assets #8: Youth as Resources, #9: Service to Others, #26: Caring, and #27: Equality and Social Justice.

● Challenge assumptions that youth are naturally irresponsible. Ask your local media to feature stories about responsible kids and teens.

● When you let someone down by not following through on a commitment, don't brush it off or make excuses. Claim responsibility, ask forgiveness, and double your efforts to be more responsible next time.

FACT:

The after-school hours are the worst!

If there's ever a time when you need to be responsible for your actions and decisions—and perhaps for those of younger siblings—it's during the hours from 2 P.M. to 8 P.M., when you're out of school and your parents are still working. Drug use escalates; teen pregnancies (and sexually transmitted diseases) skyrocket. Recent studies have shown that juvenile crime *triples* starting at 3 P.M. Even if you're not committing crimes, you're still at risk; victims outnumber perpetrators by 10 to 1.

If you're on your own during "crime time," take care of yourself. Stay home and do your homework or occupy yourself in other safe, meaningful ways. Or join an after-school program, youth program, or community service program. Check out your local Boys & Girls Club; get a mentor through Big Brothers Big Sisters of America; work with your community to start a youth center; advocate for more after-school opportunities for children and youth. Help yourself and others.

Sources: *Quality Child Care and After-School Programs: Key Weapons Against Crime* (Washington, DC: Fight Crime: Invest in Kids, 1998); *Newsweek*, April 28, 1998, pages 28–33.

In Your Faith Community

● Ask for real responsibilities within your faith community. Volunteer for specific tasks and be sure to follow through.

● Help plan workshops and discussion groups for parents, children, and teens on the topic of responsibility.

● Within your youth group, talk with each other about responsibility. Share insights, experiences, and advice.

Assets in Action

Each summer, First Chinese Baptist Church in **San Francisco, California,** *sponsors a day camp for children in the Chinatown community. About 100 children attend, and most of the leaders are youth group members. Youth leader Jerald Choy says the day camp is "where they first learn to be more responsible . . . as part of the church." The program's success is partly due to its progressive training structure. The first year, kids are counselors in training; the next year, they become junior counselors. "By the time they've been in the program three years, they're ready to be senior counselors," Choy says. "They can take a whole group of kids and plan the program with the junior counselors and counselors in training."*

With Your Friends

Talk with each other about your responsibilities. Are they fair and reasonable? Do adults expect too much of you—or too little? As a group, brainstorm ways you might take more responsibility at home, at school, in your community, and with each other. Support and encourage each other in accepting and carrying out responsibilities. Offer to help when responsibilities seem overwhelming. See Asset #15: Positive Peer Influence.

RESOURCES

For your parents:

Raising a Responsible Child: How to Prepare Your Child for Today's Complex World by Don Dinkmeyer and Gary D. McKay, rev. ed. (New York: Fireside, 1996). Practical tips on teaching responsibility from the founders of the STEP program.

Raising a Responsible Child: How Parents Can Avoid Overindulgent Behavior and Nurture Healthy Children by Elizabeth M. Ellis (Secaucus, NJ: Birch Lane Press, 1995). A family counselor explains how to motivate children and teens to succeed in school, respect authority figures, and deal with stress. Chapters offer suggestions for different age groups, from preschoolers through young adults.

For educators:

Educators for Social Responsibility
23 Garden Street
Cambridge, MA 02138
1-800-370-2515
www.esrnational.org
Dedicated to creating safe, caring, and respectful classrooms, this organization has many materials available for educators.

42% of the youth we surveyed have this asset in their lives.

RESTRAINT

You believe that it's important not to be sexually active or to use alcohol or other drugs.

IMPORTANT: *"Just say no" is a joke. Anyone who thinks three words are enough to stop teens from using drugs (or drinking, or having sex) doesn't get it. You need people who respect you enough to give you reasons; you need facts so you can make informed decisions. To learn more about sex, alcohol, and other drugs, ask an adult you trust, check out the resources listed here, visit your library, or go online (careful! much of what's on the Net about drugs is bogus). This asset is essential to your success; the risks of teen pregnancy, STDs (including HIV/AIDS), drunk driving, impaired judgment, addiction, legal consequences, and more are real. If you already have this asset, help build it for others.*

At Home

Talk with your parents.

Ask them their views on teen sex, alcohol use, other drug use, and smoking. Ask them what they expect of you; ask them to be specific and give reasons. Most teens are relieved to hear their parents say "We expect you not to have sex or drink alcohol as a teenager, and here's why. . . ."

Your parents' beliefs may be based on values. Talk about your family values and what they mean in your everyday life. See Asset #28: Integrity.

Some parents can talk openly with their kids about sex, alcohol, other drugs, and smoking. If yours can't, try some of the suggestions in Asset #2: Positive

Family Communication. If they still won't talk, find another adult who will. See Asset #3: Other Adult Relationships.

 FACT:

Some parents are clueless!

According to an ongoing study of more than 9,700 parents, children, and teens, parents are seriously out of touch with the reality of drugs in their children's lives. The study found these differences:

Parents	Teens
21% think their teens might have used marijuana	44% say they have
45% believe their children have friends who smoke pot	71% say they do
38% suspect their kids have been offered drugs	59% say they have
43% think it would be easy for their children to find marijuana	58% say it would
33% say their teenagers view marijuana as harmful	18% think it is
94% say they talked with their teens about drugs during the past year	67% remember such discussions

The study also found that drug use is significantly *lower* among children who learn about the risks of drugs at home. But only 28 percent of teens say they've learned a lot about the dangers of drugs from their parents.

Source: *1997 Partnership Attitude Tracking Study* (New York: Partnership for a Drug-Free America, 1998).

Sort out your values and beliefs.

Take time to reflect on why it's important to you not to be sexually active or to use alcohol or other drugs. (If these aren't your beliefs, reflect on why that is.) What motivates your beliefs? Experiences? Safety and health concerns? Moral or religious convictions? Your upbringing? Your environment? Other people who have been influential in your life? Be able to tell others (and remind yourself) why you believe what you do.

Be a critic.

Television programs, movies, video games, Web sites, popular music, and other media often communicate negative and even harmful messages about sex, alcohol, other drugs, and smoking. Sometimes you can get the impression that restraint isn't important. When you see and hear these messages, challenge them—even if it's just in your own head.

Strengthen your decision-making skills.

A key to restraint is strong decision-making skills. If you're feeling challenged and pressured to use alcohol or other drugs or be sexually active, see Asset #32: Planning and Decision Making.

Make a promise to yourself.

Imagine your future and everything you want to do and be. Then promise yourself that you won't be sexually active, use alcohol or other drugs, or smoke cigarettes. Write your promise in your journal or on a piece of paper you keep in your wallet or a special place. If you want, share it with your parents. *Tip:* It's hard to make and keep promises that extend far into the future, especially if you're in your early teens. Try making a six-month promise, or a year-long promise— whatever feels doable to you. Then renew your promise when that time is up.

☞ **If you're already sexually active or using alcohol or other drugs, you can stop.** Get help if you need it. Tell adults you trust; tell friends who will stand by you. Consider joining a support group; check your local Yellow Pages under Drugs and Alcohol for local chapters of Alcoholics Anonymous, Cocaine Anonymous, Marijuana Anonymous, Narcotics Anonymous, and Nicotine Anonymous. Or call a hotline.

Center for Substance Abuse Treatment (CSAT)
1-800-662-HELP (1-800-662-4357)
Part of the Substance Abuse and Mental Health Services Administration, CSAT offers counseling and referrals in emergencies.

National Drug and Alcohol Treatment and Referral Hotline
1-800-662-4357
Sponsored by the U.S. Department of Health and Human Services, this hotline offers information, referrals, and crisis counseling.

☞ **If you need support to be sexually abstinent, talk to your parents or your spiritual leader.** You might consider joining an abstinence campaign. One of the largest is True Love Waits. Initiated by Southern Baptists, this international campaign is also supported by other Christian entities. For more information, go to: *www.lifeway.com/tlw*

☞ **If you've chosen to be sexually active, be sure this is *your* choice and not the result of peer pressure, pressure from a partner, curiosity, or impulse.** Have you gotten current, accurate information about the dangers and risks involved? Have you taken this information into account? Does being sexually active fit your values and beliefs? If you can't answer yes to these questions, then maybe it's *not* your choice. Talk to an adult you trust; ask for help and support. If it truly *is* your choice, then it's also your responsibility to take precautions against sexually transmitted diseases and pregnancy. Contact:

National STD Hotline
1-800-227-8922
National HIV/AIDS Hotline
1-800-CDC-INFO (1-800-232-4636)
These information and referral hotlines are backed by the Centers for Disease Control (CDC).

Planned Parenthood Federation of America
www.plannedparenthood.org
Information about pregnancy, STDs, and more, with many links to other sites. To reach the Planned Parenthood office nearest you, call 1-800-230-7526.

Ask your parents for a promise.

There's no guarantee that others will feel the way you do or respect your decision. If you find yourself in a risky situation—with someone who wants to have sex with you, or with people who are drinking or using drugs—you may need a way out. Ask your parents to promise that if you ever call them to come and get you—from any place, at any time—they'll do it with no questions asked. Agree that you'll tell them what happened the next day (or soon after), when you're all able to talk calmly. You may want to formalize this agreement with a written contract.

At School

Stay awake in sex ed.

Many schools offer some form of sex education. Sex ed has been one of the biggest battlegrounds in the public schools for nearly 30 years. School boards, teachers, administrators, and parents struggle to make the right decision. Should sex ed be taught in schools at all? If so, how? Does giving kids information about sex make them more or less likely to choose abstinence? Which programs are most effective—those that teach about healthy sexuality, or those that focus on the negative consequences of sexual behavior? These conflicts have torn communities apart, and there's no quick fix.

If your school offers sex ed, pay attention. Tell your parents what you're learning. They may agree with the program, or they may not. Decide together what's best for you, based on your family's values. If you're getting what you need, great. If you're not, there are other sources of information available.

Join or start a SADD chapter.

Formerly Students Against Driving Drunk, SADD now stands for Students Against Destructive Decisions to reflect the organization's expanded focus on violence, tobacco, and drugs as well as alcohol. Founded in 1981, SADD has over 7 million members in more than 25,000 chapters across the country. For more information, write to: SADD, 255 Main Street, Marlborough, MA 01752, or go to *www.sadd.org*. Schools can order SADD starter kits by calling 1-877-723-3462.

Explore more ways to build restraint.

● Start a lunchtime or after-school discussion group where students can express their values, attitudes, and concerns about sex, alcohol, other drugs, and smoking. Ask a teacher or school counselor to sit in and offer guidance.

● Check your school library or media center. Are appropriate resources available on sex, alcohol, other drugs, and smoking?

● Create a school pledge about staying alcohol-, drug-, and cigarette-free. Make copies available for students to sign, and inform the local media.

FACT:

Everybody is NOT doing it!

- 50% of girls and 45% of boys ages 15–19 are *not* having sex. (After increasing steadily for more than two decades, the percentage of teenagers who are having sex is decreasing.)

- 70% of eighth graders, 52% of tenth graders, and 45% of twelfth graders have *never* used an illicit drug. (Drug use among teens is leveling off after a long rise.)

- 55% of kids in grades 6–8 and 29% of teens in grades 9–12 *don't* use alcohol.

- 63% of high school students *don't* smoke. (BUT teen smoking is on the rise. Tobacco use among teens jumped by nearly 1/3 during the past six years; smoking among African American teenagers almost doubled.)

Sources: *1995 National Survey of Family Growth; 1997 Monitoring the Future Survey; 1997 PRIDE Survey; 1997 Youth Risk Behavior Survey.*

In Your Community

Try these ideas from the National Clearinghouse for Alcohol and Drug Information (NCADI):

Promote drug-free youth. Celebrate and acknowledge the drug-free lifestyle most youth already practice. Take your positive stories to newspapers, radio and TV stations, and other groups.

Raise community awareness. Tell parents, community leaders, and other adults about problems faced by youth in your community, such as the convenience store that sells drugs and/or allows underage youth to buy alcohol. Adults need to know what youth face on a day-to-day basis so they can rally to your support.

Develop teen spokespersons. Organize a teen speakers' bureau. Many adult groups and organizations are interested in involving youth in community prevention programs.

Speak out on youth issues about drugs. Listen and call in to radio stations with talk programs that discuss issues about drugs and related problems among youth. Throw your two cents in the barrel.

Tap into the creative interests of youth. Have teens who are into the arts—dancers, actors, musicians, writers, and others—help develop messages, slogans, posters, songs, print ads, T-shirts, buttons, speeches and articles that promote and address the benefits of non-use of marijuana and other drugs.

Create positive peer pressure. Set a good example for your friends and younger brothers and sisters.

Assets in Action

The Coulee Community Action Program in **LaCrosse, Wisconsin,** *takes a relationship-building approach to preventing teen pregnancy. The One-By-One project matches older adolescent girls with pre-teen girls. The pairs attend meetings to learn about pregnancy prevention skills and developmental assets; they also participate in community service activities and have fun together. Older teens become valuable resources for younger teens, and younger teens learn restraint and resistance skills.*

In **Minneapolis, Minnesota,** *colored lights swirl, kids of all ages and races fill the dance floor, and speakers pound with the sounds of the latest music. The scene is 16-Plus Night at Tropix Beach Club in the city's fashionable Warehouse District, and the place is packed. Security is tight, police patrol the parking lots, and if you've been drinking you don't get in. The club is a safe place free of drugs, alcohol, and sex where teens can stay until midnight curfew. Other clubs in the area also offer teen nights and dance parties; teens from all over come to have fun and meet new people.*

*In **Trumbull, Connecticut,** the Trumbull Community Prevention Council had high school seniors conduct audiotaped interviews with eighth graders about marijuana use. Then the council formed a panel of community members to respond on video to the question "How do we help the young people of Trumbull grow up healthy, caring, and responsible?" Blending the audios and videos, the council made a new video called* Reality Check *for community access TV. Meanwhile, 1,200 middle school families received an advance information packet encouraging them to watch the program with their children. The packet also included a list of assets and a summary of results from an asset survey of local youth.*

In Your Faith Community

● Find out what your faith tradition teaches about sexual behavior and the use of alcohol or other drugs. Talk with your spiritual leader and youth leader.

● With your youth group, make a pledge not to have sex or use alcohol as teenagers. Support and affirm each other. Or make a personal pledge based on your values.

With Your Friends

Sex, alcohol, and drugs can be tempting. Pressure to be sexually active and get high can be almost irresistible. Especially if your friends are involved, you may feel left out if you aren't, too.

Restraint takes courage—and support. Think about and clarify your personal values, then surround yourself with friends who feel the way you do. True friends care about each other and respect each other's thoughts, feelings, and decisions. See Asset #15: Positive Peer Influence.

6 TIPS FOR STAYING SAFE

HOW TO RESIST ALMOST ANYTHING YOU DON'T WANT TO DO

1. Think ahead. Any upcoming activity deserves some advance thought and planning. Where are you going? Who'll be there? Are the parents home? Will alcohol or other drugs be available? Are you going with at least one good friend, someone you can rely on to support you? How are you getting there and back? Is there a chance you'll have to catch a ride with someone who's drunk or high? Is there an adult you can trust and call if needed?

2. Have alternate plans. If you decide to attend a party or other event, have a back-up plan ready. Sometimes the best plan is simply to leave the party. You need to be prepared for this, though. Who can you call for a ride home if you need one? Do you have money for a pay phone and a taxi? What if your friend goes off and leaves you alone in a risky situation? Can you drive yourself or have a parent drive you so you're in control of your exit? Do you have an agreement with an adult you can call?

3. Do something else. If you decide not to attend an activity or event, don't sit around moping. Make your own party. Call a few friends and do something you like.

4. Get involved. Sports, acting, singing, dance, gymnastics, writing—the list of possible activities is endless. Keep busy and you won't have time to fool around with drinking and drugs. Do things that give you a chance to show off a little; when you feel good about a skill or talent, you won't reach for alcohol and other drugs to make you feel accepted or popular.

5. Value individuality. Many teens seek safety in looking, acting, and being like everyone else. It takes self-confidence to do things differently. Ask yourself "What do I think? What do I want? Is that what or how I want to be?" When you learn to think your own thoughts, it will be easier to make good, self-caring decisions.

6. Practice saying no and don't worry about sounding rude or wimpy. Girls are often taught to please others; boys are more likely to take risks and act on dares. Saying no doesn't come naturally. Decide what words and phrases you'll use in various situations, then practice them in a mirror, with your friends, or with your parents. Start with these:

- "Thanks, but no thanks."
- "I don't drink/I don't do drugs."
- "No way! Forget it."
- "Thanks, but I'll pass."
- "Thanks, but I already have something to drink."

Adapted from *Taking Charge of My Mind & Body* by Gladys Folkers, M.A., and Jeanne Engelmann. Free Spirit Publishing Inc., 1997, pages 52–56. Used with permission.

RESOURCES

For everyone:

The Partnership at Drugfree.org
352 Park Avenue South, 9th Floor
New York, NY 10010
(212) 922-1560
www.drugfree.org
Comprehensive, accurate, up-to-date information about drugs, plus help for parents, a list of organizations, recommended readings, and more.

Substance Abuse and Mental Health Services Administration
1 Choke Cherry Road
Rockville, MD 20857
1-877-SAMHSA-7 (1-877-726-4727)
www.samhsa.gov
SAMHSA's mission is to reduce the impact of substance abuse and mental illness on communities in the United States. Check out their publications section at their Web site to find information and materials about substance abuse prevention and treatment.

For you:

Sex, Love, and You: Making the Right Decision by Thomas Lickona and Judith Lickona (Notre Dame, IN: Ave Maria Press, 1994). Food for thought, including 13 reasons why some young people choose to have sex.

Taking Charge of My Mind and Body: A Girl's Guide to Outsmarting Alcohol, Drug, Smoking, and Eating Problems by Gladys Folkers, M.A., and Jeanne Engelman (Minneapolis: Free Spirit Publishing, 1997). First-person stories, up-to-date facts, skill-building strategies, and more give girls and young women the power to make good choices.

TobaccoFree
www.tobaccofree.com
An anti-smoking resource for young people, this site offers information on the negative effects of smoking, current news items, and quitting tips.

For parents, educators, and community leaders:

Parenting for Prevention: How to Raise a Child to Say No to Alcohol/Drugs by David J. Wilmes and Cyril A. Reilly (Minneapolis: Johnson Institute, 1989). This book is available free of charge to anyone in the United States who writes for a copy. Write to: Miller Family Foundation, PO Box 831463, Stone Mountain, GA 30083.

Sex Is Not a Four-Letter Word! Talking Sex with Your Children Made Easier by Patricia Martens Miller (New York: Crossroads Publishing, 1995). A sex education and religion instructor provides a solidly scientific, psychologically empathic, and spiritually focused guide to children's sexuality from birth through young adulthood.

ParentFurther

615 First Avenue NE

Minneapolis, MN 55413

1-800-888-7828

www.parentfurther.com

Provides practical, everyday parenting tips and helpful advice for difficult situations. Check out their Technology and Media section for advice and information on cyberbullying, cell phone safety tips, the Internet, video games, teens and social media, and more.

SOCIAL COMPETENCIES

These assets are about improving yourself and your relationships—developing the skills and attitudes that will help you function as an independent, capable person in the world. They're about making plans and decisions, making friends, and getting along with all kinds of people. They're about having the strength and the smarts to avoid risky situations—and resolve conflicts without using violence of any kind.

The social competencies assets are:

32. Planning and Decision Making
33. Interpersonal Competence
34. Cultural Competence
35. Resistance Skills
36. Peaceful Conflict Resolution

PLANNING AND DECISION MAKING

You know how to plan ahead and make choices.

At Home

Find out who does what.

Have family meetings to talk about who's responsible for specific activities around your house. Use this chart to start a discussion, then talk about ways to include *all* family members in planning, deciding, and doing.

What?	Who plans?	Who decides?	Who does?
Family relaxation activities			
Meals			
Holiday celebrations			
Household chores			
Activities outside of school or work			
What else?			

Think past one day at a time.

Some teens take life as it comes. That's fine—until they miss an important deadline, opportunity, or social event. Living for today may sound like fun, but it won't make your dreams come true.

If you're a poor planner, start simple:

1. Make a daily things-to-do list.
2. Number the items, starting with 1 for the most important.
3. Check off items as you complete them.
4. Move leftover items to tomorrow's list.

Or buy your own daily planning calendar. (Inexpensive calendars are available at every office supplies store.) Keep your things-to-do lists in your calendar. Write in future things to do—dates of long-term assignments, school holidays, tests, upcoming social events, etc. Every day or so, look ahead to see what's coming up and what you need to prepare for.

FACT:

Most teens have plans for after high school!

When 1,000 students from ages 13–17 were asked what they plan to do right after high school, here's what they said:

What's next?	According to how many teens?
Attend a four-year college/university	60.6%
Get a job	46.7%
Travel	17.0%
Get married	15.2%
Attend a two-year college/university	14.7%
Go to training/vocational school	13.0%
Join the armed forces	9.6%
Join a volunteer organization	3.6%

Source: *The Mood of American Youth* (Alexandria, VA: Horatio Alger Association of Distinguished Americans and the National Association of Secondary School Principals, 1996).

Go beyond planning to goal setting.

Making plans and following through can help you get what you want. Setting goals and acting on them can help you *become* what you want. Here are five benefits of being a goal setter:*

---

* Adapted from *The Gifted Kids' Survival Guide: A Teen Handbook* by Judy Galbraith, M.A., and Jim Delisle, Ph.D. Free Spirit Publishing Inc., 1996, page 85. Used with permission.

1. You gain independence. You're not letting someone else decide your life for you.

2. You gain a sense of accomplishment. You're not just following orders or doing what's expected of you.

3. You make things happen. You're not waiting and wishing they would happen.

4. You manage your time more effectively. Getting more done gives you more freedom to explore other things you want to do.

5. People who set goals aren't bored, and they aren't boring.

Many people have a general idea of where they'd like to be 5, 10, or 20 years from now. But they don't have the discipline to do the daily goal setting needed to get there. If you train yourself to do this—and you must do it for yourself—you'll take charge of your life *and* greatly improve your chances of realizing your potential.

STEPS TO GOAL SETTING

1. Write down all the things you'd like to accomplish during the next 10 years. These are your *long-range goals*. Be specific and thorough.

2. When you've completed your list of long-range goals, prioritize them. Select the 3–4 that are most important to you.

3. Write down all the things you'd like to accomplish during the next 3–5 years. These are your *intermediate* (medium-range) *goals*. Prioritize them; select the top 3-4. Your intermediate goals should help you achieve your long-range goals.

4. Write down all the things you'd like to accomplish during the next year. These are your *immediate* (short-range) *goals*. Prioritize and select the top few. Your immediate goals should relate directly to your intermediate goals.

Tip: When setting goals, most people focus only on the serious stuff—school performance, self-improvement, career plans, life direction. Be sure to leave room on your lists for hobbies, interests, passions, friends, and fun. These shouldn't be "rewards" for reaching your "real" goals; they should *be* real goals.

5. Write your lists in a small spiral-bound notebook and date them. Carry your notebook with you and consult your lists regularly—once a day (best) or once a week (minimum). When you reach a goal, write down that date in your notebook. Feel free to revise your goals as circumstances change.

CONTINUED ON NEXT PAGE...

Tip: Share your goals with an adult you trust and respect—someone who's willing to listen and offer constructive criticism. (Finding a support person might be one of your immediate goals.)

CAUTION: Don't dismiss this process because it seems too simple. It's remarkably powerful and effective. People we know who have taken the time to think about, write down, and consult their goals report that *it really works*. Make a commitment to do this for at least three weeks; by then you'll know if it works for you.

Adapted from *The Gifted Kids' Survival Guide: A Teen Handbook* by Judy Galbraith, M.A., and Jim Delisle, Ph.D. Free Spirit Publishing Inc., 1996, pages 85–89. Used with permission.

Practice making thoughtful, deliberate decisions.

One of the best and simplest ways to do this is with Pros and Cons lists. Think of a decision you're facing, then come up with as many Pros (good things) and Cons (not-so-good things) about it as you can. If your Pros list is longer or stronger, do it. If your Cons list is longer or stronger, don't do it. *Example:*

Should I go to the party at Mark's on Friday?

PROS	CONS
—I like Mark	—I don't like some of his friends who'll probably be there
—No drinking at his parties	—Theo is having a party on the same night
—Jenny is going	—Everyone wants to watch scary movies on the big screen TV
—His last party was fun	—Allergic to Mark's cat
—My parents like Mark	—Have to get up early on Saturday
—I can wear my new shirt	
—Count on great food	
—Cool entertainment center and his parents let us use it	

If this was your list, what would you decide?

At School

Get a grip on long-range assignments.

Many students do their daily homework but drop the ball on term papers, research reports, special projects, and other long-range assignments. Avoid panic attacks and desperate acts by following this plan from *School Power* author Jeanne Shay Schumm:

1. Decide on a theme.

2. Get your teacher's approval.

3. Make a list of things you need to do to complete your assignment. Rank them in the order they need to be done.

4. Decide if you'll need help from your parents or other adults. Ask if and when they can help you. Be clear about what you want them to do . . . and don't wait until the last minute to ask. (Parents *hate* that.)

5. Set deadlines for each part of your assignment. (*Examples:* doing your research; preparing an outline; writing a first draft; writing a final draft; etc.) Write the dates in your planning calendar or assignment notebook.

6. Make a list of materials you'll need, if any. Estimate how much they will cost.

7. Send away for resource materials.

8. Contact community resources.

9. Visit the library.

10. Complete your project on schedule.

Explore more ways to plan and make decisions.

● Find someone at school—a teacher, school counselor, or coach—who can help you make long-range plans for continuing your education and/or choosing a career.

● Start a lunchtime or after-school discussion group where students can talk about tough choices they're facing or have faced in the past. Ask a school counselor to sit in and offer guidance.

● Get involved with decision-making committees and boards at your school.

● Help plan events at your school—homecoming, a dance, a new club, the annual open house, or whatever interests you.

Assets in Action

*A teacher and coach in **Cherry Creek, Colorado,** gave each of his students a list of assets. Then he taught them how to build assets, how to become the people they wanted to be, and how to develop the values they wanted to have. He also taught them how to use a personal calendar, set goals, and manage their time.*

In Your Community

● Help adults in your neighborhood plan a neighborhood event (*examples:* picnic, parade, block party, potluck dinner). Watch how they plan . . . and watch what happens when they *don't* plan.

● Interview adults you admire. Ask them how they got where they are today. (You'll probably discover that goal setting had something to do with it.) Ask if they have any goal-setting tips to share with you.

● Identify something in your community you'd like to change, then make a plan for changing it. See "10 Steps to Social Action" on pages 220–221.

● Find out if your community center offers workshops on planning, goal setting, and decision making. If it does, go.

● Get involved with decision-making committees and boards in your community.

● Put your planning skills to work and help plan something big. *Examples:* a community carnival, a series of workshops on asset building, an after-school program. *Tip:* Keep a start-to-finish journal of your experience. Afterward, summarize it on a single page, with emphasis on your responsibilities. This will look very good to prospective employers and college admissions officers.

In Your Faith Community

● Take an active part in planning the youth program. *Example:* If kids in your faith community want a basketball court on the parking lot, help make it happen.

● Are youth involved in decisions that affect the faith community as a whole? If not, ask about ways to get involved.

● Within your youth group, talk about how your faith shapes and influences your decisions.

Assets in Action

North Shore Synagogue in **Syosset, New York,** *trains teens to be planners and leaders. Starting in seventh grade, youth sit on a steering committee that helps plan the youth program. In eighth grade, they learn how to lead groups and monitor younger kids. By ninth grade, they run the youth program, with the youth director acting as an advisor.*

With Your Friends

Talk about the choices you're facing in your lives—at home, at school, in your community, with each other. Support each other in making good choices. See Asset #15: Positive Peer Influence.

STEPS TO MAKING 5 GOOD CHOICES

1. Think it through. Take all the time you need or have. Realize that your choice might have both positive and negative consequences.

2. Gather information. Find out as much about your choice as you can. Try to predict the consequences. Is your choice more likely to help someone or hurt someone?

3. Weigh your choices and the possible consequences, then make your decision. It might not be perfect, but it will be the best it can be under the circumstances.

4. Review what you did and what happened as a result. Did your choice help someone? Did it make something better? Would you make a different choice next time?

5. Learn from your choice. Use what you learn to make good choices in the future.

Note: The worst choices are the ones you make by default. Instead of making a choice, you simply allow something to happen. By not choosing, you have made a choice, and the results might not be what you wanted.

Adapted from *What Do You Stand For? For Teens* by Barbara A. Lewis. Free Spirit Publishing Inc., 1998, pages 29–30. Used with permission.

RESOURCES

For everyone:

How to Get Control of Your Time and Your Life by Alan Lakein (New York: New American Library, 1996). A classic time management book—plus it's short and easy to read.

For you:

Challenges: A Young Man's Journal for Self-Awareness and Personal Planning by Mindy Bingham and Sandy Stryker (Santa Barbara, CA: Advocacy Press, 1984) and *Choices: A Teen Woman's Journal for Self-Awareness and Personal Planning* by Mindy Bingham, Judy Edmondson, and Sandy Stryker (Santa Barbara, CA: Advocacy Press, 1983). Readings and exercises build skills in planning and decision making.

No Easy Answers: Short Stories About Teenagers Making Tough Choices, edited by Donald R. Gallo (New York: Bantam Books, 1997). Sixteen original short stories by some of today's most popular writers for teens explore choices, consequences, and what it means to do the right thing.

Day-Timers, Inc.
1-800-225-5005
www.daytimer.com
Ask about the Student Planner.

Franklin Covey Co.
1-800-819-1812
www.franklinplanner.com
Ask about the Premiere Agendas daily planners (available in elementary school, middle school, and high school editions) and the Collegiate Kit.

For your parents:

The Life-Smart Kid: Teaching Your Child to Use Good Judgment in Every Situation by Lawrence J. Greene (Rocklin, CA: Prima Publications, 1995). Practical ways to help young people develop critical thinking and decision-making skills.

43% of the youth we surveyed have this asset in their lives.

INTERPERSONAL COMPETENCE

You're good at making and keeping friends.

At Home

Talk with your parents about friendship.

Talk about your friends; ask about theirs. Be willing to learn from each other. You might start a discussion with questions like these:*

- How have your friendships changed over the years?

- What do you value in your closest friends?

- What do your friends value in you?

- Is it easy for you to make friends? If not, what seems to make it difficult?

- Is it easy for you to keep friendships going? If not, what seems to cause problems?

- Do you have friends of different ages? Races? Religions? Ethnic backgrounds? Genders?

- What are some things you and your friends have in common?

---

* Adapted from *Talk with Teens About Feelings, Family, Relationships, and the Future* by Jean Sunde Peterson, Ph.D. Free Spirit Publishing Inc., 1995, page 108. Used with permission.

- What are some things you don't have in common with your friends?

- What makes friendships different for you now than when you were younger?

- Did you have some friends your parents didn't approve of? If so, what kinds of problems did that cause for you?

- What have you learned through your friendships?

- Have you ever felt rejected by a friend? If you have, how did you handle the rejection? Do you still think about it?

- Do you develop close friendships quickly and easily, or are you hesitant to get involved in a close friendship?

- What advice would you give to someone who has a hard time making friends?

You can also ask *yourself* these questions. Think about the answers or write them in your journal, if you keep a journal.

Make your life easier.

You want your parents to like your friends (or at least tolerate their presence). Try these tips to improve your chances:

Introduce them to each other. When you have a friend over for the first time, don't race to your room. Take a moment to make introductions. *Examples:* "Mom, this is Max. We're in math class together" or "Dad, this is Dorie. We met at the Y." If you really want to impress your mom or dad, introduce your parents as Mr., Mrs., or Ms. *Examples:* "Max, this is my mom, Ms. Smith." "Dorie, this is my dad, Mr. Jones."

Tip: Most adults love it when kids call them by their last names—a sign of respect that's in short supply. Never call your friends' parents by their first names until they say it's okay. If a friend does a poor job (or no job) of making introductions, take charge. *Example:* "Hi, Mr. Brown. I'm Mark." To which Mr. Brown might reply "Nice to meet you, Mark." In which case you should keep calling him Mr. Brown. Or he might say "Nice to meet you, Mark. You can call me Tom."

Give them chances to get acquainted. Spend time talking or have dinner together. With close friends, you might suggest sharing a family outing or vacation. Parents often base their opinions on first impressions, and if your friends look or dress in ways they don't approve of, those impressions might not be good. Dreadlocks, nose rings, and tattoos are less threatening when they're attached to a friendly, interesting, funny, polite human being.

Listen when your parents voice objections about your friends. Don't brush them off or yell "They're MY friends and I don't CARE what you think!" Their objections might be valid; if your best friend has just been arrested for the third time, it makes sense to reconsider that relationship. Or their objections might be petty; so what if a friend shaves his or her head? Listen anyway and offer some reassurance that you know what you're doing. Emphasize your friend's positive qualities. *Example:* "Yeah, that head is radical. But did you know that Billy volunteers at a homeless shelter three times a week? He's really an amazing person." *Tip:* If you're wondering whether a friend is right for you, take the Friendship Test. See Asset #15: Positive Peer Influence.

Listen when your parents say nice things about your friends. Thank them for noticing. If you want to lay it on thick, you might even say "If I pick good friends, it's because you taught me well."

Know when to back off. Some parents don't like their kids' friends, no matter who they are. You could bring the Dalai Lama home for dinner and they'd criticize his clothes. If your parents aren't willing to change their opinions (even in the face of positive facts), don't try to force them. If your parents are openly rude or hostile, stop bringing your friends home. And if your parents are making it hard or impossible for you to have friends, talk to another adult you trust. You need friends in your life.

FACT:

Most teens can choose their own friends!

According to a recent nationwide survey of more than 218,000 students in grades 6–12, 92 percent say they have the freedom to pick their own friends, 87 percent can listen to whatever music they want, and 81 percent can decide how to spend their own money.

Source: "USA Weekend's 10th Annual Teen Report: Teens & Freedom," reported in *USA Weekend,* May 2–4, 1997.

At School

● Get involved with clubs, activities, and service projects at your school; these are great opportunities to make new friends and strengthen existing friendships. See assets #5: Caring School Climate, #9: Service to Others, and #24: Bonding to School.

● Reach out to newcomers and others who may not have friends.

● Take time to pay attention to younger kids.

● Start a lunchtime or after-school discussion group where students can talk about making and keeping friends, friendship problems, and related issues. Ask a teacher or school counselor to sit in and offer guidance.

● Reach out to kids you don't normally interact with. *Example:* What about sitting with a different group at lunch? If they give you the cold shoulder, at least you tried.

● Get involved in a peer helping program, which can teach you important friendship skills including listening skills, conflict resolution skills, and how to show care.

Assets in Action

At Pattonsville High School in **Maryland Heights, Missouri,** *a group of 35 students started the New Friends Club to promote awareness about disabilities and provide sensitivity training to their peers. During the first year, they brought in speakers to educate themselves, went through awareness exercises with parents of children with disabilities, and raised money for worthy organizations. During the second year, they used puppets to teach disability awareness in local elementary schools and organized a wheelchair basketball game. Current activities including meeting to talk about different types of disabilities, sponsoring special presentations, and volunteering. Many of the club's active members have physical or learning disabilities.*

In Your Community

If you can't find friends in the usual places—school, your neighborhood, your place of worship—then look at your community as a whole. Is there a club, organization, or group that matches one of your interests? Consider joining. You'll immediately have at least one thing in common with everyone else. See Asset #18: Youth Programs.

Do your best to form friendships with many different kinds of people. Diversity makes life more interesting. Valuing and appreciating diversity—which happens naturally when your friends are different ages, races, religions, ethnic backgrounds, and genders—is an essential step toward eliminating bias and prejudice. See assets #3: Other Adult Relationships, #4: Caring Neighborhood, and #34: Cultural Competence.

Friendships are built on empathy and sensitivity: knowing that other people have needs and feelings, and being aware and responsive. Empathy begins by deciding how you want to be treated—probably with kindness and respect. From there, it's not too hard to understand that other people want to be treated the same. If you remember times when you were treated unkindly, even cruelly, you can make a personal commitment not to say or do things that will cause pain to others.

TIPS FOR MAKING AND KEEPING FRIENDS

1. Reach out. Don't wait for someone else to make the first move. A simple hi and a smile go a long way.

2. Get involved. Join clubs that interest you; take special classes inside or outside of school. Seek out neighborhood and community organizations and other opportunities to serve others.

3. Let people know that you're interested in them. Don't just talk about yourself; ask questions about them and their interests. Make this a habit and you'll have mastered the art of conversation.

4. Be a good listener. This means looking at people while they're talking to you and genuinely paying attention to what they're saying.

5. Risk telling people about yourself. When it feels right, let your interests and talents be known. BUT . . .

6. Don't be a show-off. Not everyone you meet will share your interests and abilities.

7. Be honest. Tell the truth about yourself and your convictions. When asked for your opinion, be sincere. BUT . . .

8. When necessary, temper your honesty with diplomacy. The truth doesn't have to hurt. It's better to say "Gee, your new haircut is interesting" than "You actually paid money for THAT?"

9. Don't just use your friends as sounding boards for your problems and complaints. Include them in the good times, too.

10. Do your share of the work. That's right, *work*. Any relationship takes effort. Don't always depend on your friends to make the plans and carry the weight.

11. Be accepting. Not all of your friends have to think and act like you do. (Wouldn't it be boring if they did?)

12. Learn to recognize the so-called friends you can do without. Some teens get so lonely that they put up with anyone—including friends who aren't really friends at all. Follow tips 1–11 and this shouldn't happen to you.

Adapted from *The Gifted Kids' Survival Guide: A Teen Handbook* by Judy Galbraith, M.A., and Jim Delisle, Ph.D. Free Spirit Publishing Inc., 1996, page 209. Used with permission.

Assets in Action

In **Hopkins, Minnesota,** *teens are working to create a teen center where they can hang out with their friends. They started with a survey of 1,200 students to find out what kind of center they wanted and where it should be. The center will include a coffee shop with couches, dart boards, and inexpensive food.*

In Your Faith Community

When Search Institute's researchers asked teenagers what subjects they'd like to learn more about from their spiritual organization, the top response was "knowing how to make friends and to be a friend." Find out what your faith community is doing to promote and nurture friendships among youth. Does your youth program leave time for relationship building? Does it sponsor activities where teens can get to know each other and share experiences? A youth program shouldn't be all fun and games, but it shouldn't be all books and lectures, either. Ask how you can help make your faith community a place where children and teens can form positive friendships.

With Your Friends

How are your friendships? Are you doing your part to keep them healthy and strong? Rate your own relationship skills. Read each of the following statements, then decide if this is something you *never* do, *occasionally* do, or *often* do.

	NEVER	OCCASIONALLY	OFTEN
1. I call a friend on the phone just to talk.	❑	❑	❑
2. I ask a friend's opinion on an issue.	❑	❑	❑
3. I trust a friend with a confidence.	❑	❑	❑
4. I tell a friend when he or she hurts my feelings.	❑	❑	❑
5. I give a friend a compliment.	❑	❑	❑
6. I listen to a friend who needs to talk.	❑	❑	❑
7. I refuse to listen to gossip or rumors about a friend.	❑	❑	❑

CONTINUED ON NEXT PAGE...

	NEVER	OCCASIONALLY	OFTEN
8. I tell a friend how I really feel about him or her.	❑	❑	❑
9. I do something nice for a friend just because.	❑	❑	❑
10. I let a friend know that our friendship is important to me.	❑	❑	❑
11. I suggest something a friend and I can do together.	❑	❑	❑
12. I do something a friend wants to do, even if it's not something that really interests me.	❑	❑	❑
13. I treat a friend with kindness and respect.	❑	❑	❑
14. I'm there for a friend who needs me.	❑	❑	❑
15. I stick up for a friend who's being picked on or bullied.	❑	❑	❑

SCORING: You decide: What kind of friend are you? Are there relationship skills you're especially proud of? Are there others you need to work on?

RESOURCES

For everyone:

Friendshifts: The Power of Friendship and How It Shapes Our Lives by Jan Yager, Ph.D. (Stamford, CT: Hannacroix Creek Books, 1997). Sensible advice on how to make, keep, and improve friendships, plus information on how friendships change throughout our lives.

LifeStories. This game encourages people to share stories about themselves and build interpersonal competence. Play it with your family, friends, and neighbors. Check your local game store.

For you:

How Rude! The Teenagers' Guide to Good Manners, Proper Behavior, and Not Grossing People Out by Alex J. Packer, Ph.D. (Minneapolis: Free Spirit Publishing, 1997). In all of your relationships, manners matter. This serious and hilarious book guides you through the world of etiquette from A (Applause) to Z (Zits).

For your parents:

How to Raise a Child with a High EQ: A Parent's Guide to Emotional Intelligence by Lawrence E. Shapiro, Ph.D. (New York: HarperCollins, 1998). Hundreds of ways to help children develop social and emotional skills. See especially the chapter on making friends.

Asset #34

35% of the youth
we surveyed have this
asset in their lives.

CULTURAL COMPETENCE

You know and are comfortable with people of different cultural, racial, and/or ethnic backgrounds.

At Home

Know what's in it for you.

If you already have this asset, you're enjoying the benefits. If you don't, here's what you're missing:*

1. The more you know about people of different cultural, racial, and/or ethnic backgrounds, the less you fear. The less you fear, the more willing you are to explore new ideas and meet new people. Curiosity replaces suspicion, and you're not limited by ignorance or prejudice. *Tip:* It's easy to hate a stereotype, hard to hate someone you know.

2. You become more self-confident and comfortable in all kinds of situations. Studies have shown that people who get along with different kinds of people are emotionally and physically healthier—and more successful in their careers—than those who don't.

---

* Adapted from *Respecting Our Differences* by Lynn Duvall. Free Spirit Publishing Inc., 1994, pages 5–6. Used with permission.

3. **Your life becomes more interesting.** What if all of your friends and acquaintances looked, thought, and behaved exactly alike? What if everyone was the same age, religion, gender, and race? Big yawn.

If you don't already have this asset, you need it, because the world is growing more diverse each day. Nationwide, 66 percent of students in public elementary and secondary schools are white, 17 percent are black, 13 percent are Hispanic, 4 percent are Asian or Pacific Islander, and 1 percent are American Indian/Alaskan Native. Depending on where you live, these numbers are larger or smaller. The point is: Even if your world right now is relatively homogeneous, your future won't be. You'll be working with, living with, socializing with, and dealing with people of many different races. Why wait to start?

FACT:

Teens and adults see different worlds!

A nationwide poll of 1,282 adults and 601 teens ages 12–17 found that teens have different views of race than their parents. Here are some of the findings:

- 58% of white teens and 62% of black teens think racism is a big problem in the U.S. today, compared to 64% of white adults and 78% of black adults. (34% of white and black teens think racism is a *small* problem.)

- 76% of white teens and 55% of black teens think that race relations in this country will improve, compared to 60% of white adults and 43% of black adults.

Overall, teens of both races are more optimistic, and adults of both races are more skeptical.

Source: TIME/CNN poll reported in *Time*, November 24, 1997.

Boost your family's cultural competence.

● Learn about your own heritage. Ask your parents and other relatives to tell you about their cultural background and experiences. *Tip:* When you have a positive view of your own racial or ethnic group, you're more likely to have a positive view of other groups.

● Go as a family to events that celebrate different cultures and religions. Talk about them afterward.

● Include traditions from many cultures in your family celebrations. Learn words from other languages and teach them to each other; prepare meals from different cultures or eat at local ethnic restaurants.

● Invite friends and neighbors from various cultures and backgrounds into your home. Introduce them to some of your customs and traditions.

● As a family, watch TV shows that positively portray people from different cultural, racial, and/or ethnic backgrounds. Talk about what you see.

● Read positive books and stories about people from many different cultures. See Asset #25: Reading for Pleasure.

● Get a pen pal from another country or culture. Encourage your brothers and sisters to get pen pals, too. Here are two organizations you can contact:

Student Letter Exchange
1111 Broadhollow Road, Suite 329
Farmingdale, NY 11735
(631) 393-0216
www.pen-pal.com

World Pen Pals (WPP)
PO Box 337
Saugerties, NY 12477
(845) 246-7828
www.world-pen-pals.com

Assets in Action

Brian Harris, a student at Cypress High School in **Cypress, California,** *set up an international pen-pal service to promote interracial understanding. The son of an African-American father and a Caucasian mother, Brian speaks frequently at high schools, colleges, and civic organizations to spread the word about his service, and he processes a huge volume of mail to match pen pals of different races. So far, he has arranged letter-writing relationships for more than 20,000 people around the world.*

At School

Advocate for multicultural education.

Born in the wake of the Civil Rights movement of the 1960s, multicultural education was an antidote to the "melting pot" approach of simply assimilating minority groups into the dominant American culture. Today it's almost as controversial as sex education. Some educators and parents are against it, believing it divides students along racial and cultural lines. Others are for it, believing it promotes tolerance, reduces prejudice, and prepares students to live in a diverse world.

In 1996, a nationwide survey asked public school students in grades 7–12 what *they* think. A majority (71 percent) said they were either very interested or somewhat interested in learning more about other cultures. Nearly half (45 percent) said their schools place the right amount of emphasis on teaching multiculturalism; 28 percent said their schools place too little emphasis on it, and only 11 percent said too much.* You might poll the students in your school to learn their opinions.

Tip: Advocate for arts education, too (see Asset #17: Creative Activities). Multicultural understanding is stronger in schools with strong arts programs.

Go online.

If your school is on the Internet, join ePals. Classrooms around the world are participating; you can search the online database to learn who's there and add your classroom. On the Web, go to: *www.epals.com*

Learn your school's policies on racist behaviors.

What happens when one student makes a racist remark about another? When a teacher makes a racist remark? When racial tensions lead to fights between groups of students? What are the consequences for these behaviors? Are they fair? Do they work? Are they clearly spelled out in the student handbook?

Assets in Action

*Andrea Hurwitz, a student at Peabody Veterans Memorial High School in **Peabody, Massachusetts,** launched a Blue Ribbon Campaign to raise awareness of and encourage support against hate graffiti at her school. Borrowing an idea from the AIDS awareness movement (which uses red ribbons), Andrea distributed blue ribbons symbolizing zero tolerance for hate crimes. She spoke at a class assembly and recruited 50 students to help her make and distribute the ribbons. When her efforts reached the community, she began speaking at area schools and conferences on the prevention of hate crimes.*

*In response to rising school violence and racial and ethnic intolerance, schools in **Syracuse, New York,** are using the No Putdowns Project curriculum. It has three goals: 1) to create school and home environments that recognize the destructive use of putdowns, 2) to reject the use of putdowns in all interpersonal interactions, and 3) to replace putdowns with healthy communication skills. Several schools have reported that discipline referrals and student fights are down for the first time in years.*

* Source: *The Metropolitan Life Survey of the American Teacher 1996: Students Voice Their Opinions on: Learning About Multiculturalism,* conducted by Louis Harris and Associates, Inc.

WAYS TO FIGHT RACISM IN YOUR SCHOOL

1. Don't put up with it. Don't laugh at racist jokes or join in racist taunts—but don't just ignore them, either. You might say something like "I don't think that joke is very funny" or "Don't call Michael that word. Call him by his name."

Take a stand against racism and let your friends know how you feel. Set a good example by talking about and treating all people with respect.

2. Be on the lookout for racist biases. Do students from one racial or ethnic group seem to win most of the awards at school assemblies? Do they seem to get more positive attention in the classroom? Are they encouraged more to achieve? Do they receive other forms of special treatment? Do students from a particular group seem to get praised more highly—or punished more harshly—than others?

Call attention to racist biases you notice; talk with your teachers or principal.

3. If you have a conflict with a student of another race, don't immediately assume it's a racial conflict. Some conflicts are labeled "racially motivated" when they're really just *people problems*—difficulties getting along, seeing eye-to-eye, communicating, and/or respecting each other that any two people might experience, regardless of their race.

Take a deep breath before you jump to the conclusion that race is the reason for your conflict. Then try to determine the real reason. If you need help, ask an adult.

4. Widen your circle of friends. Do you tend to hang out only with people from your own racial or ethnic group? Look for an integrated club or team you can join . . . or start one if none exists.

You don't have to like everybody, but *you can only like or dislike people you know*. When you give people a chance, you may find yourself with more friends than you can count.

5. Talk about your racist feelings. Even if we don't realize it or admit it, we all have biases and prejudices. These affect the way we perceive other people and relate to them. It affects how we feel about them and treat them.

Don't just ignore your racist feelings. Talk about them with adults you trust; talk about them with your friends and classmates. Get them out in the open, where you can see them for what they are.

6. Work for positive change. Paint over racist graffiti. Banish racist words from your vocabulary. Brainstorm other ways you can fight racism in your school, choose one to start with, and enlist other people to help you.

Every action, no matter how small, makes a difference.

Adapted from *The Best of Free Spirit*. Free Spirit Publishing Inc., 1995, pages 47–48. Used with permission.

In Your Community

● Make a special effort to meet and get to know people from other cultures. You might start with your own neighbors. See Asset #4: Caring Neighborhood.

● Study community publications, advertisements, posters, and promotional materials. Do they include the images and voices of a variety of people (black, white, Latino/Latina, Native American, Asian)? If not, why not?

● Monitor newspapers and radio programs for announcements of upcoming cultural events and festivals. Go to as many as you can.

● Work with your neighborhood organization, community organization, or youth program to create a calendar of cultural events and festivals in your community. Post it on a community Web page, or get a grant to produce and print copies. If your community already publishes an events calendar, ask them to add your information.

● Propose and help plan a heritage festival that celebrates all of the cultural, racial, and ethnic groups within your community.

● Encourage your local media to feature stories about different cultures and customs within your community.

● Volunteer to tutor a neighbor who needs help learning English.

● As you're learning about differences, look for similarities—the common ground where relationships are built.

Assets in Action

Luhui Whitebear of **Otis, Oregon,** *speaks for native youth on a statewide board. As the only female youth representative on the Oregon Native Youth Council, she lets the adult members know what she thinks is best for young Natives. She talks to them about problems youth have with gangs, alcohol and other drugs, and education. She also serves as president of the Oregon Native Youth New Voices student organization.*

Anisa Kintz, a student at Whittemore Park Middle School in **Conway, South Carolina,** *organized an annual Calling All Colors conference at Coastal Carolina University to promote racial unity among young people in grades 3–8. Similar conferences have since been held around the U.S., in Canada, and in New Zealand. Andrea was invited to speak on racial unity at a United Nations conference.*

Note: *Brian Harris (page 273), Andrea Hurwitz (page 274), and Anisa Kintz have something in common besides cultural competence. All were state or national honorees in the Prudential Spirit of Community Awards program. To learn more about this program, contact The Prudential Spirit of Community Initiative; see page 84.*

In Your Faith Community

Suggest that your faith community form a relationship with another faith community that's different from yours. Help plan ways for members to meet, work, and serve together. Or get your youth group together with a group from another faith community.

Assets in Action

In **Chicago, Illinois,** *After School Action Programs (ASAP) brings together a network of ethnic associations, religious congregations, nonprofit organizations, and public housing buildings to create positive opportunities for youth in the city's ethnically diverse North Side neighborhoods. According to ASAP's executive director, Jon Schmidt, "Kids are picking up racial biases and prejudice at an early age." To deal with cultural conflict, ASAP started the UN Academy, an eight-week summer program where kids of diverse races and ethnic backgrounds meet three times a week. The program features cross-cultural arts events and discussions of topics such as immigration, religion, and racial differences.*

With Your Friends

How much contact do you currently have with people of other races, ethnic backgrounds, and cultures? How much contact do your friends have? Find out by taking this inventory.

TYPE OF CONTACT	Weekly	Monthly	Yearly	Rarely	Never
1. I see people with different cultural backgrounds in my neighborhood.	❏	❏	❏	❏	❏
2. I see people with different cultural backgrounds in my community.	❏	❏	❏	❏	❏
3. I talk to people with cultural backgrounds that are different from mine.	❏	❏	❏	❏	❏
4. I watch TV shows that positively portray people with different cultural backgrounds.	❏	❏	❏	❏	❏
5. I listen to music from other cultures.	❏	❏	❏	❏	❏

CONTINUED ON NEXT PAGE...

TYPE OF CONTACT	Weekly	Monthly	Yearly	Rarely	Never
6. I hear others talk positively about people from different cultures.	❏	❏	❏	❏	❏
7. I eat foods from other cultures.	❏	❏	❏	❏	❏
8. I study in school about people with a variety of cultural backgrounds.	❏	❏	❏	❏	❏
9. I read positive stories about people from many different cultures.	❏	❏	❏	❏	❏
10. I attend cross-cultural events.	❏	❏	❏	❏	❏

SCORING: You decide: How culturally competent are you? What are some ways you can increase your cultural competence, individually and as a group?

RESOURCES

For everyone:

Talking About People: A Guide to Fair and Accurate Language by Rosalie Maggio (Phoenix, AZ: Oryx Press, 1997). This outstanding dictionary gives respectful alternatives to the biased words and phrases we often use without thinking.

Southern Poverty Law Center
400 Washington Avenue
Montgomery, AL 36104
(334) 956-8200
www.splcenter.org
An excellent source of information and materials on intercultural and interracial understanding. SPLC is a nonprofit organization that combats hate, intolerance, and discrimination through education and litigation.

For you:

Prejudice: Stories About Hate, Ignorance, Revelation, and Transformation, edited by Daphne Muse (New York: Hyperion, 1995). An anthology of 15 fine stories by Kate Walker, Ntozake Shange, Sandra Cisneros, and others.

Respecting Our Differences: A Guide to Getting Along in a Changing World by Lynn Duvall (Minneapolis: Free Spirit Publishing, 1994). Real-life examples, activities, and resources encourage teens to become more tolerant and savor the diversity of America's ever-changing culture.

For your parents:

40 Ways to Raise a Nonracist Child by Barbara Mathis and Mary Ann French (New York: HarperCollins, 1996). Practical, age-specific advice (from infancy through the high school years) on how to teach children to shun prejudice.

For your teachers:

Celebrations Around the World by Carole S. Angell (Golden, CO: Fulcrum Publishing, 1996). Describes more than 300 celebrations, festivals, and religious holidays observed by countries and cultures from Angola to Zimbabwe.

"Teaching Tolerance." This national education project is dedicated to helping teachers foster equity, respect, and understanding in the classroom and beyond. Free or low-cost resources—including video-and-text teaching kits, posters, and *Teaching Tolerance* magazine—are available to educators at all levels. Contact the Southern Poverty Law Center (see page 278); on the Web, go to: *www.tolerance.org*

Multicultural Pavilion
www.edchange.org/multicultural
This University of Virginia Web site includes resources for educators, statistical data and article archives, awareness activities, hundreds of categorized links, and more.

RESISTANCE SKILLS

**You resist negative peer pressure
and avoid dangerous situations.**

At Home

Be aware of the pressures you face every day.

Deep sea divers know that when they enter the ocean, they're going to experience tremendous pressure. They take proper precautions so they can return to the surface safely. As a teen, you experience pressure every day of your life—and much of it comes from people you consider your friends. Negative peer pressure can be as forceful, relentless, and potentially lethal as the water that surrounds a diver.

Which of these things do you feel pressure about now?

❏ to look a certain way

❏ to wear certain types of clothes

❏ to have a certain attitude
(cool, sexy, tough, bored,
stoned, crude, rude)

❏ to listen to certain types of music

❏ to watch certain TV
programs/movies

❏ to have a girlfriend or boyfriend

❏ to have sex with your girlfriend
or boyfriend

❏ to have unprotected sex with
your girlfriend or boyfriend

❏ to get pregnant or get someone
pregnant

❏ to smoke cigarettes

❏ to use alcohol or other drugs

❏ to bend or break family rules, school rules, or laws

❏ to act less intelligent than you really are

❏ to spend more money than you have

❏ to be friends with some people but not others

❏ to drop an old friend to please new friends

❏ to join in when your friends tease or bully someone

❏ to treat authority figures (parents, teachers, etc.) disrespectfully

❏ to get involved in certain types of activities

❏ to drop out of a club, organization, or group you enjoy

❏ to not join a club, organization, or group that interests you

❏ to treat school and learning as if they aren't important to you

❏ to help someone cheat on a test

❏ to shoplift, steal, or vandalize someone else's property

❏ to join a gang

❏ to avoid, distrust, or feel superior to people of other cultural, racial, or ethnic backgrounds

❏ to laugh at bigoted jokes

❏ to treat your parents and siblings as if you can't stand them

❏ to prove yourself by doing something risky or dangerous

❏ _____ (what else?)

SCORING: Add up the number of negative pressures you feel. Ouch! Too many? (*Any* number is too many.) Read on to learn what you can do.

FACT:

If you think peer pressure is a problem, you're not alone!

When 1,000 students from ages 13–17 were asked to name the worst influences facing today's youth, peer pressure was #2—right after drugs.

Search Institute researchers found that 37 percent of young people in grades 6–12 have resistance skills, which means that 63 percent find it hard to resist negative peer pressure and avoid dangerous situations.

Source: *The Mood of American Youth* (Alexandria, VA: Horatio Alger Association of Distinguished Americans and the National Association of Secondary School Principals, 1996); Search Institute.

Be clear on what you believe and why.

Before you can decide what you won't do, you need to know what's important to you. Talk with your parents or other adults about your values and beliefs. Or make a list. Start each item with "I believe. . . ." Then read your list, make any changes, and keep revising until it feels right to you. Now you know what to stick up for, say no to, and say yes to.

Think of three people you can count on to support your values and beliefs. Ask them to be your safety net—people you can call when you're pressured or tempted to do something unsafe or unhealthy. Keep their telephone numbers with you at all times. (If you can't think of three people, see assets #1: Family Support, #3: Other Adult Relationships, #15: Positive Peer Influence, and #33: Interpersonal Competence.) Offer to be part of a friend's safety net.

Look to the future.

Choices you make today can affect you for years to come. Imagine where you'd like to be in 5 or 10 years . . . or as soon as next year. Being clear about your goals can help you resist pressures that can steer you off course.

Tip: If you think nothing bad can happen to you—that you can't get hooked on drinking, drugs, or smoking; you can't get pregnant or get someone pregnant; you can't get HIV/AIDS; you can't have an accident while driving drunk (or riding with someone who is); you can't get caught while shoplifting or cheating; you won't suffer negative consequences from doing something risky or dangerous—think again. Better yet, talk to people your age who have struggled (or are struggling) with the results of poor choices. Ask if they thought it could happen to them.

At School

● Ask your teachers if you can spend class time role-playing situations when resistance skills are needed. (This might be part of the health and prevention curriculum at your school.) *Examples:* being pressured to have sex, drink alcohol, or use drugs; being asked to ride in a car with a person who has been drinking alcohol; being invited to a party at a friend's house when the parents are away; being called a coward because you won't shoplift; being called a traitor because you won't help a friend cheat on a test.

● Start a lunchtime or after-school discussion group where students can talk about peer pressure and resistance skills. Ask a teacher or school counselor to sit in and offer guidance.

● Make a personal commitment to learning. Build and strengthen assets #21–25 so you can resist peer pressure *not* to learn—and be a positive role model for others.

FACT:

Teens are pressured to underachieve!

In a recent study of 20,000 high school teens, nearly 20 percent said they don't try as hard in school as they might because their friends might think less well of them. Seventy percent spend fewer than five hours a week on homework, and half say they don't even do the homework that's assigned. Many believe that "getting by" is good enough.

Source: *Beyond the Classroom: Why School Reform Has Failed and What Parents Need to Do* by Larry Steinberg, Bradford Brown, and Stanford M. Dornbush (New York: Simon & Schuster, 1996).

Assets in Action

Randi Pope, a student at Long Beach Middle School in **Long Beach, Mississippi,** *confronted her fear of rejection and her feelings of being an outsider at her school by forming an organization to fight negative peer pressure. After she proposed her Circle of Friends program to an assembly of nearly 1,000 fellow students, more than half signed a pledge to become COF members. Each month, the group recognizes students who perform special acts of kindness, highlighting them on the school's morning news show.*

Note: *In 1997, Randi won a special Prudential Spirit of Community Inspiration Award. To learn more about this national awards program, contact The Prudential Spirit of Community Initiative; see page 84.*

In Your Community

Spread the word.

Encourage your local media to promote resistance skills with positive messages, or start your own campaign with your club or youth group. Survey kids and teens in your community to find out what the messages should say. What would get their attention? What would turn them off? Marketing experts who study teens recommend these strategies for reaching them:

- Talk *to* them, not *at* them, and don't patronize.

- Get the language right. Avoid stale slang.

- Learn and respect what's important to them.

- Be honest; don't exaggerate. Use facts, not hyperbole. Offer substance, not fluff.

- Respect their intelligence. According to Whiton S. Paine, president of the market research firm KidToKid, teens have been "deluged with advertising since age two, and they have very accurate crap detectors."

- Talk with teen leaders—people whose opinions matter to their peers. Ask what they think and recommend.
- Talk with cool teens. Not sure who they are? Ask other teens.
- Use music and humor.
- Let kids and teens deliver the messages.

You might also use these tips to create and put on a play for younger kids about how to handle risky situations.

Be prepared.

Photocopy this page, cut out the card, and carry it with you. Consult it whenever you feel pressured to do something risky or dangerous. If you'd like a durable plastic version of this card (sized like a credit card), it's available for sale in packets of 50. You might buy a packet for your youth group. Call Search Institute at 1-800-888-7828.

after cutting out card,
fold in half ⌐

KEY QUESTIONS

Is this a risky situation?

Am I being pressured?

How would my parents
feel about this?

Is this consistent with
my values?

What effect will this have
on my future?

What other choices
do I have?

Positive Values

Caring
Equality and Social Justice
Integrity
Honesty
Responsibility
Restraint

*These values are important to me
and my relationships with others.*

_____
Signature   Date

Assets in Action

*Each year, hundreds of high school students gather at Iowa State University in **Ames, Iowa,** for the Teen Get a Grip (GAG) Conference. Over three days of events and activities, they learn to improve their leadership abilities and avoid peer pressure. Staffed by college students, former GAG graduates, and Department of Public Safety officers, funded through the Governor's Traffic Safety Bureau, the conference attracts students ages 14–18 from all over Iowa.*

FACT:

Assets protect you!

The National Longitudinal Study on Adolescent Health—a multimillion-dollar study of more than 12,000 adolescents in grades 7–12, mandated by Congress—has identified several protective factors that appear to keep teens out of trouble. These factors are directly related to the assets you're building. The two most important are:

• feeling connected to your family (Asset #1: Family Support)
• feeling connected to your school (Asset #24: Bonding to School).

Other protective factors include parents who expect you to achieve in school (#16: High Expectations), doing well in school (#21: Achievement Motivation), working fewer than 20 hours a week (#20: Time at Home), parents who disapprove of teen sex (#31: Restraint), making a pledge not to be sexually active (#31: Restraint), believing that religion and prayer are important (#19: Religious Community), and self-esteem (#38: Self-Esteem).

Source: *Journal of the American Medical Association* 278:10 (September 10, 1997), pages 823–832. *Note:* Search Institute researchers have found that the more assets young people have, the less likely they are to get involved in risky behaviors. See Why You Need Assets on pages 12–18.

In Your Faith Community

Within your youth group, talk about and role-play ways to resist negative peer pressure and avoid dangerous situations. Ask an adult leader to sit in and offer advice and suggestions. *Tip:* This would be a great topic for a weekend retreat.

With Your Friends

Resisting negative peer pressure and avoiding dangerous situations takes assertiveness skills. When you're assertive, you're firm yet respectful. You don't bully or back down. You state your position calmly and don't budge from it even when you're teased, mocked, or threatened. *Examples:* "No, I don't do drugs." "No, I don't drink." "No, I don't go to parties when parents aren't around." "No, I don't ride with drivers who have been drinking. I'll find another way home." *Tip:* Don't wait until you're in a tough situation to assert yourself. Practice when the stakes aren't as high. For example, when you're trying to choose a movie with your friends, speak up about the one you really want to see. For more on assertiveness, see Asset #37: Personal Power. See also "6 Tips for Staying Safe" in Asset #31: Restraint.

25 WAYS TO RESIST NEGATIVE PEER PRESSURE

1. Walk away.

2. Ignore the person.

3. Pretend that the person must be joking. ("What a riot! You are so funny.")

4. Say no—calmly but firmly.

5. Say no and give a reason. ("No. Cigarette smoke makes me sick.")

6. Say no and state a value or belief that's important to you. ("No. I've decided not to have sex until I get married.")

7. Say no and warn about the possible consequences. ("No way! We could all get expelled.")

8. Say no and change the subject. ("No, I'm not interested. Say, what did you think of that stunt Clarisse pulled in math class today?")

9. Say no and offer a positive alternative. ("No thanks, I'll pass. I'm going for a bike ride. Want to come?")

10. Say no and ask a question. ("No! Why would I want to do that?")

11. Say no and use humor. ("Forget it. I'd rather go play on the freeway; it's safer.")

12. Say no and apply some pressure of your own. ("No. Say, I always thought you were smarter than that.")

13. Share your feelings. ("I don't like being around people who are drinking.")

14. Use your parents as an excuse. ("My dad would kill me if I ever did that.")

CONTINUED ON NEXT PAGE...

15. Stick up for yourself. ("I'm not going to do that. It wouldn't be good for me.")

16. Confront the person. ("I can't believe you'd ask me to do that. I thought you were my friend.")

17. Call another friend to help you.

18. Always have an out—a Plan B. ("Sorry, I can't come to the party. I promised my sister I'd take her to a movie.")

19. Lie. ("Gotta run. I told my mom I'd clean out the garage.")

20. Laugh.

21. Hang out with people who don't pressure you to do risky things.

22. Ask a peer mediator to help.

23. Tell an adult.

24. Trust your instincts. If something doesn't feel right, it probably isn't right.

25. Avoid the person from then on.

RESOURCES

For you:

Coping with Peer Pressure by Leslie S. Kaplan (Center City, MN: Hazelden, 1997). Discusses the positive and negative effects members of a peer group can have on each other and explores ways to handle the pressures you face.

How to Say No and Keep Your Friends: Peer Pressure Reversal for Teens and Preteens by Sharon Scott (Amherst, MA: Human Resource Development Press, 1997). Describes a step-by-step way to deal with peer pressure without putting friendships in jeopardy; helps you notice peer pressure before it turns into trouble; teaches you how to make logical decisions; and suggests things to do or say in specific situations.

For your parents:

Helping Kids Learn Refusal Skills by David J. Wilmes (Minneapolis, MN: Johnson Institute). This booklet gives creative, practical advice on how to help kids develop resistance skills.

Teen Tips: A Practical Survival Guide for Parents with Kids 11–19 by Tom McMahon (New York: Pocket Books, 1996). Parenting expert Tom McMahon has gone straight to the source—veteran moms and dads—for tips on talking and listening, setting limits, handling peer pressure, promoting a healthy self-concept, and more.

Asset #36

44% of the youth we surveyed have this asset in their lives.

PEACEFUL CONFLICT RESOLUTION

You try to resolve conflicts nonviolently.

At Home

Know the difference between conflict and violence.

Sometimes we think being peaceful means never having conflicts. Not true . . . and impossible besides. Conflicts, arguments, and disagreements are normal between people who think, act, and believe differently. Some conflict is even healthy. The point of this asset is not to avoid conflict or anger, but to resolve it peacefully. This means:

- never using physical force in a conflict
- not saying or doing things that put the other person down
- recognizing that working through conflicts—even when it's difficult—has its rewards (strengthening relationships, building understanding)
- knowing that a conflict doesn't have to end a relationship. You can talk about it later, when tempers have cooled and everyone involved is willing to hear both sides.

Practice peaceful conflict resolution.

When a conflict arises at home—no matter what it's about—try these steps from Myrna B. Shure, Ph.D., a developmental psychologist and creator of the I Can Problem Solve (ICPS) program:

1. Identify the conflict. Have each person talk about what happened. Each person's account is equally important.

2. Talk about the events that led to the conflict. What happened first? Second? What escalated the conflict?

3. Name how you feel. Ask others involved to identify how they feel. Encourage people to be honest about how they feel without blaming others.

4. Listen carefully to each person's feelings and accounts of the conflict. Use empathy skills. Try to understand each person's point of view.

5. Brainstorm solutions. Be creative. Affirm each person's ideas, but keep encouraging people to think of different solutions.

6. Evaluate each solution. Choose one solution that everyone agrees on.

7. Monitor how the solution works. If something needs to change, start again.

Tips: Before starting this process, identify a time and place that works for everyone. (Some families have a 24-hour rule; they wait a day before addressing a conflict, giving everyone a chance to cool down.) Stay focused on the conflict at hand; don't bring up other problems or old grievances. Negotiate a win-win solution that offers something for everyone. If tempers flare or you reach a dead end, allow family members to leave the discussion. Agree on a time to reconvene and try again.

Use I-messages.

The basic formula for an I-message is:

> *"I feel _____ when _____, because _____.*
> *I want you to _____."*

I-messages are simple but powerful. Rather than blaming the other person (which puts him or her on the defensive), you're honest about your feelings, wants, and needs. *Example:* Instead of "YOU make me so mad when you borrow my jacket without asking," try "I feel angry and upset when you borrow my jacket without asking, because then I can't wear it. I want you to ask me first."

Set up a Peace Place in your home.

This might be a room or a corner of a room where family members can go when they need to resolve a conflict. The rules of your Peace Place might be:

1. Go there if someone asks you to.

2. Use respectful words.

3. Take turns talking and listening.

4. Use I-messages.

5. If the problem is too big for you to solve, get help.

Explore more ways to keep the peace.

● Talk about small conflicts before they become big problems.

● When you're angry, try talking more *quietly* than usual. The other person may respond by lowering his or her voice, too. Instead of shouting at each other, you can have a real conversation.

● Many conflicts fade away when people really listen to each other. Look at other people when they're speaking; acknowledge what they're saying; don't interrupt, but ask questions if you need more information.

● If you're too angry to talk (or the other person is too angry to listen), go to a quiet place and write about how angry you are. Or go for a walk, run, or bike ride.

● Read books about peace and peaceful conflict resolution, individually or as a family. Talk about what you read. See Asset #25: Reading for Pleasure.

● Make a family pact never to use violent words or actions against each other. This means no abusive language, name-calling, hitting, pushing, kicking, or other hurtful behaviors. You might want to formalize your pact with a contract that everyone signs—parents included.

● Spend time each day in quiet meditation. Get to know yourself and your feelings; practice talking about them with others.

IMPORTANT: *If you experience violence at home, you need to know that this is NOT normal or acceptable. You should never be disciplined or attacked with violence. If you are, talk to an adult you trust—a school counselor, teacher, youth leader, or religious leader. Or call a hotline. The Boys Town National Hotline at 1-800-448-3000 is open 24 hours a day, every day, and free of charge to everyone in all 50 states, the District of Columbia, U.S. Territories, and Canada. You'll talk to a highly trained, professional, sympathetic counselor who will listen to you and give you "right now" answers. If you're hearing impaired, you can call the TTY line at 1-800-448-1833. For a list of more crisis hotlines, see page 88.*

At School

Work to make your school more peaceful.

Ideas to try:

● Pass a petition calling for a peaceful school. Invite everyone—students, teachers, administrators, staff—to sign it; post it where all can see it every day.

● Set up a Peace Place in your school or classroom. See the suggestions under At Home above. You might make this a place where students can go whenever they want to be quiet, thoughtful, and calm. Decorate it with artwork and posters; stock it with books about peace and tapes of soothing music.

● Have class meetings to address conflicts that arise among students (and between students and teachers). Make it a class rule to resolve conflicts fairly and nonviolently.

FACT:

If you think schools are getting more violent, you're right!

According to a recent government survey of 10,000 students ages 12–19, violent crime is a serious problem at U.S. schools today—and it's on the rise.

- 15% of students say they have been crime victims; 4% say the offenses involved violence.
- 13% say they know students who bring guns to school.
- 28% of students report gangs at their schools.
- 10% of public schools reported one or more serious violent crimes during the 1996–97 school year. There were nearly 11,000 physical attacks or fights with weapons . . . and nearly 190,000 physical attacks or fights without weapons.

Source: *Students' Reports of School Crime: 1989 and 1995* (Washington, DC: U.S. Departments of Education and Justice, 1998).

Learn about peacemakers past and present.

Examples: Martin Luther King Jr., Mother Teresa, Nelson Mandela, Elie Wiesel, Rosa Parks, Mikhail Gorbachev, Jody Williams, the Dalai Lama, Sojourner Truth, Bishop Desmond Tutu, Dorothy Day, Albert Schweitzer, President Jimmy Carter. See the latest edition of *The World Almanac* for a list of Nobel Peace Prize winners, or go online to learn about these courageous men and women:

The Nobel Foundation
www.nobelprize.org

The Nobel Prize Internet Archive
www.almaz.com

Assets in Action

When the construction of two new school buildings took away part of the playground at Franklin Elementary School in **Franklin, Nebraska,** *quarrels and fights at recess became common. The kids on the school's Community Problem-Solving Team noticed students shoving, pushing, grabbing balls, and arguing over rules. Calling themselves the Conflict Busters, they decided to help. First, they wrote a rule book so everyone on the playground would follow the same rules. Next, they wrote a conflict resolution book with worksheets for every grade. Then they lobbied for playground improvements, eventually convincing the City Council to allocate money for a new basketball court.*

Join or start a S.A.V.E. chapter.

Students Against Violence Everywhere (S.A.V.E.) teaches nonviolence through experiential learning while students have fun. Members have painted peace murals, planted peace gardens, presented skits on conflict resolution, staged violence-free Teen Nights, hosted forums and speakouts against violence, surveyed and reported on TV violence, and more. S.A.V.E. programs in middle and high schools are led by students and facilitated by adult advisors. For more information, contact:

S.A.V.E.
322 Chapanoke Road, Suite 110
Raleigh, NC 27603
1-866-343-7283
www.nationalsave.org

Advocate for conflict resolution education.

Peaceful conflict resolution is a skill you can learn. Actually, it's a skill you must learn—like talking, writing, or riding a bicycle—since you're not born knowing how to do it. Often, kids and teens don't learn it at home, so many schools have made violence prevention, conflict resolution, and peer mediation part of the curriculum. Find out what your school offers. If it doesn't offer anything, talk with your parents, teachers, and principal; go to your PTA/PTO or school board if necessary. With violence increasing in our schools and communities, these programs are more important than ever.

FACT:

Conflict resolution programs work!

Researchers at the University of Minnesota surveyed a wide range of evaluations of school-based conflict resolution and peer mediation programs. They found that, by and large, these programs have a positive impact. While untrained students tend to withdraw or use force in conflict situations, trained students are more likely to face the conflict and to use problem-solving to negotiate a solution. Also, trained students tend to have a more positive attitude toward school and fewer disciplinary problems and suspensions.

Source: *Review of Educational Research* 66: 4 (1996), pages 459–506.

Be a mediator.

Intervene in conflicts and help the people involved find a solution. Start by asking yourself:*

• Am I the right person?
• Can I assist without taking sides?
• Will both parties let me assist?
• Is this the right time to intervene?
• Are the parties relatively calm?
• Do we have enough time?
• Is this the right place?

If you can answer yes to these questions, continue with the Steps for Mediation on page 294.

Assets in Action

In **Las Vegas, Nevada,** the Clark County School Board and Clark County Social Services provide a school-based mediation program for some 2,500 students at one middle and three elementary schools. An evaluation of the 1995 program found that:

· peer mediators successfully resolved 86% of the conflicts they mediated
· there were fewer conflicts and physical fights on school grounds
· mediators' mediation skills and self-esteem increased.

---

* Reprinted with the permission of Educators for Social Responsibility © 1997 Educators for Social Responsibility, Cambridge, MA.

STEPS FOR MEDIATION

from the Resolving Conflict Creatively Program

I. Introduction

1. Introduce yourselves as a mediator.

2. Ask those in the conflict if they would like your help in solving the problem.

3. Find a quiet area to hold the mediation.

4. Ask for agreement to the following:
—try to solve the problem
—no name calling
—let the other person finish talking
—confidentiality

II. Listening

5. Ask the first person "What happened?" Paraphrase.

6. Ask the first person how she or he feels. Reflect the feelings.

7. Ask the second person "What happened?" Paraphrase.

8. Ask the second person how he or she feels. Reflect the feelings.

III. Looking for Solutions

9. Ask the first person what she or he could have done differently. Paraphrase.

10. Ask the second person what she or he could have done differently. Paraphrase.

11. Ask the first person what she or he can do here and now to help solve the problem. Paraphrase.

12. Ask the second person what she or he can do here and now to help solve the problem. Paraphrase.

13. Use creative questioning to bring disputants closer to a solution.

IV. Finding Solutions

14. Help both disputants find a solution they feel good about.

15. Repeat the solution and all of its parts to both disputants and ask if each agrees.

16. Congratulate both people on a successful mediation.

Reprinted with the permission of Educators for Social Responsibility © 1997 Educators for Social Responsibility, Cambridge, MA.

In Your Community

Work to make your community more peaceful.

Ideas to try:

● Learn the power of politeness. Simple words and phrases like *please, thank you, excuse me, I'm sorry,* and *no problem* can defuse countless conflicts before they explode into violence. So you sacrifice a little pride; it's worth it to keep the peace.

● Find out if your neighborhood or community has a dispute resolution center. If it doesn't, work with community leaders to start one.

● Find out if your community offers classes and workshops on conflict resolution. If it does, get involved. Learn everything you can about resolving conflicts peacefully. Teach younger kids what you learn.

● If you see conflicts starting among younger kids in your neighborhood, don't just let them escalate. Use your mediation skills (see page 293) and help them learn to resolve their own conflicts peacefully.

● Encourage your local media to promote and publicize the efforts of community members who are working for peace.

Assets in Action

When Marieo Henry was a student at Earhard Middle School in **Detroit, Michigan,** *his baseball coach was shot to death on his way home from Detroit's Westside Cultural & Athletic Club, where he volunteered. "There were five to ten violent deaths a year in the neighborhood," Marieo remembers. "I was sad because my coach had been my mentor." Marieo helped his school counselor write a conflict resolution book, then wondered if there was a way to share his research with the athletic club. He worked with the club director to write a proposal for a conflict resolution program; the club liked the idea so much that it named Marieo director of the program. Now he trains kids from ages 5–16 in conflict resolution skills. The amount of violence among teenagers in the club has dramatically decreased, and Marieo's program has helped thousands of kids.*

In **New Haven, Connecticut,** *undergraduate students at Yale University help middle school students learn conflict resolution skills. The college kids run a program called Peace Games that teaches cooperative problem solving by having younger kids create and play noncompetitive games. More than 1,500 middle school students in the Greater New Haven area have taken part in the program.*

Take part in a national day of nonviolence.

It's exciting to join people across the country who are working for a common cause. You might get involved in one or both of these:

● **Martin Luther King Jr. Day.** *Date:* The third Monday of January. This holiday has become a national day of service, interracial cooperation, and youth anti-violence initiatives. For more information, contact the Office of Public Liaison at the Corporation for National Service; see page 80.

● **Turn Off the Violence Day.** *Date:* The second Thursday of October. Begun in Minnesota in 1991, Turn Off the Violence Day has spread to all 50 states. The idea is simple: just for one day, you refuse to be entertained by violence—meaning no violent music, movies, videos, TV shows, or computer games. No censorship or boycotting is involved; each individual decides what he or she should avoid. Brochures, violence prevention curricula for grades K–12, Community Action Kits, and other materials are available. For more information, contact: Turn Off the Violence, PO Box 27321, Minneapolis, MN 55427, *www.turnofftheviolence.org*

Join a national organization that works for peace.

See assets #9: Service to Others, #10: Safety, and #27: Equality and Social Justice. Several of the organizations listed in those chapters also have peace and non-violence programs and initiatives. Or contact:

Fellowship of Reconciliation
PO Box 271
Nyack, NY 10960
(845) 358-4601
www.forusa.org
A spiritually based network of people committed to active nonviolence as a means of personal, social, and political change, FOR has about 60 local groups in the U.S. and chapters and affiliates in 40 countries. Ask about the Peacemaker Training Institute.

Many youth organizations offer training in conflict resolution skills, so see Asset #18: Youth Programs, too.

Know the laws that affect you.

When a disagreement turns into a fight, you're at risk of breaking the law. Depending on what happens, you may be charged with assault, disorderly conduct, disturbing the peace, or worse. Depending on where it happens, you might be suspended or expelled from school, arrested, fined, and even sent to prison. People are sick of violence and crime; communities, states, and the U.S.

government are cracking down on offenders of all ages, and some juveniles are being tried and sentenced as adults. More and more, the focus is on enforcement, not prevention.

Learn and know the laws that affect you—not so you can get around them, but so you'll understand the seriousness of what might not seem like a big deal to you.

In Your Faith Community

● Learn what your faith tradition says about peace and conflict resolution.

● Find out about conflict resolution programs that are a good fit with your faith tradition. If your faith community doesn't already offer one or more of these programs, talk to your youth leader about getting one started.

● Join a religious fellowship that works for peace and nonviolence. Contact the Fellowship of Reconciliation (see page 296) or visit the Web site for information on the Baptist Peace Fellowship, Buddhist Peace Fellowship, Episcopal Peace Fellowship, Jewish Peace Fellowship, Muslim Peace Fellowship, and Orthodox Peace Fellowship. Ask leaders in your faith community about other faith-based organizations.

● Establish a peer mediation system so kids and teens can help each other.

With Your Friends

Think about a time in your past when you and a friend had a major argument or fight. Ask yourself these questions:

• What was the conflict about?
• What was my view of the situation?
• What was my friend's view?
• Did we resolve the conflict? Why or why not?
• If I was facing this conflict now, would I do anything differently? What? Why?

If you're still friends, talk together about what happened and what you might have done differently. What did you learn from the conflict? From your attempts to resolve it? Has your relationship changed because of the conflict? If so, in what ways?

Make a pact with your friends to do a better job of resolving conflicts in the future. Promise that you'll tell each other when you're angry, not just bury your feelings. Pledge to help each other resolve conflicts peacefully and creatively.

RESOURCES

For everyone:

The Eight Essential Steps to Conflict Resolution: Preserving Relationships at Work, at Home, and in the Community by Dudley Weeks, Ph.D. (New York: Putnam, 1994). A leading expert in conflict resolution explains how to turn conflict into lasting partnerships.

For educators and other adult leaders:

Conflict Resolution Education: A Guide to Implementing Programs in Schools, Youth-Serving Organizations, and Community and Juvenile Justice Settings (Washington, DC: U.S. Departments of Justice and Education, 1996). A collaboration between the Office of Juvenile Justice and Delinquency Prevention and the Safe and Drug-Free Schools Program, this comprehensive guide tells you everything you need to know about choosing and implementing a conflict resolution education program. Call the Juvenile Justice Clearinghouse at 1-800-851-3420 (reference document number NCJ 160935). Or download a copy from: *www.ncjrs.org*

Waging Peace in Our Schools by Linda Lantieri and Janet Patti (New York: Ballantine Books, 1998). Filled with stories, voices, ideas, and advice, this practical guide to creating peaceable classrooms was written by two prominent activists in the fields of conflict resolution and emotional literacy (Lantieri is National Director of the Resolving Conflict Creatively Program; Patti is a Senior Program Associate).

Resolving Conflict Creatively Program (RCCP)
23 Garden Street
Cambridge, MA 02138
1-800-370-2515
www.esrnational.org
This highly acclaimed program has taught thousands of teachers and students how to respond non-violently to conflict. It's now being used in some 350 schools nationwide.

POSITIVE IDENTITY

These assets are about knowing who and what you are: a valuable, worthwhile person with talents, skills, abilities, and promise. You know your personal power—and your limits. You have positive self-esteem without being boastful or arrogant. You have a sense of purpose in life; you're not just taking up space in the world. And you look ahead to the future with optimism and excitement, because you know it's going to be *good*.

The positive identity assets are:

37. Personal Power
38. Self-Esteem
39. Sense of Purpose
40. Positive View of Personal Future

Asset #37

45% of the youth we surveyed have this asset in their lives.

PERSONAL POWER

You feel that you have control over many things that happen to you.

At Home

Know what it means to have personal power.

Having personal power doesn't mean being bigger, stronger, smarter, richer, or more popular than everyone else. It doesn't mean you're the boss of the world. It means you're the boss of *yourself*.

When you have personal power, you feel secure and confident inside yourself. You know you have choices; you know you can make decisions; you know what you can and can't control. If something good happens to you, you don't think "I got lucky." You're aware that you helped make it happen. If something bad happens to you, you don't think "It's my fault." You do what you can to remedy the situation.

Tip: Psychologist and author Martin Seligman has studied personal power. He says that when good things happen to us, it's best to interpret them globally; when bad things happen to us, it's best to interpret them specifically. *Examples:* If you get an A in math, tell yourself "I'm a smart person," not "I'm just smart in math." If someone you're dating breaks up with you, tell yourself "He (or she) doesn't want to date me," not "Nobody likes me."

Know your rights.

Having and using your personal power means knowing and defending your rights. You have:

1. the right to think for yourself

2. the right to express your views and opinions

3. the right to make decisions about your life

4. the right to say no

5. the right to say yes

6. the right to act as you choose, as long as you don't hurt yourself or others

7. the right to have your needs taken seriously

8. the right to stand up to people who criticize you or put you down

9. the right to share your feelings of anger, frustration, confusion, and fear—as well as your feelings of love and joy

10. the right to respond to violations of your rights.

You also have other rights—civil rights, legal rights, and basic human rights (see Asset #27: Equality and Social Justice). But the rights listed here are the ones you may want to focus on most as you build your personal power.

Assets in Action

Bryan Drapp, 19, got fed up with the McDonald's in **Macedonia, Ohio,** *where he worked. So he walked out—and started the first successful strike against a U.S. McDonald's franchise. Drapp and a coworker, 20-year-old Jamal Nickens, were soon joined by 15 more McDonald's workers. Five days into the strike, the franchise owner agreed to most of their demands, including higher base pay, work schedules posted four days in advance, a week's paid vacation after a year on the job—and a requirement that managers attend workshops on people skills.*

Know your limits.

You *can* control the kind of person you are and how you live your life. You're responsible for your own behavior and your own feelings.

You *can't* control the choices other people make, how they behave, or what they feel. When a friend makes a good choice, you don't get to take the credit—even if you offered advice along the way. On the other hand, when a friend makes a poor choice, you don't have to take the blame.

For years, millions of people around the world have used the Serenity Prayer to remind them of their limits and their power. You might find it helpful, too.

God, grant me the serenity to accept the things I can't change, the courage to change the things I can, and the wisdom to know the difference.

What if you believe that other people control too many things in your life? Talk to your parents, teachers, and other adults who have power over you. See if they'll agree to let you make more decisions for yourself. Then, when you make a decision, follow through. This shows that you're responsible and mature—which usually leads to more control for you.

Build your skills.

Developmental Assets give you all kinds of personal power. The more assets you build, the more personal power you'll have. You'll also want to build stress-reduction and assertiveness skills. See pages 303–304 and 306–307.

WAYS TO BUILD YOUR PERSONAL POWER

1. Decide that you really *want* to have control over many things that happen to you. When there's something you want, you work to get it.

2. Make a commitment to develop and strengthen your personal power. Write down specific things you'll do. *Examples:* "I'll tell Sam I won't ride with him when he's been drinking." "I'll cut back on my work hours so I have more time for homework." Tell someone you trust about your commitment and your progress.

3. Learn the rules that affect you. Family rules, school rules, community rules, laws, the rules of your culture, heritage, traditions, and/or faith—find out what they are and follow them. Then you won't waste your personal power fighting things you can't control. *Exceptions:* You might work to change rules that are unjust or unfair.

4. Be accountable. Accept responsibility for your choices. Don't blame others for your actions and decisions.

5. Practice. New skills don't form on their own. Having and using personal power is something you can learn and practice.

6. Do activities that make you a stronger person—inside and out. Strengthen your body by exercising. Strengthen your mind by reading, practicing a musical instrument, or learning something new. Strengthen your spirit by practicing your faith.

CONTINUED ON NEXT PAGE...

7. Eliminate harmful habits. *Example:* If you spend several hours each week watching violent TV programs, make a conscious decision to spend your time in healthier, more productive ways. You might start by watching different programs, then gradually cut back on your TV time.

8. Start a support group. Tell a few close friends about your commitment to build your personal power. Ask if they'd like to join you. Talk together about your plans, problems, hopes, dreams, and experiences. Plan and do activities that strengthen your commitment.

Adapted from *What Do You Stand For? For Teens* by Barbara A. Lewis. Free Spirit Publishing Inc., 1998, pages 246–247. Used with permission.

Know how to handle stress.

Stress is a fact of life. Not all stress is bad; there are times when stress can make you more alert, productive, and creative. But too much stress can leave you feeling confused, exhausted, frustrated, helpless, anxious, overwhelmed, restless, trapped, sick, and depressed . . . and it can seriously cramp your personal power. You can't cure stress by worrying or wishing it away. But you *can* reduce the stress in your life.

7 WAYS TO LESSEN STRESS

1. Think back to other times when you've successfully coped with a difficult situation, person, or event. What did you say? What did you do? Recycle winning strategies.

2. Find a sounding board—someone who will listen and, if you want, offer honest, respectful, and trustworthy advice.

3. If you don't know how to relax, learn how. Try deep breathing exercises or meditation; do something you enjoy that makes you feel peaceful and calm. *Examples:* go for a walk; wander through a bookstore; sit on a bench in the park; call a friend on the phone. Spend part of each day slowing down.

4. Develop and maintain your sense of humor. Laughter is a proven stress reducer.

5. Stock up on stress reduction techniques. If one doesn't work for a particular situation, you can always try another.

6. Don't give up. Handling stress is a learned skill and an ongoing endeavor. Few of us are taught it in school; either we learn it on our own, or we find people who help us at various points in our lives.

CONTINUED ON NEXT PAGE...

7. Always remember that you don't have to go it alone. Even in your darkest, most stressful hour, there's someone or somewhere you can turn to for help. *Suggestions:* a supportive adult; a teen clinic; a crisis intervention center; a hotline; the public library; a stress management class; a close friend; a counselor.

Adapted from *The Gifted Kids' Survival Guide: A Teen Handbook* by Judy Galbraith, M.A., and Jim Delisle, Ph.D. Free Spirit Publishing Inc., 1996, pages 130–131. Used with permission.

FACT:

Tests stress teens the most!

When M&M/Mars surveyed teens ages 12–17 about what causes stress in their lives, here's what they said:

- taking SAT and ACT tests (59%)
- getting into college (54%)
- getting a job after high school or college (50%)
- school (40%).

How do teens cope with stress? According to the survey:

- 46% listen to music
- 23% go out with friends
- 22% exercise/work out
- 15% watch TV
- 9% party
- 8% play video games
- 5% go to a movie.

Source: *Minneapolis StarTribune,* May 12, 1998.

Build personal power within your family.

● Hold a family meeting to talk about each other's abilities and responsibilities. Get everyone involved in family decisions. See Asset #32: Planning and Decision Making.

● Learn how to prepare a balanced meal, pay bills, do laundry, etc.—skills you'll need once you're on your own. Take on some of the responsibilities around the house.

● Serve others as a family. People who believe they can make a difference in the world have a tremendous sense of personal power. See Asset #9: Service to Others.

● Help your younger brothers and sisters build personal power. Praise their abilities; encourage them to try new things; show you have confidence in them. When they have problems or difficulties, don't just rush in and rescue them. Instead, ask "What can you do about this?"

At School

● When you're given a choice—about which assignment to do, which project to work on, whether to write an essay or make a video—think it through. Don't just choose the easiest option.

● Join a club or organization that has power or influence in your school.

● Use your personal power to make your school a better place for everyone. Work for a more caring school climate (see Asset #6), a safer school (#10), and a school where boundaries are clear and respected (#12).

● When something at school seems unreasonable or unfair—a rule, boundary, policy, or procedure—work with your friends to brainstorm solutions and present them to your teacher or principal.

In Your Community

● Use your personal power to make your community a better place for everyone. Work for a more caring neighborhood (see Asset #4), a safer community (#10), and a neighborhood where boundaries are clear and respected (#13). Find or create a useful role for yourself (#8) and serve others (#9).

● Get involved with an organization that promotes an issue or addresses a problem you care about. See assets #18: Youth Programs, #26: Caring, and #27: Equality and Social Justice.

● Take community education classes that build your personal power. You might look for classes on assertiveness, time management, self-defense, problem solving, and relaxation techniques—or cooking, car maintenance, and bicycle repair. (Knowledge is power!)

● Speak out about issues that matter to you.

Assets in Action

Aja Henderson of **Baton Rouge, Louisiana,** *noticed a problem. A lot of her friends and the neighborhood children didn't have anyone to take them to the library. Many parents worked, and by the time they got home, the libraries were closed. Aja could have felt helpless; instead, at the age of 12, she opened her own library—in the den of her home. Today her library has more than 3,000 titles, and young children, teenagers, and adults all use it. The library doesn't have any set hours, and it's open seven days a week. "Sometimes people knock on our door early in the morning," Aja says, "or someone stops by pretty late at night. I never turn anyone away."*

In Your Faith Community

● Help plan activities for the youth program.

● Volunteer to serve on decision-making boards and committees.

● Encourage your faith community to offer many ways for youth to get involved—so they can choose what fits them.

With Your Friends

Practice assertiveness skills as a group—and don't hesitate to use them with people who violate your rights. The ASSERT Formula is a simple mnemonic that can help you frame assertive responses on the spot.*

A stands for **Attention.** Before you can address a problem you're having with another person, you have to get his or her attention. *Example:* "Sean, I need to talk to you about something. Is now a good time?"

S stands for **Soon, Simple, and Short.** Speak up as soon as you realize that your rights have been violated. Look the person in the eye and keep your comments brief and to the point. *Example:* "It's about something you said at softball practice today."

S stands for **Specific Behavior.** What has the person done to violate your rights? Focus on the behavior, not the person. Be as specific as you can. *Example:* "I didn't like it when you told the catcher to watch his head when it was my turn to bat."

E stands for **Effect on Me.** Share the feelings you experienced as a result of the person's behavior. *Example:* "I got embarrassed because I've been working hard on my swing lately. I think I'm making progress."

R stands for **Response.** Wait for a response from the other person. *Example:* "Sorry, dude."

T stands for **Terms.** Suggest a solution to the problem. *Example:* "You can give me a hard time in private, but not in front of the team, okay?" Your friend might agree ("Sure, fine") or not ("What's the big deal? Can't you take a joke?"). But at least you spoke your piece calmly, reasonably, and respectfully. That in itself feels better than keeping quiet.

---

* Adapted from *Fighting Invisible Tigers: A Stress Management Guide for Teens* by Earl Hipp. Minneapolis: Free Spirit Publishing, 1995, page 96. Used with permission.

Note: It's important to understand the difference between being assertive and being aggressive. Assertiveness is positive and affirming; aggressiveness is negative and demanding. Assertiveness bargains; aggressiveness bullies. Assertiveness invites the other person to have a dialogue with you; aggressiveness puts him or her on the defensive.

RESOURCES

For everyone:

Your Perfect Right: A Guide to Assertive Living by Robert E. Alberti and Michael L. Emmons (San Luis Obispo, CA: Impact Publishers, 1995). Step-by-step procedures, detailed examples, and exercises for building assertiveness and equal relationships.

For you:

Fighting Invisible Tigers: Stress Management for Teens by Earl Hipp (Minneapolis: Free Spirit Publishing, 2008). Proven, practical advice on coping with stress, being assertive, taking risks, making decisions, building relationships, and more.

Life Happens: A Teenager's Guide to Friends, Failure, Sexuality, Love, Rejection, Addiction, Peer Pressure, Families, Loss, Depression, Change, and Other Challenges of Living by Kathy McCoy, Ph.D., and Charles Wibbelsman, M.D. (New York: Perigee, 1996). The award-winning authors of *The New Teenage Body Book* explore common crises (depression, failure, stress) and suggest ways to get past problems and move on with life.

Stick Up for Yourself! Every Kid's Guide to Personal Power and Positive Self-Esteem by Gershen Kaufman, Ph.D., Lev Raphael, Ph.D., and Pamela Espeland (Minneapolis: Free Spirit Publishing, 1999). Strategies for building personal power, assertiveness skills, and self-esteem. A Teacher's Guide is available.

47% of the youth
we surveyed have this
asset in their lives.

SELF-ESTEEM

You feel good about yourself.

At Home

Know where self-esteem comes from.

We know what pulls us down . . . guilt, prejudice, rejection, neglect, disrespect, putdowns, ridicule, exploitation. But what pulls us up? According to psychologist, educator, and author Dr. Louise Hart, self-esteem comes from:

- love, respect, and acceptance
- being taken seriously
- being listened to
- having your needs met and taken seriously
- honoring uniqueness
- being healthy and fit
- having meaning and purpose in life
- a sense of humor, laughter, and play
- taking pride in your cultural heritage
- having choices and a sense of personal power
- feeling safe and secure
- doing good
- competence and achievement.*

---

* Many of these self-esteem builders are also Developmental Assets. Can you tell which ones?

Alex J. Packer—also a psychologist, educator, and author—has this to say about self-esteem:

Some adults believe that the way to build self-esteem is by looking in a mirror and repeating self-congratulatory mantras. They teach kids to tell themselves "I'm great at math, I'm lovable and good." This can, in fact, raise self-esteem—to the point at which many nasty, selfish kids who are flunking math start to feel good about themselves. But this is just a mind trick. The way to build genuine self-esteem is by doing esteemable things. Care, give, treat others with kindness and tolerance, be honest but gentle with yourself, do the best you can in the things that really matter. You'll build your self-esteem—and it will be genuine and deserved.

FACT:

Teens have high self-esteem!

According to a recent nationwide survey of 272,400 students in grades 6–12, most kids (93%) feel good about themselves. But look what happens when the results are broken down by gender and race:

- 58% of the boys feel really good about themselves . . . compared to 43% of the girls.

- 46% of the white teens feel really good about themselves . . . compared to 56% of the minority-group teens. More than 70% of all teens who responded to the survey say that their race or ethnicity has no impact on the way they feel about themselves. When it does make a difference, it's usually positive.

High self-esteem seems *less* related to looks than people might think. When the teens surveyed were asked "How satisfied are you with your looks?" only 31% said very, 63% said somewhat, and 6% said not at all.

Source: "USA Weekend's 11th Annual Teen Survey: Teens & Self-Image," reported in *USA Weekend,* May 1–3, 1998.

Watch your self-talk.

Self-talk—the messages we give ourselves—can profoundly affect our self-esteem. When you make a mistake, what do you tell yourself? "Everybody makes mistakes" or "I'm so stupid"? When you succeed at something, do you think "I did it!" or "I could have done better"?

Whenever you have a negative thought about yourself—when your self-talk makes you feel bad—change it to a positive thought. Do this immediately. You'll feel better and you'll form the habit of self-affirmation, which most successful people share.

Focus on the good side.

Sometimes we focus more on the negative side of our personality traits than on the positive side. Make a conscious effort to focus on the good side. You'll feel better about yourself—and you'll realize you have more positive than negative traits. *Examples:*

Instead of thinking . . .	*Try thinking . . .*
"I'm too emotional."	"I'm in touch with my feelings."
"I'm too shy."	"I'm reserved and thoughtful."
"I'm too pushy."	"I'm assertive, and I get things done."
"I'm too nosy."	"I'm curious and I love learning new things."
"I work too hard."	"I'm focused and goal-oriented."
"I'm too conservative."	"I live by my values and beliefs."
"I'm unconventional."	"I'm creative."
"I'm arrogant."	"I have high self-esteem."

Start a happiness savings account.

You can collect and store good feelings. Follow these suggestions from counselors Gershen Kaufman and Lev Raphael:*

1. Make a list of five things you feel good about that happened today. These can be big things (finishing a school project, making a new friend) or small things (the sun on your face, a favorite song).

2. Do this every day—weekdays and weekends, school days and holidays.

3. Keep your lists in a special notebook, folder, or journal. This is your happiness savings account.

4. Whenever you need a boost, dip into your savings account and read a list or two. Enjoy your good feelings all over again.

Tip: Suggest that your whole family try this. Even very young children (and jaded parents) can benefit from keeping happiness savings accounts.

Build self-esteem with your family.

● Ask your parents what makes them proud of you. What do they think are your best qualities? Your greatest achievements? Tell them what makes *you* proud of *them.* See assets #1: Family Support and #2: Positive Family Communication.

---

* Adapted from *Stick Up for Yourself! Every Kid's Guide to Personal Power and Positive Self-Esteem* by Gershen Kaufman, Ph.D., and Lev Raphael, Ph.D. Minneapolis: Free Spirit Publishing, 1990, pages 62–63. Used with permission.

● Find something good in every family member, whether it's a sense of humor, computer skills, singing voice, or wonderful smile. Tell them you love them and why. You might write specific things you like about each other on sticky notes and post them around the house—or hide them to be discovered later.

● Start a We Did It! family journal. At family meetings or dinners, have parents, teens, and younger kids name things they've accomplished or things they noticed other family members accomplish. Celebrate each other's successes.

● Talk with each other about self-esteem problems. What makes you feel sad or bad? Listen, support each other, and offer constructive criticism if it seems appropriate.

CARDINAL MISTAKES OF SELF-ESTEEM

by Sol Gordon, Ph.D.

1. Comparing yourself unfavorably to others. There will always be people who appear to be handsomer, prettier, richer, luckier, and better-educated than you. What's the point of comparing? We are all created equal. We are all created to serve in a special way.

2. Feeling you won't amount to much unless. . . . Choose your favorite ending to this sentence: a) someone falls for you, b) someone marries you, c) someone needs you, d) you earn a lot of money, e) your parents are satisfied with your achievements. In fact, you have to be someone to be attractive to someone else. You have to be self-accepting before you can please someone you care about. If you don't amount to anything before someone wants you, you won't amount to much afterwards, either.

3. Thinking you must please everyone. You must first please yourself . . . and there-after, only people you care about. Those who try to please everyone end up pleasing no one.

4. Setting unreasonable goals for yourself. Lower your standards to improve your performance. You can always advance beyond today—tomorrow is always another day.

5. Looking for THE meaning of life. Life is not a meaning, it is an opportunity. You can only find the meaning of life at the end of it. Life is made up of meaningful experiences—mainly of short duration, but repeatable.

6. Being bored. If you are bored, then it is boring to be with you. If you are bored, don't announce it. It is especially unattractive to bemoan how you don't like yourself, or that you have "nothing to do." If you have nothing to do, don't do it in company.

CONTINUED ON NEXT PAGE...

7. Deciding that your fate is determined by forces outside yourself. Mainly, *you* are in control of your life.

Sol Gordon, Ph.D., has been a professor of Child and Family Studies at Syracuse University and director of the University's Institute for Family Research and Education. He is the author of *When Living Hurts, The Teenage Survival Book*, and many more books for adults and young people. From *The Best of Free Spirit*. Free Spirit Publishing Inc., 1995, pages 47–48. Used with permission.

At School

● Make an effort to affirm the people you see at school each day—your teachers, administrators, staff members, other students. Affirmation can be as simple as a friendly smile or a few kind words. *Examples:* "I like your smile," "You're a great listener," "I admire your ability to do well in math," "You're always willing to help—I appreciate that."

● Don't judge others by their looks, the way they talk, where they live, their race, socioeconomic status, or any other reason. In fact, don't judge others, period. Be tolerant and accepting. See assets #33: Interpersonal Competence and #34: Cultural Competence.

● With your class or club, set rules for how people are expected to treat each other, emphasizing the positive. See assets #12: School Boundaries and #24: Bonding to School.

● Start a self-esteem club at your school. Or start a lunchtime or after-school discussion group where students can explore ways to build self-esteem. Ask a teacher or school counselor to sit in and offer guidance.

Assets in Action

In **Boone, Iowa,** *Susan Mowrer leads a theater group of junior and senior high school students who take prevention messages to schools and community groups. One of their shows, called "We're Not Buying It," made it clear that they weren't buying alcohol, tobacco, irresponsibility, or a negative view of themselves. "We talk about assets a lot," Mowrer says, "to give the kids a grasp of what self-esteem is about and where it comes from—and if it's not coming from the environment, how they can get it."*

In Your Community

● See if your community offers classes and workshops for young people on building self-esteem. Topics might include positive self-talk, learning from mistakes, being assertive, and more. If classes are available, sign up. If no classes are available, suggest that your community center offer some.

● Build positive, supportive relationship with other caring adults, or find a mentor. See Asset #3: Other Adult Relationships.

● Look for opportunities to do community service. Doing good for others is a great self-esteem builder. See Asset #9: Service to Others.

● Take time to pay attention to younger kids—while waiting in line at the movie theater, walking through the park, or hanging out in your neighborhood. Show by your attitude and behavior that you value them. See "55 Ways to Show Kids You Care" on page 66.

Assets in Action

In **Nashville, Tennessee,** retired juvenile probation officer Don McGehee started a school-wide program at two inner-city schools called "I Am Somebody." The program promotes self-esteem and builds character by focusing on the value of diverse abilities and trying to be the best one can be. All children have the opportunity to prove themselves in at least one of the nine components of the program: academics, altruism, art, athletics, attitude, character, creativeness, music, and perseverance. McGehee provides most of the funding for the program—about $1,000 for each school of 300 to 400 students.

In Your Faith Community

● Does your faith community offer workshops for parents on building self-esteem in children and teens? If not, offer to help start something.

● Visit your public library and local bookstores to find books about self-esteem for children, teens, and parents. Make a list of books that look interesting. Suggest that these books be added to the library in your place of worship.

● Work with your youth leader to plan a Self-Esteem Retreat for teens in your faith community.

With Your Friends

● Because negative peer pressure is so powerful, make a special effort to build each other up, not tear each other down. Tell your friends what you like and admire about them; ask them what they like and admire about you. Be a positive influence in each other's lives. See Asset #15: Positive Peer Influence.

● Collect a stack of teen magazines and zero in on the ads. Really *look* at them. Think about and talk about these questions together:

— Do the ads imply that most teens have high self-esteem or low self-esteem?
— Are the ads aimed at boys different from the ads aimed at girls? If so, in what ways are they different? What messages are they sending?
— Do the ads try to make teens feel good about themselves or bad about themselves? How can you tell?
— Do *you* feel better or worse about yourself after looking at the ads? Why?

FOR GIRLS ONLY: *Research has shown that girls' self-esteem drops significantly during early adolescence. Starting about age 11, strong, self-confident girls become insecure about their abilities, emotions, and decisions. Their appearance—and how boys perceive them—become all-important. They're afraid of giving the wrong answers in class; they stop competing and start deferring. If you're a girl or young woman with low self-esteem, get help. Ask a teacher or school counselor; check with your local Girl Scouts, YWCA, or Boys & Girls Club. Don't give up!*

Assets in Action

In 1993, the Ms. Foundation in **New York, New York** launched Take Our Daughters to Work Day to help girls stay strong and confident. The Foundation believed that a day at work— particularly a day watching women in the workplace—would help boost girls' aspirations. The program spread from New York to the nation. In 1997, 15.4 million people took part in the fifth annual TODTW day.

RESOURCES

For you:

The Girls' Guide to Life: How to Take Charge of the Issues That Affect You by Catherine Dee (Boston, MA: Little, Brown & Co., 1997). Go, girls! This supportive, informative, fun and savvy guide explains how to cultivate a healthy self-image and expand your horizons at school, at work, and at home.

Making Every Day Count: Daily Readings for Young People on Solving Problems, Setting Goals, and Feeling Good About Yourself by Pamela Espeland and Elizabeth Verdick (Minneapolis: Free Spirit Publishing, 1998) and *Making the Most of Today: Daily Readings for Young People on Self-Awareness, Creativity, and Self-Esteem* by Pamela Espeland and Rosemary Wallner (Minneapolis: Free Spirit Publishing, 1991). Each offers a year's worth of inspiration, affirmation, and respectful, practical advice.

For your parents:

Raising Your Child's Inner Self-Esteem: The Authoritative Guide from Infancy Through the Teen Years by Karen Owens (New York: Plenum Publishing, 1995). Explains what to expect from children at each developmental stage; covers topics including shyness, aggression, and children with special needs.

The Winning Family: Increasing Self-Esteem in Your Children and Yourself by Louise Hart, Ph.D. (Berkeley, CA: Celestial Arts, 1993). Simple, practical advice for parents—especially those without much time to read.

55% of the youth
we surveyed have this
asset in their lives.

SENSE OF PURPOSE

You believe that your life has a purpose.

At Home

Think about your life purpose.

Why was I born?   *Why am I here?*   *What's the point?*

These are all great questions . . . so why do we usually save them for times when we're frustrated, depressed, or angry at the world? We can also ask them when we're focused, motivated, and feeling good about ourselves. That's when we *know* we're here for a reason, whatever that reason might be.

Socrates once said "The unexamined life is not worth living." This asset challenges you to examine your life. No one is here by accident; every life has meaning. If you believe this, then you already have this asset. Keep strengthening it by the choices you make and the actions you take. *Tip:* People and purposes can change. Don't be locked into a goal or dream that no longer feels right to you.

If you're clueless about your purpose, find some quiet time and just think. Ask yourself questions like these:

- What matters to me?
- What gets me excited about each new day?
- What are my talents? Interests? Passions?
- What dreams do I have for the future?
- If I could do only one thing with my life, what would it be?

For inspiration, you might want to ponder these words by Joseph Campbell, a great teacher and storyteller:

You have a success in life, but then just think of it—what kind of life was it? What good was it that you've never done the thing you wanted to do in all your life? I always tell my students, go where your body and soul want to go. . . . Follow your bliss and don't be afraid, and doors will open where you didn't know they were going to be.

Assets in Action

Kelly Huegel of **Philadelphia, Pennsylvania,** *was 12 years old when she learned she had Crohn's disease, an incurable illness that affects the digestive system. Frightened and confused, she searched in vain for books that might help her understand and deal with her disease. When she was 23, she wrote her own book,* Young People and Chronic Illness. *It's full of practical advice and inspiring true stories. If you'd like to read Kelly's book, check your library.*

Like Kelly Huegel, 17-year-old Matthew Green of **Titusville, Florida,** *has Crohn's disease. Also like Kelly, he looked for information about Crohn's but found that it was all geared toward adults. When a flare-up kept him out of school for almost three months, he used his free time to start a Web site for teens with Crohn's. It's packed with facts, links, encouragement, advice, recipes, a chat room—even jokes. Thousands of people from all over the world have visited Matthew's site. If you'd like to see it, go to:* pages.prodigy.net/mattgreen

Talk with your parents.

● Talk about your life goals, priorities, and dreams. You might do this in casual conversation, over dinner, or during a family meeting. Ask your parents about their life purpose. (They may be surprised by the question; many people never take time to consider this seriously.)

● Talk about your family values. (See Asset #28: Integrity.) How is your purpose related to your values? Have your values helped to shape your purpose?

● Try this with your family: Have everyone list five things they're passionate about. (Young children can name things they like a lot or care about, and older siblings or parents can write them down.) Compare and discuss your lists. If two or more family members share a passion, maybe they can pursue it together.

Explore more ways to find your life purpose.

● Interview a family member, neighbor, or mentor who seems to have a strong sense of purpose. What advice can he or she give you?

● Write one sentence that describes the kind of person you want to be. Keep it in your wallet, daily planner, or backpack.

● Brainstorm a list of reasons to get up in the morning. Include simple pleasures (to feel the sun on your face, to see a friend) and more purposeful reasons (to learn something new, to work toward a goal).

● Boxing champ Sugar Ray Robinson once defined a dream as "something that you feel so strongly about that you see yourself accomplishing it." Visualize yourself doing something meaningful and important.

● Find inspiring quotations about purpose, meaning, and goals. Collect them in a notebook or journal.

● Learn how to set goals and make good choices. See Asset #32: Planning and Decision Making.

● Limit the hours you spend watching TV, playing video games, surfing the Net, or talking on the phone. Use that time to develop and pursue other interests. See assets #17: Creative Activities, #18: Youth Programs, and #25: Reading for Pleasure.

Don't let anyone or anything distract you from your purpose.

When someone says "you can't" or "you shouldn't," stay focused on your purpose. When society says "you must" or "you should," weigh those assumptions against your purpose and decide what's right for you. Chances are you'll grow up hearing that everyone should work a 9-to-5 job, get married, buy a house, have kids, etc. Be open to unique purposes. (Mother Teresa had nothing . . . and everything.)

PEOPLE WHO WOULDN'T LISTEN

Marian Anderson wanted to sing in Washington's Constitution Hall on Easter Sunday, 1939, but she was barred because she was black. So she gave her concert on the steps of the Lincoln Memorial and drew a crowd of 75,000.

Lucille Ball was a would-be actress when the head of a drama school advised her to "try another profession. *Any* other." She went on to become one of the most popular and beloved comedians of our time.

Walt Disney was fired by a newspaper editor because he had "no good ideas" and he "doodled too much."

CONTINUED ON NEXT PAGE...

Thomas Edison was told by his teachers that he was too stupid to learn anything. He read all the books in his local library and became the greatest inventor of all time, with more than 1,000 patents issued in his name.

Madeleine L'Engle's book, *A Wrinkle in Time,* was rejected by almost every major publisher before one accepted it—after warning that the book probably wouldn't sell. It won the Newbery Medal.

Theodor Geisel's first book, *And to Think That I Saw It on Mulberry Street,* was rejected by 23 publishers. You know Geisel by his pen name: Dr. Seuss.

John Horner's teachers thought he was lazy. He had trouble with every subject in school and flunked out of college. Today he's a world-famous paleontologist and winner of a MacArthur Foundation "Genius Award." Dr. Horner was the real-life model for the paleontologist in the movie *Jurassic Park.*

Dr. Robert Jarvick was rejected by 15 American medical schools. He later invented an artificial heart.

Michael Jordan was a gangly kid when he got beat out for North Carolina High School Player of the Year. His teachers told him to go into math, "where the money is."

Paul Orfalea was placed in a class for retarded students after he failed second grade due to dyslexia. He later founded a company called Kinko's, Inc. You probably have a Kinko's in your community.

Rosa Parks was told to move to the back of the bus because she was black. She refused, forcing the police to remove, arrest, and imprison her—and sparking the Montgomery bus boycott. She became known as the mother of the American civil rights movement.

Aung San Suu Kyi has spent her life working for democracy and human rights in her country of Myanmar (formerly Burma). From 1989–1995, the government placed her under house arrest, hoping that would shut her up. She won the Sakharov Prize for Freedom of Thought in 1990 and the Nobel Peace Prize in 1991.

At School

Study people with purpose.

Read biographies of notable people from the past and present. (You might start with the 12 People Who Wouldn't Listen above.) Learn what drove them and who influenced them. *Example:* George Washington Carver simply wanted "to be of the greatest good to the greatest number of my people."

Create a People with Purpose bulletin board. Post pictures, brief biographies, and quotes. Each week, feature a different Person with Purpose who's part of your school—a student, teacher, administrator, staff person, or volunteer.

FACT:

Teens have many life goals!

When 1,000 students from ages 13–17 were asked to name the one thing they want most out of life, here's what they said:

What?	According to how many teens?
Happiness	27.7%
Long/enjoyable life	15.9%
Marriage/family	9.3%
Financial success	7.8%
Career success	7.6%
Religious satisfaction	7.5%
Love	6.5%
Personal success	5.7%
Personal contribution to society	2.2%
Friends	1.9%
Health	1.7%
Education	1.6%

Source: *The Mood of American Youth* (Alexandria, VA: Horatio Alger Association of Distinguished Americans and the National Association of Secondary School Principals, 1996).

Find purpose in what you're learning in school.

This might be hard at first—especially in classes that seem utterly meaningless or boring—but give it a try. *Examples:* Why read literature? Because it gives you a better understanding of yourself and other people. Why learn about music or art? See Asset #17: Creative Activities for a whole list of reasons.

Draw connections between what you're learning in school and what's happening in the world. Good teachers can help you do this.

Advocate for service learning in your school. See Asset #9: Service to Others. People who make a difference in the world know that their lives have purpose.

In Your Community

● Choose something you really like to do. Find an organization or place where you can do it. See Asset #18: Youth Programs.

● Don't wait for a purpose to come to you. Do something positive for another person or many people. See assets #9: Service to Others, #26: Caring, and #27: Equality and Social Justice.

● Interview notable people in your community—leaders, volunteers, celebrities, and others. Ask them about their life purpose(s). Write stories about them for your school or community newspaper.

● Be active in your community. See assets #4: Caring Neighborhood, #7: Community Values Youth, and #8: Youth as Resources.

Assets in Action

High school senior Michael Harris of **Arapaho, Oklahoma,** *has spent half his life working to preserve natural resources and educate others about what he calls environmental "resuscitation." When he was nine years old, he started collecting aluminum and plastic for recycling; later he began recycling Christmas trees, telephone books, clothing, and more. He's given educational programs to students and community groups, and promoted conservation awareness through newspaper articles, public service announcements, a calendar, and a newsletter.*

Jenny Hungerford, a student at Parkview High School in **Orfordville, Wisconsin,** *wasted nearly three years of her life hooked on drugs and running away from home. When she finally recovered, she decided to help others resist the temptation of drugs. Working with her mother, she scripted a reenactment called "Jenny—A Day in the Life of a Teenage Addict," which she and her mom have presented to schools, youth conferences, treatment facilities, and community groups.*

Note: *Michael and Jenny have more in common besides a sense of purpose. They were both National Honorees in the 1998 Prudential Spirit of Community Awards program. To learn more about this program, contact The Prudential Spirit of Community Initiative; see page 84.*

In Your Faith Community

Tap the resources of your faith.

For many people of faith, their religious convictions are key to giving them a sense of meaning and purpose in life. If religious convictions are important to you, seek guidance and support from spiritual leaders in finding a sense of purpose that ties your unique gifts and abilities to the values and priorities of your faith. Explore purpose not only in terms of career, but also family, friendships, volunteering, how you use money, and other issues.

Encourage an ongoing focus on purpose.

Make sure that your faith community regularly explores issues of meaning and purpose. Ideas to try:

● Talk about purpose within your youth group. Ask your youth director what gives meaning to his or her life. Explore what your faith tradition says about meaning and purpose.

● As you work with younger kids in your faith community, invite them to tell you about their hopes, dreams, and goals.

● Ask your spiritual leader to give sermons and homilies about finding meaning and purpose in life.

With Your Friends

As you're sitting around, driving around, or hanging out with each other, talking (as friends do) about anything and everything, consider these questions:

Why was I born?	*Why am I here?*	*What's the point?*

And, if you feel like getting more specific, try:

What am I good at?	*Who needs me?*	*What worries me?*
What makes me happy?	*What would I like to make better?*	*What are my dreams?*

Close friends are great sounding boards for the wildest, craziest ideas—some of which might contain clues to your purpose.

IMPORTANT: *If you really, truly can't imagine why you're here—if your life doesn't seem to have meaning or purpose—talk with an adult you trust and respect. Explain how you feel and ask for support and guidance in finding your purpose. You're here for a reason!*

RESOURCES

For everyone:

Man's Search for Meaning by Viktor Frankl (New York: Washington Square Press, 1998). Internationally renowned psychiatrist Viktor Frankl endured years of unspeakable horror in Nazi death camps. During, and partly because of, his suffering, he developed a revolutionary approach to psychotherapy known as logotherapy. At the core of his theory is the belief that humankind's primary motivational force is its search for meaning. Give this thought-provoking book a try.

The Web of Life: Weaving the Values That Sustain Us by Richard Louv (Berkeley, CA: Conari Press, 1996). A collection of gentle reflections on family, friendship, neighborhood, community, and other topics, Louv's book invites us to see ourselves as strands in a web, connecting and supporting each other and the world.

Asset #40

70% of the youth
we surveyed have this
asset in their lives.

POSITIVE VIEW OF PERSONAL FUTURE

You're optimistic about your future.

At Home

Picture a positive future for yourself.

What do you see when you picture your future? Are you happy or sad? In a job you enjoy or bored out of your gourd? Do you have healthy, loving relationships, or are you lonely? Studies have shown that when people envision themselves reaching their goals, they're more likely to make it happen. That's why it's important for you to picture a positive future for yourself. Even if you're not sure how to achieve your dreams, try to see them in your mind.

Start planning your future today.

Try these ideas or come up with your own:

● Talk to your parents about your dreams for after high school and beyond. Ask for their help in preparing to make those dreams come true. Are you planning to continue your education after high school? Do you want to go to college, trade school, or technical school? Will you have the credits, grades, and test scores you need? Will you be able to afford it? Ask other adults for guidance and advice—a school counselor, a mentor, alumni of colleges or schools you'd like to consider. *Tip:* If you don't plan to continue your education right after high school, there are plenty of other choices available—internships, apprenticeships, volunteer opportunities, the military.

● Write a letter to yourself about what your life will be like 5, 10, 15, or 20 years from now. Or write a story about yourself at age 20 or 30.

● Keep a journal about your hopes and plans for the future.

● Read biographies and autobiographies of interesting people to get new ideas about how you might live your life.

● Practice setting and reaching goals. This builds optimism, enthusiasm, and self-confidence. See Asset #32: Planning and Decision Making.

● Keep building and strengthening assets. Remember that the more you have, the better. Decide that you're going to have them all. Why not?

● Learn how to manage your money. According to a recent national survey, 75 percent of college freshmen are concerned about their future financial security, compared with 44 percent in 1970. You can start a savings and investment program now. If you don't know how, ask your parents, a teacher, a mentor, or someone else who knows about managing money—perhaps a neighbor, a friend of your parents, or a helpful person at your bank. Some money management firms have special programs for young investors.

Have a positive attitude.

Viktor Frankl could easily have lost all hope. During World War II, he was held in the Nazi concentration camp at Auschwitz for three years. His father, mother, brother, and wife all died in the camps. Yet Frankl stayed optimistic about his future. In *Man's Search for Meaning,* he wrote: "Everything can be taken from a man but one thing: the last of human freedoms—to choose one's own attitude in any given set of circumstances." If Frankl believed he had this choice—despite being imprisoned, tortured, and degraded, his life turned upside down and his loved ones dead—what about you?

12 WAYS TO BE MORE POSITIVE

1. You can choose to be optimistic. A pessimist sees a glass of water as half empty; an optimist sees it as half full. Who has a more positive attitude? Who's likely to be happier, more confident and sure?

CONTINUED ON NEXT PAGE...

2. You can choose to accept things as they are. This doesn't mean that you give up and back down when things don't go your way. It means that you don't bang your head against a brick wall. Instead, you get on with your life.

3. You can choose to be resilient. Trees that bend with the wind survive even the worst storms. Like a tree, you can bend and sway as life batters you—then bounce back again, supported by your strong, deep roots. When you're resilient, you can survive almost anything—being hurt, frustrated, or let down, losing friends, making mistakes, and much more.

4. You can choose to be cheerful. Start by refusing to say gloomy things. Bite your tongue. Count to 10. Pull up the corners of your mouth. When you send out positive words, thoughts, and feelings, positive people (and things) are attracted to you.

5. You can choose to be enthusiastic. Greet each new day with excitement. Approach tasks and chores with zest. Enthusiasm is catching; the more upbeat you are, the more people around you will feel and act the same.

6. You can choose to be more alert. When you're alert, you're better prepared to confront or avoid problems. You can also be alert to positive experiences and act on them.

7. You can choose to have a sense of humor. If you laugh a lot, you'll be healthier. Laughter releases chemicals in your body that stimulate you and can help you grow. When you do something silly, don't miss the opportunity to laugh at yourself.

8. You can choose to be a good sport. This attitude can win you friends even if you don't win the game or competition. When you lose, do it gracefully. Smile, shake hands with the winner, and don't blame other people or circumstances for your loss. When you win, don't brag or gloat.

9. You can choose to be humble. People who toot their own horns seldom attract an audience. If you're genuinely interested in others, they'll see your good qualities even if you don't advertise them.

10. You can choose to be grateful. You probably have a lot to be grateful for. Gratitude puts a smile on your face. It makes you feel good about your life—and other people feel good about being around you.

11. You can choose to have faith. For some people, this means believing in God or another Higher Being/Higher Power. Others put their faith in their country, other people, or themselves. Having faith means believing that things will work out for you—and that you can work things out for yourself.

12. You can choose to have hope. Without hope, life has no meaning or point. We expect nothing, plan nothing, and don't set goals for ourselves (why bother?). Hope may be your most important positive attitude—the basis for all the others. What do you hope for? What are your ambitions? Your purpose in life? If you're willing to consider these questions, you're already a hopeful person.

Adapted from *What Do You Stand For? For Teens* by Barbara A. Lewis. Free Spirit Publishing Inc., 1998, pages 15–16. Used with permission.

Take reasonable risks.

A man named Frederick Wilcox once said "You can't steal second base and still keep your foot on first." To get where you want to go, you'll need to take risks. Not stupid, reckless, impetuous risks, but planned, thought-out, *reasonable* risks—ones where the chance of something good happening is greater than the chance of something bad happening. When you're considering taking a risk, ask yourself these questions before you act:

• What are the risks involved?
• What have I got to gain?
• What have I got to lose?
• Do the things I might gain justify the things I might lose? Do the positives outweigh the negatives?
• What are my chances of succeeding?

Risking and succeeding builds optimism and confidence. Risking and failing builds resilience; you learn to deal with frustration and failure. Either way, you win!

What if you're afraid to take risks? You may be a perfectionist or someone who fears making mistakes. See Asset #16: High Expectations.

Watch for signs of depression.

Read each of the following statements and decide if it's true for you.*

	TRUE	NOT TRUE
1. I often feel sad and anxious.	❏	❏
2. I feel worthless and/or guilty.	❏	❏
3. I'm easily irritated.	❏	❏
4. My appetite has changed drastically.	❏	❏
5. I don't enjoy things I used to like to do.	❏	❏
6. I have little or no energy.	❏	❏
7. I sleep too little or too much.	❏	❏
8. I have trouble concentrating/making decisions.	❏	❏
9. I have violent outbursts/trouble with self-control.	❏	❏
10. Some people think I'm loud and obnoxious.	❏	❏
11. I skip school or have dropped school activities.	❏	❏

CONTINUED ON NEXT PAGE...

* Adapted from *When Nothing Matters Anymore: A Survival Guide for Depressed Teens* by Bev Cobain, R.N.,C. Minneapolis: Free Spirit Publishing, 1998, page 15. Used with permission.

	TRUE	NOT TRUE
12. I often have headaches or other aches.	❏	❏
13. I use alcohol or other drugs to help myself feel better.	❏	❏
14. I feel hopeless about the future.	❏	❏
15. I feel helpless to change my situation.	❏	❏
16. I think about death, suicide, or harming myself.	❏	❏

SCORING: If four or more of these statements are true for you and you've felt this way almost continuously for two or more weeks, you might be depressed. Talk with a trusted adult ASAP. If #16 is true for you, please talk to someone *immediately*. Confide in an adult or call a suicide hotline. Check your Yellow Pages or call the Covenant House Nineline at 1-800-999-9999. Someone there will listen to you.

FACT:

Depression is real—and treatable!

Some 17.6 million American adults—10 percent of the population—suffer from a depressive illness. It's estimated that anywhere between 112,000 and 2.3 million children and teens in the U.S. are depressed.

Depression is not the same as a passing blue mood. It's not a sign of personal weakness or a condition you can will or wish away. People with a depressive illness can't just pull themselves together and get better. Depression affects your body, mood, and thoughts, and it can seriously cramp your present and future.

Untreated depression is the #1 cause of suicide—and suicide rates are rising for kids and teens. In a nationwide study of 16,000 high school students, 1 in 12 said he or she had attempted suicide in the previous year.

The good news is: *Most people with depression can be helped.* If you think you might be depressed, talk to your parents. Tell them how you feel and that you need to see a doctor.

Sources: National Institute of Mental Health; American Academy of Child & Adolescent Psychiatry; Centers for Disease Control and Prevention; Suicide Awareness Voices of Education (SAVE); "Suicide's Shadow," *Time,* July 22, 1996, pages 40–43.

At School

● Make a personal commitment to learning; build assets #21–25. Corny as it sounds, education really *is* the key to your future. Do your part to create a caring, safe school with clear rules and consequences for everyone's behavior. See assets #5: Caring School Climate, #10: Safety, and #12: School Boundaries.

● Get to know your school counselor. He or she can help you choose courses that will benefit you the most—either in preparing for college or, if you plan to work right out of high school, finding a job that's right for you. (If you're working now, limit your hours. See Asset #20: Time at Home for reasons why.)

● Get to know the people in the college and career planning center. They can give you the scoop on colleges, scholarships, and training programs. If your school doesn't have a planning center, offer to help start one. You can also go online to learn about, virtually visit, and apply to colleges and other schools. There are *many* resources on the Web. Here are four good ones to try:

CollegeNet
www.collegenet.com

Go College
www.gocollege.com

Peterson's Education & Career Center
www.petersons.com

The Princeton Review
www.princetonreview.com

● If your school offers Junior Achievement classes, sign up. (If it doesn't, find out why—and lobby to bring this respected program into your school.) JA classes are taught by volunteers from the business community who work to improve students' economic literacy, prepare them for careers, and teach them the importance of success in business. Currently JA reaches more than 2.6 million U.S. students in grades K–12 each year. For more information, contact:

Junior Achievement Inc.
One Education Way
Colorado Springs, CO 80906
(719) 540-8000
www.ja.org

FACT:

Employers think teens aren't prepared for the workforce!

According to a nationwide survey of 300 businesses and 1,000 high school seniors, most seniors feel they're ready to join the workforce. But most employers don't agree. Employers find that:

• 60% of high school seniors don't know much about how business works.
• 50% can't communicate very well in writing.
• 35% aren't very punctual or dependable.
• 30% don't understand the importance of getting work done on time.
• 27% don't have good basic math skills.
• 27% barely get by when communicating verbally.
• 24% can barely read a training manual, if at all.
• 21% don't work well with people of varying backgrounds.
• 21% have only minimal computer skills.

Source: Roper Starch Worldwide survey for Junior Achievement, Amway Corporation, and Newsweek, Inc.

In Your Community

• Talk to adults you admire. Ask them about their teenage years and how they got where they are today.

• Find positive role models whose backgrounds are similar to yours. This is especially important if you come from a less than ideal family situation. It will give you hope for your own future. See assets #3: Other Adult Relationships and #14: Adult Role Models.

• Volunteer. Serve. Make a difference. When the 104 national honorees in the 1996 Prudential Spirit of Community Awards program—all outstanding volunteers—were asked "Do you feel optimistic or hopeful about the future?" 83 percent said yes. (Hmmm . . . maybe there's a connection.) See assets #9: Service to Others, #26: Caring, and #27: Equality and Social Justice.

• Look for opportunities to play a useful role in your community. You might get clues about your future direction—and you'll make great contacts among adult leaders in your community. These are people you can turn to later for advice, employment opportunities—and college recommendations. See Asset #8: Youth as Resources.

• Learn what your community offers to help teens prepare for the future. Are there programs that match teens with adults for mentorship and guidance? Programs that teach job skills? You might gather information and create a directory. Get a grant to publish it, or post it on a community Web site.

• If you must work during the school year, try to find a job in an organization or business that means something to you. Is this somewhere you might want to work full-time as an adult?

• Talk to younger kids about positive things they can do and be in the future. Help them to feel optimistic and hopeful.

Assets in Action

According to Dedric Doolin, director of the Area Substance Abuse Council (ASAC) in **Cedar Rapids, Iowa,** *African-American kids who "have only heard negatives about being African American" may find it hard to develop a positive view of the future. So ASAC runs a mentorship project with an ethnocultural bent. African American Mentors Reaching Out works with black volunteer mentors who are trained to help youth gain a new perspective of their potential. "If you're an African-American youth pulled up to a stoplight, think about how your outlook changes if you know that a black man—Garret Morgan—invented it," Doolin says. "Knowing about the contributions of African Americans can help kids know where they've come from, who they are, and what's possible for them.*

"At Drew University in **Madison, New Jersey,** 130 college students mentor more than 110 at-risk children and teens who are bussed to the university once a week. The kids started out with a feeling of hopelessness; the mentors have given them hope that they can make a better life for themselves. Many of the kids have expressed an interest in someday going to college.

In Your Faith Community

● Invite other youth who have graduated to come back and talk to your group. Find out what they're doing and how they planned for the future.

● Within your youth group, talk about the future—with emphasis on the bright side. This might be a good topic for a youth retreat.

● Get to know the adult leaders in your faith community. Seek their advice and encouragement as you plan for your future.

With Your Friends

Talk with your friends about the future. You might start by asking each other questions like these:

• What do you want to do with your life? What's your dream job or career?

• How much money do you want to earn?

• What kind of car do you want to drive?

• Where do you want to live?

• How will you get where you want to go?

• Will you need to go to college? Technical school? Graduate school?

• Do you think you'll get married? Have children?

• Do you see yourself doing any kind of volunteer work? If so, what kind?

• What are the biggest challenges you're facing as you plan for your future? The greatest opportunities?

• What's the one thing that worries you the most about your future?

• What's the one thing you look forward to the most?

RESOURCES

For everyone:

Learned Optimism by Martin E.P. Seligman, Ph.D. (New York: Pocket Books, 1992). How to choose optimism and gain the freedom to build a life of real rewards and lasting fulfillment.

Mental Help Net
www.mentalhelp.net
Substance Abuse and Mental Health Services Administration
www.samhsa.gov
Two big collections of mental health information.

For you:

Get a Financial Life: Personal Finance in Your Twenties and Thirties by Beth Kobliner (St. Louis, MO: Fireside, 1996). This survival guide for the financially inclined (or challenged) teaches you how to manage your money with the smallest possible investment of time and effort. And you don't have to wait until your 20s to read it.

Real Kids Taking the Right Risks: Plus How You Can, Too! by Arlene Erlbach (Minneapolis: Free Spirit Publishing, 1998). In a time when risktaking is usually associated with dangerous behavior (drugs, gangs, daredevil stunts), this book points out the benefits of taking a chance and facing the possibility of rejection or failure.

When Nothing Matters Anymore: A Survival Guide for Depressed Teens by Bev Cobain, R.N., C. (Minneapolis: Free Spirit Publishing, 1998). Defines and explains depression, describes the symptoms, emphasizes that depression is treatable, and talks about treatment options in clear, accessible language.

My Future
www.myfuture.com
Information on career options, financial aid, scholarships, building a résumé, managing your money, and more.

For your parents and teachers:

"Help Me, I'm Sad": Recognizing, Treating, and Preventing Childhood and Adolescent Depression by David G. Fassler, M.D., and Lynn S. Dumas (New York: Viking Press, 1997). Explains with wisdom and empathy how parents can play a vital role in helping a child overcome and often prevent depression. Includes chapters on suicide, choosing a therapist, and getting treatment.

TOOLS
AND
RESOURCES

WHAT'S YOUR STORY?

We want to hear from you! Photocopy this page and use it to tell us your Assets in Action stories—ways you've built assets for yourself or others; ways your parents, teachers, and community are building assets; and other proof that assets are making a positive difference in people's lives. Share your asset-building ideas; let us know what has worked (or is working) for you. Your stories and ideas might appear in a future book, so be sure to let us know where we can contact you. If you run out of space on this page, write on the back or attach more pages.

Your Assets in Action stories:

Your asset-building ideas:

Contact information: **Name:** _____

Address: _____
Street

_____
City   State   ZIP

_____
Daytime phone   Email address

Send this form to: **What Teens Need**
Free Spirit Publishing Inc.   You can also share your stories and ideas by
217 Fifth Avenue North, Suite 200   email (help4kids@freespirit.com) or through
Minneapolis, MN 55401-1299   our Web site *(www.freespirit.com)*.

40 DEVELOPMENTAL ASSETS

These building blocks of healthy development help young people grow up healthy, caring, and responsible.

Support

1. **Family support**—Family life provides high levels of love and support.
2. **Positive family communication**—Young person and her or his parent(s) communicate positively, and young person is willing to seek advice and counsel from parent(s).
3. **Other adult relationships**—Young person receives support from three or more nonparent adults.
4. **Caring neighborhood**—Young person experiences caring neighbors.
5. **Caring school climate**—School provides a caring, encouraging environment.
6. **Parent involvement in schooling**—Parent(s) are actively involved in helping young person succeed in school.

Empowerment

7. **Community values youth**—Young person perceives that adults in the community value youth.
8. **Youth as resources**—Young people are given useful roles in the community.
9. **Service to others**—Young person serves in the community one hour or more per week.
10. **Safety**—Young person feels safe at home, school, and in the neighborhood.

Boundaries and Expectations

11. **Family boundaries**—Family has clear rules and consequences and monitors the young person's whereabouts.
12. **School boundaries**—School provides clear rules and consequences.
13. **Neighborhood boundaries**—Neighbors take responsibility for monitoring young people's behavior.
14. **Adult role models**—Parent(s) and other adults model positive, responsible behavior.
15. **Positive peer influence**—Young person's best friends model responsible behavior.
16. **High expectations**—Both parent(s) and teachers encourage the young person to do well.

Constructive Use of Time

17. **Creative activities**—Young person spends three or more hours per week in lessons or practice in music, theater, or other arts.
18. **Youth programs**—Young person spends three or more hours per week in sports, clubs, or organizations at school and/or in the community.
19. **Religious community**—Young person spends one or more hours per week in activities in a religious institution.
20. **Time at home**—Young person is out with friends "with nothing special to do" two or fewer nights per week.

CONTINUED ON NEXT PAGE...

Commitment to Learning

21. **Achievement motivation**—Young person is motivated to do well in school.

22. **School engagement**—Young person is actively engaged in learning.

23. **Homework**—Young person reports doing at least one hour of homework every school day.

24. **Bonding to school**—Young person cares about his or her school.

25. **Reading for pleasure**—Young person reads for pleasure three or more hours per week.

Positive Values

26. **Caring**—Young person places high value on helping other people.

27. **Equality and social justice**—Young person places high value on promoting equality and reducing hunger and poverty.

28. **Integrity**—Young person acts on convictions and stands up for his or her beliefs.

29. **Honesty**—Young person "tells the truth even when it is not easy."

30. **Responsibility**—Young person accepts and takes personal responsibility.

31. **Restraint**—Young person believes it is important not to be sexually active or to use alcohol or other drugs.

Social Competencies

32. **Planning and decision making**—Young person knows how to plan ahead and make choices.

33. **Interpersonal competence**—Young person has empathy, sensitivity, and friendship skills.

34. **Cultural competence**—Young person has knowledge of and comfort with people of different cultural/racial/ethnic backgrounds.

35. **Resistance skills**—Young person can resist negative peer pressure and dangerous situations.

36. **Peaceful conflict resolution**—Young person seeks to resolve conflict nonviolently.

Positive Identity

37. **Personal power**—Young person feels he or she has control over "things that happen to me."

38. **Self-esteem**—Young person reports having a high self-esteem.

39. **Sense of purpose**—Young person reports that "my life has a purpose."

40. **Positive view of personal future**—Young person is optimistic about her or his personal future.

ASSET-BUILDING IDEAS
FOR ADULTS

- Learn the names of the children and teenagers who live near you. Whenever you see them, look at them and greet them by name.

- Take time to play or talk with young people who live near you or work with you.

- Pay attention to young people instead of ignoring them.

- Listen to children and teenagers.

- Build at least one sustained, caring relationship with a child or adolescent, either informally or through a mentoring program.

- Encourage friends and neighbors to get to know the young people who live around them and to make young people a priority.

- Expect young people to behave responsibly. When they don't, enforce boundaries appropriately.

- Support initiatives designed to expand opportunities for young people to participate in teams, clubs, and organizations.

- Never allow the quality of schools or youth programs to suffer because of a lack of financial resources.

- Thank people who work with children and youth (teachers, youth group leaders, social service providers, clergy, etc.).

- Volunteer to lead or support a youth program in your neighborhood, a community center, a youth organization, or a faith community.

- Volunteer in a school as a tutor, club leader, reader to young students, or other helping roles.

- Model chemical restraint. Support efforts to reduce or eliminate kids' access to alcohol and tobacco.

- Proudly play the role of elder in your community, passing on the wisdom you have learned from others.

- Look at the list of 40 assets at least once a week and commit to at least one act of asset building every day.

- Affirm asset-building gestures you see other people make.

ASSET-BUILDING IDEAS
FOR FAMILIES

- Develop a family mission statement that focuses on building assets. Use it as a guide for family decisions and priorities.

- Post the list of 40 assets on your refrigerator door. Each day, purposefully nurture at least one asset.

- Model and talk about the values and priorities you wish to pass on to your children.

- Take time to nurture your own assets by spending time with supportive people, using your time constructively, and reflecting on your own values and commitments.

- Regularly do things with your children, including projects around the house, recreational activities, and service projects.

- Talk to your children about assets. Ask them for suggestions on ways to strengthen assets.

- Actively seek support from your extended family, from neighbors, from a faith community, and from others in your network of friends.

- Eat at least one meal together every day.

- Limit television watching.

- Read to or with your children.

- Be active in your child's education through school activities, monitoring homework, and conversations about school and learning.

- Provide a positive learning environment in your home.

- Negotiate appropriate boundaries and consequences for everyone in your family. Affirm when boundaries are followed, and enforce agreed-to consequences when they are broken.

- Model the assets, including reading for pleasure, positive values, good decision making, and clear boundaries about responsible alcohol use.

- Articulate your values.

- Encourage active involvement in organizations, teams, and clubs at school, in the community, or in a faith community. Keep a balance so activities don't overwhelm your ability to meet other needs.

- Limit the amount of time your children spend at home alone.

- Monitor where your children are, even when they are teenagers.

- Serve others in the community together with your children.

- Be a friend and asset builder for the friends of your children; welcome them into your home.

ASSET-BUILDING IDEAS FOR SCHOOLS AND YOUTH ORGANIZATIONS

Schools:

- Make it a priority to provide caring environments for all students.
- Train support staff, teachers, paraprofessionals, administrators, and other school staff in their role in asset building.
- Provide additional opportunities to nurture values considered important by your community.
- Expand, diversify, and strengthen cocurricular activities for all youth.
- Develop mentoring relationships between teenagers and children.
- Reward asset-building activities.
- Provide opportunities for staff to share best practices for providing support, establishing boundaries, nurturing values, and teaching social skills and competencies.
- Expand efforts to promote chemical and sexual health.
- Integrate service learning, values development, relationship building, the development of social competencies, and other asset-building strategies into the curriculum.
- Use schools' connections to parents to increase parental involvement and to educate parents in asset building.
- Provide opportunities for adults to volunteer.

Youth organizations:

- Involve youth in leadership and program planning.
- Provide a range of structured activities for youth with diverse interests and needs.
- Provide opportunities where young people feel supported and safe.
- Develop expectations, boundaries, and consequences with youth; enforce appropriate consequences when boundaries are not respected.
- Train volunteers, leaders, and coaches in asset building and in young people's developmental needs.
- Sponsor celebrations of children and families.
- Focus on asset building in programming, including building social competencies, engaging youth in service, and strengthening personal identity.
- Support young people's educational development through tutoring, computer skills, literacy programs, and other forms of academic enrichment.
- Coordinate activities and priorities with other youth-serving organizations.
- Advocate for young people in the community.
- Maintain programming for youth of all ages.

ASSET-BUILDING IDEAS FOR FAITH COMMUNITIES AND NEIGHBORHOOD GROUPS

Faith communities:

- Intentionally foster intergenerational relationships by providing activities for all ages within the faith community.
- Listen to what youth say they want.
- Regularly offer parent education as part of the faith community's educational programs.
- Focus attention on values development.
- Make community service a central component of youth programming.
- Network with other faith communities and institutions in the area for mutual learning, support, and coordination.
- Maintain year-round connections with youth. Don't lose contact over the summer.
- Involve youth in caring for and teaching younger children.
- Emphasize maintaining strong programs for youth throughout middle and high school.
- Sponsor celebrations of children and families.
- Provide many opportunities for youth to be leaders in and contributors to the faith community.

Neighborhood groups:

- Create neighborhood service projects linking adults and children.
- Make asset building a criterion for setting priorities for action in the neighborhood.
- Sponsor creative activities and events that help people get to know their neighbors.
- Coordinate residents to provide safe places where young people can go after school if they would be home alone or if they feel unsafe.
- Organize informal activities (such as pick-up basketball) for young people in the neighborhood.
- Use neighborhood meetings and other settings to educate people about their responsibility and power for asset building.
- Work with children and teenagers to create a neighborhood garden, playground, or park.
- Mobilize to promote a safe and drug-free neighborhood.

ASSET-BUILDING IDEAS FOR BUSINESSES AND GOVERNMENT

Businesses:

- Develop family-friendly policies that allow parents to be active in their children's lives.
- Provide opportunities for employees to build relationships with youth through mentoring and other volunteer programs, flexible scheduling, and internships for youth.
- Be intentional about nurturing assets in the lives of teenagers employed by the company.
- Become partners in and advocates for initiatives designed to create healthy communities for children and youth.
- Provide resources (donations, in-kind contributions, etc.) to youth development programs and to community-wide efforts on behalf of youth.

Government:

- Through policy, training, and resource allocation, make asset development a top priority in the city.
- Become a champion for asset building throughout the city. Convene both public and private stakeholders to begin efforts to coordinate a neighborhood or city-wide vision for asset building.
- Initiate community-wide efforts to name shared values and boundaries.
- Partner with other organizations in creating child-friendly public places and safe places for teenagers to gather.
- Build asset-building approaches into law enforcement and juvenile justice.
- Help to coordinate and publicize after-school, weekend, and summer opportunities for youth in the city.
- Strengthen or develop ordinances that reduce or eliminate youth access to alcohol and tobacco.
- Develop ordinances to place day care centers, schools, and after-school programs in places where senior citizens live and spend time.
- Build the capacity of community-based organizations to serve children and families.
- Support and expand neighborhood-building initiatives.

BIBLIOGRAPHY

Articles

Andersen, Ross E., Ph.D., and others, "Relationship of Physical Activity and Television Watching with Body Weight and Level of Fatness Among Children: Results From the Third National Health and Nutrition Examination Survey," *Journal of the American Medical Association,* 279 (1998); Abstracts, March 25, 1998.

"Asset-Building: A City Mobilizes Around Kids," *The Christian Science Monitor,* November 4, 1996.

Birmaher, Boris, and others, "Childhood and Adolescent Depression: A Review of the Past 10 Years, Part I," *Journal of the American Academy of Child and Adolescent Psychiatry* 35, November, 1996.

"The Day That Makes a Difference," *USA Weekend,* April 17–19, 1998.

"Healthy Youth, Healthy Cities," *Minnesota Cities,* 82:8, August, 1997.

"Homework Doesn't Help," *Newsweek,* March 30, 1998.

"Invincible Kids," *U.S. News & World Report,* November 11, 1996.

"It's 4:00 p.m. Do You Know Where Your Children Are?" *Newsweek,* April 28, 1998.

"It's the *Love* of Learning That Matters," *The Public Pulse,* Roper Starch Worldwide, 1997.

"Kids and Race," *Time,* November 24, 1997.

"Kids tell parents: We want you to listen to us," *Minneapolis StarTribune,* July 21, 1997.

"Lessons in Positive Values," *Lutheran Brotherhood Bond,* July/August 1997.

"McHoffa," *People,* May 18, 1998.

"Meet 10 Teen Heroes," *Minneapolis StarTribune,* April 23, 1998.

"Neighborhood Defense: Watchful Eyes, Caring Hearts," *Christian Science Monitor,* October 21, 1996.

O'Neill, Margaret A., "All Students Can Serve," *Education Week,* May 1, 1966.

"Peer pressure among young teens usually for better, not worse," University of Michigan News and Information Services, June 26, 1996.

Rauscher, Frances H., Gordon L. Shaw, and Katherine N. Ky, "Music and Spatial Task Performance" (Irvine, CA: University of California, Center for the Neurobiology of Learning and Memory, 1993).

"Renewed friendship forms base for faith-based partnerships," *Minneapolis StarTribune,* October 25, 1997.

Resnick, Michael, Ph.D., and others, "Protecting Adolescents from Harm: Findings from the National Longitudinal Study on Adolescent Health," *Journal of the American Medical Association* 278 (1997); Abstracts, September 10, 1997.

"Schools Get Results with Gun-Free Zones," *Christian Science Monitor,* October 7, 1996.

"Suicide's Shadow," *Time,* July 22, 1996.

"Survey tallies crime figures at schools across U.S.," *Minneapolis StarTribune,* March 20, 1998.

"Teen Angst," *Minneapolis StarTribune,* May 12, 1998.

"Teen Jobs: How Much Is Too Much?" *Christian Science Monitor,* November 21, 1998.

"Teens Are Lighting Up in Increasing Numbers," *Washington Post,* April 3, 1998.

"Teens get down to 16+ nights," *Minnesota Youth News (Minneapolis StarTribune),* April 30, 1998.

"USA Weekend's 10th Annual Teen Report: Teens & Freedom," *USA Weekend,* May 2–4, 1997.

"USA Weekend's 11th Annual Teen Survey: Teens & Self-Image," *USA Weekend,* May 1–3, 1998.

"Will Johnny Get A's?" *Newsweek,* July 8, 1996.

"Working with Young People to Make Their Lives Safer," *Christian Science Monitor,* March 15, 1998.

"Young spend little of purchasing power on giving," *Minneapolis StarTribune,* April 5, 1997.

Books and Publications

Adderholdt-Elliott, Miriam, Ph.D., *Perfectionism: What's Bad About Being Too Good?* (Minneapolis: Free Spirit Publishing, 1987).

Arnold, Chandler, *Read With Me: A Guide for Student Volunteers Starting Early Childhood Literacy Programs* (Washington, DC: U.S. Department of Education, 1997).

Assets: The Magazine of Ideas for Healthy Communities & Healthy Youth (Minneapolis: Search Institute, 1996—).

Becher, R., *Parent Involvement: A Review of Research and Principles of Successful Practice,* ERIC Abstract (Washington, DC: National Institute of Education, 1984).

Benson, Peter L., Ph.D., *All Kids Are Our Kids: What Communities Must Do to Raise Caring and Responsible Children and Adolescents* (San Francisco: Jossey-Bass Publishers, 1997).

———, *Developmental Assets Among Albuquerque Youth and Study Highlights* (Minneapolis: Search Institute, 1996).

———, *Developmental Assets Among Minneapolis Youth and Study Highlights* (Minneapolis: Search Institute, 1996).

———, *The Troubled Journey: A Portrait of 6th–12th Grade Youth* (Minneapolis: Search Institute, 1993).

Benson, Peter L., Ph.D., Judy Galbraith, M.A., and Pamela Espeland, *What Kids Need to Succeed: Proven, Practical Ways to Raise Good Kids,* rev. ed. (Minneapolis: Free Spirit Publishing, 1998).

The Best of Free Spirit (Minneapolis: Free Spirit Publishing, 1995).

Building Knowledge for a Nation of Learners: A Framework for Education Research 1997 (Washington, DC: U.S. Department of Education, Office of Educational Research and Improvement, 1996).

Catch the Spirit! A Student's Guide to Community Service (Newark, NJ: The Prudential in Cooperation with the U.S. Department of Education, 1996).

Cobain, Bev, R.N., C. *When Nothing Matters Anymore: A Survival Guide for Depressed Teens* (Minneapolis: Free Spirit Publishing, 1998).

Condition of Education 1996 (Washington, DC: U.S. Department of Education, National Center for Education Statistics, 1996).

Conflict Resolution Education: A Guide to Implementing Programs in Schools, Youth-Serving Organizations, and Community and Juvenile Justice Settings (Washington, DC: U.S. Departments of Justice and Education, 1996).

Creative America: A Report to the President (Washington, DC: President's Committee on the Arts and the Humanities, 1997).

Dropout Rates in the United States: 1994 (Washington, DC: U.S. Department of Education, National Center for Education Statistics, 1994).

Dropout Rates in the United States: 1996 (Washington, DC: U.S. Department of Education, National Center for Education Statistics, 1997)

Duvall, Lynn, *Respecting Our Differences: A Guide to Getting Along in a Changing World* (Minneapolis: Free Spirit Publishing, 1994).

Erickson, Judith B., Ph.D., *1998–1999 Directory of American Youth Organizations* (Minneapolis: Free Spirit Publishing, 1998).

Erlbach, Arlene, *The Best Friends Book* (Minneapolis: Free Spirit Publishing, 1995).

———, *The Families Book* (Minneapolis: Free Spirit Publishing , 1996).

Espeland, Pamela, and Rosemary Wallner, *Making the Most of Today: Daily Readings for Young People on Self-Awareness, Creativity, and Self-Esteem* (Minneapolis: Free Spirit Publishing, 1991).

Fathers' Involvement in Their Children's Schools (Washington, DC: National Center for Education Statistics, 1997).

Folkers, Gladys, M.A., and Jeanne Engelmann, *Taking Charge of My Mind & Body: A Girls' Guide to Outsmarting Alcohol, Drug, Smoking, and Eating Problems* (Minneapolis: Free Spirit Publishing, 1997).

Galbraith, Judy, M.A., and Jim Delisle, Ph.D., *The Gifted Kids' Survival Guide: A Teen Handbook* (Minneapolis: Free Spirit Publishing, 1996).

Heacox, Diane, *Up from Underachievement: How Teachers, Students, and Parents Can Work Together to Promote Student Success* (Minneapolis: Free Spirit Publishing, 1991).

Healthy Communities, Healthy Youth: A National Initiative of Search Institute to Unite Communities for Children and Adolescents (Minneapolis: Search Institute, 1996 and 1997).

Healthy Communities, Healthy Youth Speaker's Kit: Sharing the Asset Message (Minneapolis: Search Institute, 1997).

Healthy Communities, Healthy Youth Tool Kit (Minneapolis: Search Institute, 1997).

Henderson, A. T., and N. Berla, *A New Generation of Evidence: The Family Is Critical to Student Achievement* (Washington, DC: National Committee for Citizens in Education, 1994).

Hipp, Earl, *Fighting Invisible Tigers: A Stress Management Guide for Teens*, rev. ed. (Minneapolis: Free Spirit Publishing, 1995).

Huegel, Kelly, *Young People and Chronic Illness: True Stories, Help, and Hope* (Minneapolis: Free Spirit Publishing, 1998).

Ideas for Parents: Practical Suggestions for Building Assets in Your Child, newsletters 1–50 (Minneapolis: Search Institute, 1997).

Jacobs, Thomas A., J.D., *What Are My Rights? 95 Questions and Answers About Teens and the Law* (Minneapolis: Free Spirit Publishing, 1997).

Johnson, Jean, and Steve Farkas with Ali Bers, *Getting By: What American Teenagers Really Think About Their Schools* (New York: Public Agenda, 1997).

Juvenile Offenders and Victims: 1997 Update on Violence (Washington, DC: Office of Juvenile Justice and Delinquency Prevention, 1997).

Kaufman, Gershen, Ph.D., and Lev Raphael, Ph.D., *Stick Up For Yourself! Every Kid's Guide to Personal Power and Positive Self-Esteem* (Minneapolis: Free Spirit Publishing, 1990).

Kids These Days: What Americans Really Think About the Next Generation (New York: Public Agenda, 1997).

Kincher, Jonni, *The First Honest Book About Lies* (Minneapolis: Free Spirit Publishing, 1992).

———, *Psychology for Kids: 40 Fun Tests That Help You Learn About Yourself* (Minneapolis: Free Spirit Publishing, 1995).

Larson, Gary O., *American Canvas* (Washington, DC: National Endowment for the Arts, 1997).

Leffert, Nancy, Ph.D., and others, *Making the Case: Measuring the Impact of Youth Development Programs* (Minneapolis: Search Institute, 1996).

Lewis, Barbara A., *The Kid's Guide to Service Projects* (Minneapolis: Free Spirit Publishing, 1995).

———, *The Kid's Guide to Social Action*, rev. ed. (Minneapolis: Free Spirit Publishing, 1998).

———, *Kids with Courage* (Minneapolis: Free Spirit Publishing, 1992).

———, *What Do You Stand For? For Teens: A Guide to Building Character* (Minneapolis: Free Spirit Publishing, 1998).

Louv, Richard, *101 Things You Can Do for Our Children's Future* (New York: Anchor, 1994).

Ma, Xuan, *A Guide to Resources on Youth as Leaders and Partners: Strategies, Programs, and Information* (Indianapolis: Indiana Youth Institute, 1995).

A Matter of Time: Risk and Opportunity in the Out-of-School Hours (New York: Carnegie Council on Adolescent Development, 1994).

McCutcheon, Randall, *Get Off My Brain: A Survival Guide for Lazy Students*, rev. ed. (Minneapolis: Free Spirit Publishing, 1998).

The Metropolitan Life Survey of the American Teacher 1996: Students Voice Their Opinions On: Learning About Multiculturalism (New York: Louis Harris and Associates, Inc., 1996).

The Metropolitan Life Survey of the American Teacher 1996: Students Voice Their Opinions On: Learning About Values and Principles in School (New York: Louis Harris and Associates, Inc., 1996)

The Metropolitan Life Survey of the American Teacher 1996: Students Voice Their Opinions On: Violence, Social Tension and Equality Among Teens, Part I (New York: Louis Harris and Associates, Inc., 1996).

The Mood of American Youth (Alexandria, VA: Horatio Alger Association of Distinguished Americans and the National Association of Secondary School Principals, 1996).

National Household Education Survey, School Safety and Discipline Component (Washington, DC: U.S. Department of Education, National Center for Education Statistics, 1993).

1995 National Survey of Family Growth (Washington, DC: U.S. Department of Health and Human Services, National Center for Health Statistics, 1997).

1997 Partnership Attitude Tracking Study (PATS) (New York: Partnership for a Drug-Free America, 1998).

1997 PRIDE Survey (Atlanta, GA: Parents' Resource Institute for Drug Education, 1997).

1997 Profile of College-Bound Seniors National Report (Reston, VA: College Board, 1997).

1997 Youth Risk Behavior Survey (Atlanta, GA: Centers for Disease Control and Prevention, 1998).

Packer, Alex J., Ph.D., *Bringing Up Parents: The Teenager's Handbook* (Minneapolis: Free Spirit Publishing, 1992).

———, *How Rude! The Teenagers' Guide to Good Manners, Proper Behavior, and Not Grossing People Out* (Minneapolis: Free Spirit Publishing, 1997).

Peterson, Jean Sunde, Ph.D., *Talk with Teens About Feelings, Family, Relationships, and the Future* (Minneapolis: Free Spirit Publishing, 1995).

———, *Talk with Teens About Self and Stress* (Minneapolis: Free Spirit Publishing, 1993).

Plain Talk About Depression (U.S. Department of Health and Human Services: National Institutes of Health, National Institute of Mental Health, 1994).

Quality Child Care and After-School Programs: Key Weapons Against Crime (Washington, DC: Fight Crime: Invest in Kids, 1998).

Reinventing the Wheel: A Design for Student Achievement in the 21st Century (Los Angeles: The Getty Center and The National Conference of State Legislatures, 1992).

Roehlkepartain, Eugene, *Building Assets in Congregations: A Practical Guide to Helping Youth Grow Up Healthy* (Minneapolis: Search Institute, 1998).

Roehlkepartain, Jolene L., *Building Assets Together: 135 Group Activities for Helping Youth Succeed* (Minneapolis: Search Institute, 1997).

———, *Creating Intergenerational Community: 75 Ideas for Building Relationships Between Youth and Adults* (Minneapolis: Search Institute, 1996).

———, *150 Ways to Show Kids You Care* (Minneapolis: Search Institute, 1996).

Saunders, Carol Silverman, *Safe at School: Awareness and Action for Parents of Kids Grades K–12* (Minneapolis: Free Spirit Publishing, 1994).

Scales, Peter C., *Boxed In and Bored: How Middle Schools Continue to Fail Young Adolescents and What Good Middle Schools Do Right* (Minneapolis: Search Institute, 1996).

Schank, Roger C., and Chip Cleary, *Engines for Education* (Mahwah, NJ: Lawrence Erlbaum Associates, 1995).

Schumm, Jeanne Shay, Ph.D., and Marguerite Radencich, Ph.D., *How to Help Your Child with Homework: Every Caring Parent's Guide to Encouraging Good Study Habits and Ending the Homework Wars*, rev. ed. (Minneapolis: Free Spirit Publishing, 1997).

———, *School Power: Strategies for Succeeding in School* (Minneapolis: Free Spirit Publishing, 1992).

Simple Things You Can Do to Help All Children Read Well and Independently by the End of Third Grade (Washington, DC: America Reads Challenge: Read Write Now!, U.S. Department of Education, 1997).

Source: A Quarterly Newsletter of Practical Research Benefiting Children and Youth (Minneapolis: Search Institute, 1995–).

The State of Our Nation's Youth 1997–1998 (Alexandria, VA: Horatio Alger Association of Distinguished Americans, 1997).

A Status Report on Youth Curfews in America's Cities: A 347-City Survey (Washington, DC: The United States Conference of Mayors, 1997).

Steinberg, Larry, Bradford Brown, and Sanford M. Dornbush, *Beyond the Classroom: Why School Reform Has Failed and What Parents Need to Do* (New York: Simon & Schuster, 1996).

Strauss, Susan, with Pamela Espeland, *Sexual Harassment and Teens: A Program for Positive Change* (Minneapolis: Free Spirit Publishing, 1992).

Students' Reports of School Crime: 1989 and 1995 (Washington, DC: U.S. Departments of Education and Justice, 1998).

23rd Annual Monitoring the Future Survey (Ann Arbor, MI: University of Michigan Institute for Social Research, 1997).

The 27th Annual Survey of High Achievers (Lake Forest, IL: Educational Communications, Inc., 1996).

Volunteering and Giving Among American Teenagers 12 to 17 Years of Age (Washington, DC: Independent Sector, 1996).

Weitz, Judith Humphreys, *Coming Up Taller: Arts and Humanities Programs for Children and Youth at Risk* (Washington, DC: President's Committee on the Arts and the Humanities with Americans for the Arts, 1996).

Who's Who Among American High School Students 28th Annual Survey (Lake Forest, IL: Educational Communications, Inc., 1997).

Youth Indicators 1996: Trends in the Well-Being of American Youth (Washington, DC: National Center for Education Statistics, 1996).

Zill, Nicholas, and Christine Wingquist Nord, *Running in Place: How American Families Are Faring in a Changing Economy and an Individualistic Society* (Washington, DC: Child Trends, Inc., 1994).

Web Sites

Adbusters: *www.adbusters.org*

America's Promise Alliance: *www.americaspromise.org*

American Academy of Child and Adolescent Psychiatry: *www.aacap.org*

American Civil Liberties Union: *www.aclu.org*

American Library Association: *www.ala.org*

American Literacy Council: *www.americanliteracy.com*

American Medical Association: *www.ama-assn.org*

American Red Cross: *www.redcross.org*

Americans for the Arts: *www.artsusa.org*

Amnesty International USA: *www.amnesty-usa.org*

ArtsEdNet: *www.getty.edu/education*

Arts Education Partnership: *aep-arts.org*

Big Brothers Big Sisters: *www.bbbs.org*

Brady Campaign to Prevent Gun Violence: *www.bradycampaign.org*

The Center for the Book: *read.gov/cfb*

The Center for Public Integrity: *www.publicintegrity.org*

Centers for Disease Control and Prevention: *www.cdc.gov*

Character Counts: *www.charactercounts.org*

Child Trends, Inc.: *www.childtrends.org*

The Christian Science Monitor: *www.csmonitor.com*

CNN Interactive: *www.cnn.com*

The College Board: *www.collegeboard.org*

Corporation for National & Community Service: *www.nationalservice.gov*

Energize, Inc.: *www.energizeinc.com*

Habitat for Humanity International: *www.habitat.org*

Human Rights Resource Center: *www.hrusa.org*

Human Rights Watch: *www.hrw.org*

Independent Sector: *www.independentsector.org*

Indiana Youth Institute: *www.iyi.org*

Junior Achievement Inc.: *www.ja.org*

Justice Information Center (National Criminal Justice Reference Service): *www.ncjrs.org*

Kids Care Clubs: *www.kidscare.org*

Maryland Student Service Alliance: *mdservice-learning.org*

MENTOR/The National Mentoring Partnership: *www.mentoring.org*

Ms. Foundation for Women: *www.ms.foundation.org*

National Association of Secondary School Principals: *www.nassp.org*

National Center for Education Statistics (NCES): *nces.ed.gov*

National Center for Health Statistics: *www.cdc.gov/nchs*

National Conference of State Legislators: *www.ncsl.org*

National Crime Prevention Council (NCPC): *www.ncpc.org*

National Endowment for the Arts: *arts.endow.gov*

National Institute of Food and Agriculture: *www.csrees.usda.gov*

National Institute of Mental Health: *www.nimh.nih.gov*

National School Safety Center: *www.schoolsafety.us*

The Nonviolence Web: *www.nonviolence.org*

Page Education Foundation: *www.page-ed.org*

The Partnership at Drugfree.org: *www.drugfree.org*

People for the American Way: *www.pfaw.org*

Phi Delta Kappa: *www.pdkintl.org*

Planned Parenthood Federation of America: *www.plannedparenthood.org*

Points of Light Institute: *www.pointsoflight.org*

The Prudential Spirit of Community Initiative: *www.prudential.com/community*

Public Agenda: *www.publicagenda.org*

Resolving Conflict Creatively Program (RCCP): *www.esrnational.org*

Safe and Drug-Free Schools Program: *www2.ed.gov/osdfs*

Search Institute: *www.search-institute.org*

ServeNet: *www.servenet.org*

Students Against Violence Everywhere (S.A.V.E.): *www.nationalsave.org*

Substance Abuse and Mental Health Services Administration: *www.samhsa.gov*

Suicide Awareness Voices of Education (SAVE): *www.save.org*

Thrivent Lutheran: *www.thrivent.com*

U.S. Department of Education: *www.ed.gov*

Unicef U.S.A.: *www.unicefusa.org*

United Nations: *www.un.org*

United States Conference of Mayors: *www.usmayors.org*

University at Buffalo Counseling Center (State University of New York): *ub-counseling.buffalo.edu*

University of Minnesota Human Rights Library: *www.umn.edu/humanrts*

USA Weekend: *www.usaweekend.com*

VolunteerMatch: *www.volunteermatch.org*

Washington Post: *www.washingtonpost.com*

Youth Service America: *www.ysa.org*

INDEX

ABOUT THE AUTHORS

Peter L. Benson, Ph.D., has been president of Search Institute since 1985. He received his Ph.D. in social psychology from the University of Denver, his M.A. in psychology from Yale, and his B.A. in psychology from Augustana College. He is the author of several books and publications including *All Kids Are Our Kids: What Communities Must Do to Raise Caring and Responsible Children and Adolescents; The Troubled Journey: A Portrait of 6th–12th Grade Youth;* and *The Quicksilver Years: The Hopes and Fears of Early Adolescence.*

Judy Galbraith, M.A., is the founder and president of Free Spirit Publishing Inc. in Minneapolis, creators of Self-Help for Kids® and Self-Help for Teens® books and learning materials. A former classroom teacher, she received an education degree from the University of Wisconsin at Steven's Point and holds a master's degree in guidance and counseling of the gifted from Norwich University in Vermont. She is the author of *The Gifted Kids' Survival Guides* and *You Know Your Child Is Gifted When...* and coauthor of *When Gifted Kids Don't Have All the Answers,* published by Free Spirit.

Pamela Espeland has authored and coauthored many books for children, teens, and adults including *See You Later, Procrastinator!; Dude, That's Rude!; Life Lists for Teens;* and *Making the Most of Today.* She received her B.A. in English from Carleton College in Northfield, Minnesota.

Peter, Judy, and Pamela are the coauthors of *What Kids Need to Succeed: Proven, Practical Ways to Raise Good Kids.*

Other Great Books from Free Spirit

The Teen Guide to Global Action

How to Connect with Others (Near & Far) to Create Social Change

by Barbara A. Lewis

This book includes real-life stories to inspire young readers, plus a rich menu of opportunities for service, fast facts, hands-on activities, user-friendly tools, and up-to-date resources kids can use to put their own volunteer spirit into practice. It also spotlights young people from the past whose efforts led to significant positive change. Upbeat, practical, and highly motivating, this book has the power to rouse young readers everywhere. For ages 12 & up. *144 pp.; softcover; two-color illust.; 7" x 9"*

Life Lists for Teens

Tips, Steps, Hints, and How-Tos for Growing Up, Getting Along, Learning, and Having Fun

by Pamela Espeland

More than 200 powerful self-help lists cover topics ranging from health to cyberspace, school success to personal safety, friendship to fun. A 4-1-1 for tweens and teens, *Life Lists* is an inviting read, a place to go for quick advice, and a ready source of guidance for all kinds of situations. For ages 11 & up. *272 pp.; softcover; 6" x 9"*

What Do You Stand For? For Teens

A Guide to Building Character

by Barbara A. Lewis

This book empowers teens to identify and build character traits. Inspiring quotations, background information, activities, true stories, and resources make this book timely, comprehensive, and fun. For ages 11 & up. *288 pp.; softcover; B&W photos and illust.; 8½" x 11"*

What Kids Need to Succeed

Proven, Practical Ways to Raise Good Kids *(Revised, Expanded, Updated Edition)*

by Peter L. Benson, Ph.D., Judy Galbraith, M.A., and Pamela Espeland

Based on groundbreaking nationwide studies, this book has over 900 specific, concrete suggestions for building Developmental Assets at home, at school, in the community, and in the faith community. For parents, teachers, and community and youth leaders. *Parents' Choice* approved. *256 pp.; softcover; 4⅛" x 6⅞"*

Interested in purchasing multiple quantities?

Contact edsales@freespirit.com or call 1.800.735.7323 and ask for Education Sales.

Many Free Spirit authors are available for speaking engagements, workshops, and keynotes. Contact speakers@freespirit.com or call 1.800.735.7323.

For pricing information, to place an order, or to request a free catalog, contact:

Free Spirit Publishing Inc.
217 Fifth Avenue North • Suite 200 • Minneapolis, MN 55401-1299
toll-free 800.735.7323 • local 612.338.2068 • fax 612.337.5050
help4kids@freespirit.com • www.freespirit.com